PRAISE FOR DAVIS BUNN'S PAST NOVELS

"Superb writing . . . so well executed and plotted that it deserves consideration in a class by itself."

—*Providence Journal*

"Spellbinding."

—NBC-TV

"Bunn's dialogue is racehorse fast. The tale zips along without any lulls and has a nicely drawn good vs. evil plot . . . That's some feat."

—*New York Post*

"A feast of suspense. Highly recommended."

—*Library Journal*

"The story is irresistible. Aside from the next morning's demands, there's little to stop the reader from going for an all-nighter. The story is edgy and compelling, and its realistic plot is close enough to recent headlines to keep you wondering whether Bunn himself will get sued, kidnapped, or worse."

—Ganett News Service

"Written with amazing foresight and ingenuity . . . great entertainment reading."

—*Librarian's World*

"This beautifully crafted story is destined to become a holiday classic."

—*A Closer Look*

"Another wonderful story full of people you care about . . . You'll reread this book every year."

—*Grand Rapids Press*

"One of the year's most memorable books."

—The Oxford Times

"Bunn skillfully paces action, dialogue, and background and keeps readers wondering what will happen next. The story has everything that popular Christian fiction should have; adventure, a love story, and characters who mature in Christ."

—Bookstore Journal

"A thoroughly satisfying story . . . Bunn casts an adult coming to grips with faith against a backdrop in which faith is the key factor of survival."

—Catholic Bulletin

"Bunn uses a fresh approach for fiction and turns readers towards the presence of God. Compelling writing blends humor with a stirring plot."

—Moody Monthly

"FANTASTIC—4½ stars! An engrossing, neatly plotted story. The authors' skill at evoking the flavor of the issues and mores of Regency England shine through."

—Romantic Times

"This is it. This story goes to the heart of a great moral dilemma . . . A compulsive read."

—BBC Television (UK)

"Heart-stopping, harrowing . . . Bunn is known for novels that are both moving and gripping, and this is no exception. Populated with memorable characters and tackling one of today's most contentious issues—international labor relations—it's sure to be one of the summer's hottest reads."

—Palo Alto Daily News

IMPOSTER

 # IMPOSTER

DAVIS BUNN

WestBow
P R E S S

A Division of Thomas Nelson Publishers
Since 1798

visit us at www.westbowpress.com

Published in Nashville, Tennessee, by WestBow Press, a division of Thomas Nelson, Inc.

WestBow Press books may be purchased in bulk for educational, business, fund-raising, or sales promotional use. For information, please e-mail SpecialMarkets@ ThomasNelson.com.

Publisher's Note: This novel is a work of fiction. Names, characters, places, and inci-dents are either products of the author's imagination or used fictitiously. All characters are fictional, and any similarity to people living or dead is purely coincidental.

Library of Congress Cataloging-in-Publication Data

Bunn, T. Davis, 1952–
    Imposter / Davis Bunn.
      p. cm.
    ISBN 0-8499-4486-4
    I. Title.
    PS3552.U4718I47 2006
    813'.54—dc22

2005019798

Printed in the United States of America

06 07 08 09 10 QW 6 5 4 3 2 1

This book is dedicated to

Sam Gornto
Julio Marin
Monty McCart
Jeff Wallace

Friends in high places

M egan Kelly strolled the central aisle of Lexington Market like a
star. Hers was the role of a lifetime, the waif from Fells Point
finally gaining the spotlight. Her audience knew it, of course. Half the
stalls bore posters with her husband's picture. The other half weren't
worth noticing and certainly would never see any of her trade. She was
accompanied by her son, Matt, which made the afternoon truly perfect.
Matt had a profile made for Mount Rushmore and a personality made
for concealment. Most men as handsome as her son were destined for
leadership. Matt, however, hated any kind of attention. Even fawning
women left him uncomfortable. Matt Kelly had honed a talent for hiding in plain daylight. Which seemed odd only to those who did not
know the reasons. And Megan Kelly knew her son very well.

So Megan did what only she could do for Matt, which was to draw
him out, at least a little. She moved more slowly and shone more brilliantly, so that even Matt was illuminated by her presence. At every stall
she shook the patron's hand and then said the same words, singing
them with pride, "Have you met my handsome young man?"

Baltimore's Lexington Market was the oldest still operating in
America, founded just after the Revolutionary War and seldom cleaned
since. Early in the last century, when Baltimore's port serviced a bur-
geoning population, Lexington Market was the upscale place to shop.
This neighborhood boasted the first skyscrapers south of New York,
with their lower floors reserved for fashionable stores. From dawn to
dusk the area served as America's first pedestrian zone.

But nothing remained the same for long in Baltimore. The high-rises had stood empty for a generation, and the acres of diamonds and furs had been replaced by pawnshops and dollar stores. The pedestrian streets were lined with hawkers and grifters and bums. Lexington Market stood as a citadel against the worst a modern world could offer.

Yet Baltimore remained the perpetual fighter, knocked about but never defeated. Megan's husband led a new consortium that had declared a block-by-block war. Downtown, as their development was called, was the largest inner-city project in Baltimore's history. Nine city blocks—thirty-three derelict skyscrapers—with Lexington Market at its heart. Small wonder the stallholders backed her husband's bid for the United States Senate.

Megan stopped by Polish Johnny's to buy a yard of kielbasa, sausage guaranteed to lift the diner's cholesterol level by double figures. The manager made a process of wiping his hands before reaching across to shake her own. She introduced her son, stating, "Matt has just graduated from some secret agent school I can never remember the name of. I went down for the ceremony, of course. He graduated first in his class. The head of the Secret Service himself pinned the medal on Matt's chest."

Megan had to shout against the market's din. But anybody raised in Fells Point, the worst of Baltimore's waterfront slums, knew how to make themselves heard. She pretended not to see her son's embarrassment as he shook the stallholder's hand and accepted congratulations from admirers on all sides. She handed Matt her latest purchase, started down the aisle, and asked her son, "What would you like for dinner tonight?"

"Peace and quiet."

"Don't be silly. What could be grander than this?" she asked.

Megan Kelly was overdressed, as always. Fashionable attire was her signature. Today it was a coarsely woven linen jacket with gold brocade and buttons, black silk dress, matching alligator purse and shoes. Her hair was sculpted gray, her eyes merry. They stopped for chocolate at Mary's, where the manager drew out her best wares from hidden shelves and proudly served this strange lady from another era. In this place, Megan Kelly could have worn the crown jewels and remained safe. Lexington Market protected its own.

Megan Kelly had worked equally as hard on her voice. The Fells Point slang had been left behind with the rags and the beer buckets and the stench of unfulfilled dreams. She introduced Matt to the next outstretched hand, "My son, the federal agent. Off to save the world."

As they left the market, Matt asked the inevitable, "How goes the race?"

"Same as when we talked last week. Neck and neck."

"Last week Zelbert was five points behind you." Rolf Zelbert was the Republican candidate, a dental surgeon and alderman from Annapolis.

Megan watched Matt stow the last of her packages in the trunk. "There are bound to be bumps here and there."

Matt stepped two paces away from the car as Megan greeted three passersby. No man as virile as Megan Kelly's son could make himself vanish entirely. But he tried. The cause of Matt's withdrawn nature was the one battle that left her perpetually defeated. Megan hid her sorrow behind an even grander smile, urged the ladies to vote for her husband, and found herself recalling a secret from Matt's childhood. In the lonely evenings when Paul Kelly was off fighting his dragons and she and Matt were alone, Matt would make her laugh for hours with his ability as a mimic. He could copy almost anyone's voice and stance, male or female. But Matt had refused to ever imitate his father. The few times she had made the request, he had frozen solid. Megan Kelly had become adept at not mentioning Paul Kelly any more than necessary around her son. She hid the sadness behind her laughter, down with all the other flaws knitted into both their lives.

But she would not dwell on such impossibilities now. Not with her son home and Washington beckoning. So when they were safely seated in the car and the world was locked outside, she replied to his repeated query with the truth. "Zelbert has gained four points."

"Zelbert's share has lifted four points in a week?"

"Your father has never lost a race."

"Two terms in the state legislature doesn't make for much of a history. Come on, Mom. The television cameras are off. It's just us here."

Matt Kelly could not have cared less about politics. Megan knew this. Matt asked because Megan Kelly loved politics with a ferocity that baffled her son. Megan Kelly *lived* for this. She could turn the latest opinion poll into a three-hour conversation. She looked forward to November like a child awaiting Christmas. Her voice rose two octaves just saying the word out loud: *Washington.*

And she could be far more honest with her son than she could ever be with her husband. These days, Paul Kelly was a volatile mixture of confidence and panic. He needed stroking on an hourly basis. If not from her, then from Sol, Paul's campaign manager and best friend. Megan said, "The national party is throwing money at Zelbert. He's got double our airtime. Sol is very worried."

"What about the DNC?"

"Our people keep promising funds but so far they haven't delivered." She banged her fist on a silk-clad leg. "We're right on Washington's doorstep. But all they can see is how Maryland has gone Democrat in every off-year election since the First World War. I'm out there every day, Matt. I hear what people are saying. The state is going red before our very eyes. I can't get anybody at national headquarters to listen."

Megan watched her son drive past Maryland General, headed for Martin Luther King Boulevard and home. Matt had an unflappable steadiness that was utterly at odds with her husband's explosive nature. Like so much else they did not hold in common. "Enough politics. Tell me what's happening in your life."

Matt deflected, as usual. "You just saw me at the graduation ceremony."

"I was so proud of you, Matt. Your father was immensely sorry he had to miss it, but you know the pressures he faces."

Matt glared. "I know all right."

She kept her tone bright. "First in your class, being honored by that general, what was his name?"

"Walton. He prefers to be called Ambassador."

"He's your new boss; is that right?"

"He's director of State Department Intelligence. He is also universally loathed. Word is, he eats young careers like Cheerios." Matt glanced over. "I've been approached by the CIA."

This was new. And unwelcome. "Surely you'd prefer to stay where you are."

"CIA has offered me a posting in ops."

"And this is a good thing?"

"It means action. And foreign assignments. Both of which I want."

Megan Kelly almost succeeded in suppressing her shudder. "But if you stay at State at least there is the possibility of moving in a civilized direction."

"Exactly what I want to avoid at all costs."

"Even at the risk of worrying your old mother to death?"

"You're not old."

It was a familiar argument, one she had already lost. She changed course with, "How is your young lady? I'm sorry, I don't remember . . ."

"Trish. She's fine. We're not." Matt drove slowly down Eutaw, hung a right on Wilson and then a left into the alley behind their home. He pulled up beside the carport and parked. "But it's okay."

Megan touched her son's arm, stopping him from opening his door. "I know you'd like the world to think you don't care about this stream of young ladies who treat your life like just another revolving door. I also know something is bothering you very deeply."

Matt had emerald eyes that changed in depth and tone. Which was odd, given that both her and her husband's gazes were gray. She always claimed Matt had inherited her mother's eyes, which had been a secret lifelong joke. Her mother had been a bartender since she was eleven, working in her own mother's corner dive. The only color Megan Kelly could recall in her mother's eyes was red.

Matt replied, "Trish says every time we get together it's like a first date."

Megan Kelly's phone rang. She could not turn it off, not with the election only five weeks away. She slipped it from her purse, checked the readout, and then clicked it shut. "I'm sorry. Please go on." When he remained silent, she softly pressed, "This is not the first time a young lady has accused you of being unreachable."

"No."

Megan wished she could do something about her son's desire to vanish. But he was a man now and had a man's inflexibility. Which truly frightened her. "Have I ever apologized for your early years?"

"Many times."

Matt could melt into any setting and become unseen. Which did not bode well in a society that rewarded the brash and the bold. Women were attracted to Matt's looks and his calm manner. And repelled by his ability to deflect. "You do go through young ladies at an astonishing rate."

Matt responded in his normal fashion to probing conversation. He opened his door and rose from the car.

Their pre–Civil War brownstone fronted Eutaw Place, a shaded lane that ran along the crest of Bolton Hill. When Paul Kelly had purchased the place, it had been just another ruin in a long line of once-grand town-homes. Now it was a singular prize and worth a small fortune.

The Kelly home had two entrances: double front doors on Eutaw, which no one used, and through a wrought-iron gate on Wilson. The house was built on a small incline, such that the basement became the ground floor in the rear and had been converted into a private apart-ment for Matt. The home's side entrance was up closer to the front, which made for quite a hike in the rain. Paul Kelly was always going on about building stairs to the wrought-iron kitchen balcony and a covered walk from the carport. But it was one of many chores that had to wait because of the campaign.

Matt collected the shopping bags from the car and followed his mother through the side gate. Then he stopped and looked back.

Megan thought she had seen it as well, an apparition drawn from a past so distant it belonged to another woman. "What is it?"

Matt must have noted the tremor in her voice. He shifted the pack-ages to his other arm and reached inside his jacket.

"Matt?"

"I left my gun in the car."

Her mind was racing now. She had a politico's ability to think of a dozen items and keep them all separate. The spot on the other side of the street was empty now, the place so quiet she could easily have told herself it was just stress. But she heard the worry in her son's voice, and something more. Matt was suddenly a different man. A professional who considered it natural to walk through life armed.

Matt set the packages on the ground. "I want you to go inside, Mom."

"What's the matter?"

"Probably nothing." But it was a stranger talking now, a man who charged the air with lethal tension.

"But why—"

"Do what I said." Matt passed back through the rear gate. "Now."

Megan hesitated, but not for long. She was a city girl, after all. She climbed the two stairs. She fumbled for her keys, her hands unwilling to obey the simplest command. She fitted them into the door. And her phone rang.

She turned the knob with one hand and opened her phone with the other.

Then the entire world erupted in a blast of flame.

———

The bomb blast hurled Matt Kelly over a line of parked cars and onto the street. He was aware of landing hard. But he felt nothing. He lay surrounded by the smell of explosive, staring at an afternoon sky stained by oily smoke. He tried to move his head, but couldn't, and soon forgot why it mattered.

There was a gentle tearing sensation. He found himself drifting in the air above his parents' home. Just another cloud, unnoticed in the mayhem and the screaming he could no longer hear. He hung there one instant only. Not even long enough to draw the entire vista into focus. He was a newborn all over again—staring down at a billion images, none of which made any sense. Even when he told himself he had to look carefully because something vitally important had happened. Even then. He could not bring himself to care.

Then the instant was over. Gone so fast he could easily have denied it had happened at all. He was back on the pavement and staring at the billowing smoke. He remained there long enough to hear the sirens wail in the distance and voices wail closer to where he lay. Long enough to feel the pain begin to seep into his awareness. Pain so intense it was hard to claim it as his own. Then he was gone.

The ease with which he drifted away made him certain that things were very bad indeed. Matt Kelly was not a quitter. Yet he released his hold on the sky and the pavement with a total absence of concern. Not even the screams and the sirens could keep him there. He did not shut his eyes. He simply stopped seeing.

He knew what had happened to him. There had been an explosion. He could no longer see. But he could hear, as though he were in some transitory phase and sound was either the last faculty to depart or the first to connect him to whatever it was that lay beyond.

The next sound Matt heard was wind chimes. He recognized the chimes instantly as being handblown crystal and antique. They had formed a vivid component of his early childhood. The chimes had hung from his grandparents' back porch near the Fells Point marina. His thoughts were not so clear on anything else.

He felt himself drifting off again. Matt used all his remaining time to decide he was okay with being dead.

Lucas D'Amico stood on the front steps of his daughter's school when he heard the distant blast. Katy, being the daughter of a cop and a child of Baltimore, hovered just inside the door and watched her father with worried eyes.

Lucas saw that his daughter was frightened, so he turned to her and asked, "Who is your daddy?"

She responded in the low voice she used when either worried or sad. "The best policeman in the whole wide world."

"That's right. And what is your daddy's job?"

"To keep the world safe and me happy."

"Right again. Big smile, now." Nowadays it wrenched Lucas to hear Katy talk like that, because she had used that low voice for almost five months after his wife had been taken from them. "Come on, that's no smile. Give me something to take with me out on the street. That's my sweetheart. You go have a great day, Katy-girl."

Ian Reeves waited for the school doors to close behind Katy before asking, "What was that noise?"

"Hard to say."

Ian was pastor of Mount Vernon Methodist and head of Katy's school. "Could it have been an exploding gas main?"

"Maybe." But Lucas didn't think so. He was fairly certain it was a bomb. Echoes off the surrounding buildings made it hard to pinpoint direction and distance. But it had seemed to come from the north. Which might mean the National Guard Armory. Lucas fervently hoped so. A bomb in a military compound was not his worry. "What did you want to see me about?"

But the pastor was listening to several hundred car alarms wailing in the distance. His eyes nervously tracked clouds of birds wheeling overhead in frightened unison. "Don't you need to be somewhere?"

"I have a couple of minutes."

"Right." Ian Reeves was a remarkably unattractive man. He was tall and stooped at the same time. His face was almost comical. "You have the most incredible daughter it has ever been my joy to know."

Lucas nodded. Where most saw an overweight girl with dull eyes and shapeless clothes, Ian managed to see Katy for what she was. "Something wrong?"

"Not with the school or Katy. She is a favorite with almost everybody inside. No, my concern is with you."

"Why is that?" Sirens whooped in the distance. But none appeared to be headed in his direction. Mount Vernon was a haven of civil respectability, but the church stood equidistant from Maryland General and Mercy Hospital, which held the state's two busiest ER units. Sirens were a normal part of the scenery. Then his phone rang. "Excuse me."

He flipped it from the leather holster. "This is D'Amico."

His partner asked, "Where are you?"

"Front steps of Katy's school."

"Then I guess you heard it."

"Roger that. You got an ID?"

"You're gonna love this."

D'Amico turned from the pastor. "So it wasn't the armory?"

Clarence Bledsoe laughed out loud. "In your dreams, pal."

D'Amico sighed. "I'm two minutes out."

"Swing by the front; I'll be waiting. Bernstein has handed us some serious trouble this time. I hate trouble worse than Mondays."

D'Amico cut off his phone and told the pastor, "I have to go."

"Call me, Lucas. We need to talk."

"I'm doing fine, Ian."

Normally this was enough to stifle the pastor's concern. But not today. He brought his uneven features in closer and said, "Call me."

———

Lucas went code one, rolling with siren and lights. He swung by Mercy and headed down Fayette. His partner jogged out headquarters' front doors and slipped in before D'Amico pulled to the curb. "Eutaw Place."

"You have got to be joking."

"It gets worse. Paul Kelly."

Their siren cleaved through rush hour. "I know that name."

"Running for the U.S. Senate."

Of course. Lucas's wife had called Megan Kelly a friend. "They murdered a candidate? Isn't that federal?"

"I wish." Bledsoe plucked a freshly ironed handkerchief from his jacket and sneezed. He was a slender man with café au lait skin and a penchant for Egyptian cotton shirts with French cuffs. His nickname around the department was Prince. Bledsoe also had notorious allergies. "I've got a bad attack coming. I can feel it."

"Tell me why this isn't federal, Clarence." The law governing their work was supposedly simple. Federal agencies took control when a federal law had been broken. Otherwise, it was a local police case. Murder was a state crime, not a federal crime. But the antiterrorism laws were broad enough for Homeland Security to insert itself almost anywhere it wished. Such as when a senatorial candidate got himself blown up.

"Because Homeland has spoken." He sneezed again. "My throat feels like it's sandblasted."

Lucas crossed Charles Street and headed for Martin Luther King Boulevard. "You talked to the feds?"

"Not me, man. The chief." Major Hannah Bernstein had been the chief of Baltimore's homicide division for just under six months. Lucas and Clarence were still in watch-and-wait mode about their new boss. "I got to hand it to the lady. She fought the good fight. But Homeland says unless the guy is actually elected, he's just another local joe. Besides which, it wasn't the guy. It was his wife."

Lucas parked behind a lone fire truck and three foam-encrusted cars. A brick wall between the house and the street had partially protected the SUVs. Above that level, the vehicles looked decapitated. Yellow police tape was already in place. A crowd was gathering. Eutaw

Place was the very pinnacle of upmarket, the highest-priced street within the region known as Bolton Hill. But the areas to either side were heavy crime districts. Druid Lake, less than a mile to the north of where D'Amico stood, was a notorious dumping ground for gang-related violence. But here everything shouted money and a world where bombs did not demolish cars and homes and lives.

Clarence rose from the car and started for the tape, until Lucas said softly, "Hang on a sec."

His partner halted and reached for his handkerchief. Lucas did a slow circle there beside the car. His absorption of the scene was not a conscious process. It just happened. Later he would start going back over what he was now taking in. When he wrote up his reports or listened to the 911 tape or sat in a meeting, his mind would hit replay. Now that he slept alone, he sometimes went over things at night. But for Katy's sake he didn't like to bring his work home.

As he scanned the scene, his gaze did not rest anywhere for more than a few seconds. Clarence waited patiently. They had been partners for seven years. Long enough for Clarence to know that if he needed to check something later, Lucas would know. Clarence didn't scan because he wasn't good at it; therefore, Lucas scanned for both of them. Clarence coughed and sneezed and waited.

The Kelly house was one of Bolton Hill's few stand-alones, a three-story brownstone that probably dated from the early 1800s. The carriage house at the back had formerly been a garage but now housed election staff offices. A carport stood in the corner where the rear alley met Wilson. A waist-high brick wall ran along Wilson Avenue, plastered now with "Paul Kelly for U.S. Senate" election posters. A larger poster covered the carriage house's entire side wall. The poster had been partly ripped free of the wall by the blast, such that a rumpled candidate glared at the mayhem in his side lawn.

The narrow park running down the center of Eutaw Place sprouted elms in autumn finery and a fountain that actually worked. The people clustered beyond the tape displayed the area's neurotic nature. Well-heeled neighbors talked worriedly. Youths in serious street gear stood by a lavender Escalade, gold chains thumping on their chests as they did the fist-on-fist thing, probably complimenting the bomber for his handiwork. Beyond them, bums drifted and laughed, their insanity pricked by the day's cataclysm.

"Okay. I'm done." Lucas ducked under the tape and felt the same thing he always did when approaching a new crime scene. Another shard had been torn from the world's fabric. No one understood life's fragility better than a homicide cop.

Clarence said, "Get a load, will you?"

The female officer who approached them was definitely made to turn heads. Dark, slender, and so attractive her standard-issue patrol uniform looked ready for a magazine cover. But her attitude was strictly professional. "Help you gents?"

"I'm D'Amico and this is Bledsoe." They flashed their badges. Lucas read the officer's nametag. "Morales?"

"Yes sir. Sure glad to see you guys." She motioned toward the house. "We've got some serious strangeness here."

The house was surprisingly intact, except for the ten-foot hole in the side facing them. "You here alone?"

"No sir. Officer Brodski was first on scene. He's inside with the board."

Board was patrol-speak for anything to do with the fire squad and EMS. "You got a fire marshal on hand?"

"Not yet. Everybody's pretty stretched today. We've been asking for more backup. The medical examiner hasn't even gotten here. One ambo came and left with the guy."

"Guy?"

"Matthew Kelly. That's his mother over there." She pointed to the black plastic tarp draped over a rumpled form, midway between the blasted house and the side wall. "I did that because of the people. But I didn't move anything. It's just—she's in bad shape."

"You did fine." The blast had torn a sizable chunk out of the brick wall and pitted the surrounding area with what looked like a spray of bullets. "How did the kid survive that?"

"Best I can figure it, he was standing over there." She indicated a point beyond the wall. "Pretty much out of the blast pattern."

D'Amico nodded. "So right now it's just us and one engine and your partner inside."

"Brodski isn't my partner, sir." Something about that left her looking tense. "We've been radioing in pretty regular, but it sounds like the whole force is thin on the ground today. The duty sergeant's supposed to be on his way . . . I guess that must be him now."

A patrol car pulled around the corner and parked in front of the fountain. The sergeant was a twenty-year street vet Lucas knew vaguely, but couldn't for the moment remember his name. The sergeant nodded at the two homicide detectives but addressed the young officer. "What are you doing off desk, Morales?"

The young woman was attractive even when pained. "We've got two officers in Division One pulling light duty, Sarge. They said—"

"That's not what I asked."

Morales was clearly embarrassed to be discussing the matter in front of two senior detectives, which Lucas could well understand. Desk duty was assigned to an active officer only when their powers of arrest had been suspended by Internal Affairs pending an investigation, or when placed on punishment detail. "Come on, Sarge, cut me a break. You know how stretched we are."

"You heard the lieutenant same as me. You're strictly on desk duty for the duration."

Morales kicked the dirt at her feet. Shifted her belt. Was definitely tempted to argue. Instead, she wheeled about and left without another word.

The sergeant watched her climb into the car and peel rubber down the street before asking, "Homicide claiming this one?"

"Assuming there's a body under that tarp." Lucas pointed at the empty space Morales had left behind. "What was that all about?"

"You don't want to know."

D'Amico waited while his partner went through another coughing fit. "You okay?"

"Definitely not." Bledsoe wheezed as they walked toward the gaping hole. "You ever seen anything like this before?"

"Can't say that I have." A crack ran up the brownstone wall from the hole to the ornate stucco cornice along the roofline. Other than that, the house looked intact. More than that. The room Lucas could see beyond the hole appeared almost untouched. "Why don't you examine the victim; I'll check inside."

"Give me a simple gang war any day." Clarence pointed at the poster flapping on the side of the carriage house. The candidate's patented thousand-yard stare was violently skewed by the day's calamity. "I read trouble in letters ten feet tall."

Matt Kelly came around to the constant beeping of a hospital monitor. The sound of crystal chimes seemed to follow him into wakefulness, then vanish upon an astringent wind. He sensed a gradual reconnection to his physical body. He felt neither satisfaction nor sorrow over the awareness that he was alive. He knew he could open his eyes if he wanted. But there was a question he would have to ask as soon as the world realized he was awake. Even if he did not shape the words, the first set of eyes would tell him anyway. And Matt was not ready. Neither for the question, nor for the risk that his mother was gone.

So he lay as still as the death he would probably have preferred. He kept his eyes shut. He lay in the fragmented reality of a hollow world, surrounded by electronic chimes and the whispers of deadly winds. Finally he drifted away once more.

He dozed and woke and dozed again, fighting off consciousness as long as he could. Then a nurse came and woke him with hands that took his pulse and eyes that told him the tragic news. A doctor arrived, a slender, olive-skinned male named Krishnamurti. His voice was soft and his concern very professional. He too offered Matt both the message and the condolences without saying a word.

Matt ate what the nurse brought him without tasting anything. Then the doctor returned with Matt's father. Matt was as ready as he could be for that encounter. He endured the tears and the words for a brief time, and then he shut it all out—his father and the doctor and the news. He wrestled himself back into sleep, wishing he knew how to make it permanent.

He dreamed again of being blown free of his body. He struggled from the depths, followed into wakefulness by the faint tremor of crystal chimes. He fled them by focusing on sounds of other voices. Deep voices with the hard insistence of a world that would no longer be denied. He opened his eyes.

"Mr. Kelly, I'm Detective Lucas D'Amico. This is my partner, Detective Bledsoe. We're sorry to bother you. But we need to ask some questions."

Matt welcomed their official lack of emotion. He waited while the nurse raised his bed and gave him a cup of water and warned the cops not to take too long. When the nurse departed, Detective D'Amico said, "You're a federal agent, and before that you were a cop, right?"

Matt nodded.

Detective D'Amico was clearly the guy in charge, a solid block of a man with the patient air of someone built to wait forever to get what he wanted. He wore the typical cop's suit, wrinkled and cheap. "Then you know the drill. Tell us what happened."

Matt walked them through the afternoon. Meeting his mother at Lexington Market, driving home, the explosion. Five sentences. Agony.

D'Amico listened and watched. His partner, an African-American dressed in a fashionable tweed jacket and dark slacks, took notes with a gold pen and coughed. The man did not look well. When Matt stopped speaking, D'Amico gave him a few moments of silence, then, "What did you do before you met your mother?"

"The details won't help you, Detective."

"What say you let us be the judge."

"I drove back from FLETSE."

"Where?"

"Federal training academy. Outside Savannah."

D'Amico and his partner exchanged glances. "I thought you feds trained at Quantico."

"All nondefense agencies except FBI have been relocated."

"So you drove back and went straight to Lexington Market?"

"First I stopped off at a dojo in Tenth Ward and worked out."

Bledsoe, the other cop, spoke for the first time. "Vic Wright's place?"

"Yes."

Bledsoe coughed hard. His voice sounded sandpapery. "I know it. Full-contact karate." To Matt, "Korean, right?"

"Yes."

"How long you been going there?"

"Since I was twelve."

"How old are you now?"

"Thirty-one."

Bledsoe said, "If this guy's survived nineteen years with Vic Wright, he's good."

D'Amico said, "So you worked out at the dojo, then what?"

"I drove to the market and met my mother."

"Nothing else?"

"I called my girlfriend."

"Her name?"

"Trish. It doesn't matter. She wasn't in. And we've broken up."

D'Amico spoke with a soft, relentless pressure. "How do you know if she wasn't there?"

"We split up before."

"Before."

"Yes."

D'Amico and his partner exchanged a look. "Are you always this talkative?"

"Yes."

"Is there anything more you can tell us about the time from when you arrived home to when the blast took place?"

"We got out of the car. We started toward the door. I had the shopping bags and was behind her. The bomb went off. I survived."

D'Amico rose to his feet. "I wish I could say this has been helpful."

Bledsoe coughed his way across the room. "Tell Vic that Clarence said hello."

Matt watched the door sigh shut behind them, enclosing him in memories and guilt. What should he have told the detectives, that he might as well be laid out there beside his mother? That he should have done more to protect her? The nurse returned and lowered his bed and spoke words he could not hear. Matt tried to lose himself in sleep, but the memories were too harsh in their demands. So he lay there with his eyes shut, helpless to do anything but watch his past scroll toward doom and regret.

———

The day before the bombing, Matt should have been feasting on success. Ambassador Walton, head of State Department Intel, was due down that afternoon to give the valedictory address and present Matt his top-cadet medal. Instead, Matt was trapped in the headlights of public calamity, trying hard not to tell Trish good-bye.

Matt stood in the duty room using the only pay phone reserved for cadets. Cell phones did not work on the FLETSE base. This lone pay phone was the cadets' only connection to the outside world. A dozen other off-duty cadets pretended not to listen as Matt begged Trish not to make a long-distance break.

According to Trish, Matt Kelly was the handsomest mystery she had ever met. He was a trace over six feet and permanently lean. His dark blond hair was cut to agency guidelines. Even in standard cadet sweats Matt looked buttoned down and serious about stuff like life and career and a future. But Matt's appeal had faded as far as Trish was concerned, and she was showing little interest in one last chance.

"What's the point, Matt? We've been through this a dozen times already. Which is silly, since we've only been together, what, six months? Less. Most of which—"

"I'd just like to talk it through together."

"You've been away training for a job I've never understood why you wanted to take in the first place." She sighed away that particular argument. "Look. We both know it was over before it ever really started. It's best if we let go now, okay?"

"Please, Trish."

She became impatient. "Matt, I've argued with you more than I did in the previous five years with the guy I almost married. Which is insane, because you don't argue back." Her voice rose in stages. "You don't show me *anything*. I've seen you almost every day you've been in town, and I don't know you any better now than I did when we first met!

You're a complete enigma! I didn't even know what that word meant before I met you, and now I feel like it's branded to my tongue!"

The hand holding the receiver was clammy from mashing the phone to his ear, keeping the others from hearing her words. "Graduation ceremonies are this evening. I'll leave first thing tomorrow morning and drive up. Okay?"

She might have said, "Whatever." Or she might have just sighed as she hung up.

Which was why he coasted through the ceremony and skipped out on the celebrations and finally gave up on sleep at four the next morning. He made the journey back to Baltimore in seven and a half hours. He called her four times from the road, but Trish let the answering machine pick up. Then her office said she was in a meeting until two that afternoon. So Matt admitted temporary defeat and made the next call. The one to Megan Kelly, agreeing to meet her at Lexington Market after she finished some political gig, which left him two hours to kill. So Matt left the interstate at Tenth Ward and headed for Vic Wright's dojo.

Full-contact dojos, or karate studios, sprouted from the wretched soil of bad neighborhoods. Tenth Ward wasn't the worst Baltimore had to offer. But with the state pen six blocks to the west, this area was bad enough. The dojo shared the mall with a Latino grocery store, a bail bondsman, a check-cashing shop, and a bar. Halfway houses occupied several neighboring townhomes.

Matt had first come here at age twelve. This had been the closest dojo to Matt's home. Biking through Tenth Ward at age twelve had been a trip. Matt had come once by bus, but only once. He had been too pretty for the bus. Whenever his father moved the family back to Baltimore from wherever his latest project had taken them, Matt returned to the dojo. While away, he practiced on his own. He practiced very hard.

Matt switched off the engine and sat waiting for the world to stop moving at eighty-five miles an hour. Autumn had distilled Baltimore's cloying summer heat to a pristine blue-sky wrap. In Tenth Ward, however, few people looked up long enough to notice.

"Hey, hey, watcha know." A bearded man in leather vest and tattoos leaned against the dojo's front window. He nudged his buddy. "Somebody's brought us lunch."

Vic Wright appeared in the studio's doorway. He was a former Lejeune drill sergeant and D.C. cop. Black and big. "Leave it alone, Calvin."

"What, I'm supposed to let this cupcake just waltz in here?"

"He's gonna own you, you don't watch out." Vic offered Matt his hand. "How're you doing, kid?"

"So-so."

Calvin demanded, "You telling me you know this guy?"

"Better than I want to know you." Vic motioned for Matt to follow him inside. "Back off, Calvin."

But the bearded guy followed Matt into the dojo making kissy sounds. "Hey, cupcake. I'm talking to you."

Matt nodded hello to several of the older students as he crossed the front room. He needed to focus on the man tracking him. But he could not get the battle after this one out of his head—the one with Trish. The one he was bound to lose.

The studio comprised two derelict stores connected by a broad hall. The front had been split into a shop for karate gear and a changing area. The changing area had lockers and bathrooms and a wall of mirrors where students could practice while waiting their turn on the mats. The entrance area and the changing room were packed with kids. The practice room took up the entire second store. A small viewing area was nestled against the east wall. Square sawdust cushions lined the other three walls, where students sat or knelt during instruction.

Vic looked up from where he led a morning class through their first routine. "Calvin, I'm telling you to let it go."

"What, a guy comes in, I'm not allowed to challenge?" Calvin had taken his styling tips from inside the pen. Shaved head on top, full beard covering a tree trunk of a neck. Shoulder tats. Three silver-and-turquoise rings on each hand. Matt saw in the side mirror how the rings formed a solid metal wall when the man formed a fist. The rings' outer surfaces were pitted and scarred. He tapped Matt in the back. Probing. "That's what you're here for, right? A challenge?"

Matt kept his face toward the practice room as he slipped off his shoes. The students waiting their turn clustered well back and watched the confrontation with knowing eyes.

Vic asked, "How long do you have?"

Matt straightened. "Couple of hours."

Calvin tapped his shoulder again. Harder. "What, he'll talk to you and not to me?"

Vic wore what he always did, black sweats with the sleeves cut out of the shirt. His face and shoulders were pockmarked, like he had met a barrage of hot metal, little gray pinpricks all over his dark skin. Matt had wondered about the scars but had never asked. Vic said, "Calvin, go grab a tamale from next door. Tell Carlos it's on me. Save yourself some pain."

But everybody was watching them now. Calvin's pride was on the line. "You know the rules. What am I saying? You *wrote* them."

The rules were simple. Anyone who stepped onto the tatami mats was open to challenge. Vic protected his younger charges. And he did not permit the advanced to prey upon beginners. His tactics were simple. If an unfair challenge was made, the contender first had to fight Vic. Otherwise, the studio ran by street rules: Be strong; be wise; survive.

There were mirrors in the studio as well, two of them. They flanked the small area for observers on the far wall and were easy to miss. One, however, offered a sideways warning to anyone stepping through the entrance. Matt had learned early to glance that way without moving his head. Which was how he saw Calvin's strike.

Calvin attacked the instant Matt's foot touched the woven tatami mat. He came in high, a jab for the point where Matt's skull met his spine. With the rings reinforcing Calvin's fist, the punch would have temporarily paralyzed Matt. But Matt responded as Vic had taught. Strike first, strike hard.

He spun and deflected the strike with his left forearm, and put his entire body into a single punch. Straight into the ribs over the guy's heart. The muscles and the flab were enough to keep Calvin's ribs from cracking. But his breath whooshed out in a fetid cloud. Calvin's eyes went unfocused as his heartbeat faltered.

"Here, let me help." Matt grabbed Calvin by his greasy beard. He kicked the guy behind his knees and flipped him down. Calvin landed hard on the nearest sawdust-filled cushion.

Matt held the guy's head down on the tatami for a minute, just staring him in the eye. Showing him there was more if he wanted it. "Comfy?"

Vic remained leaning against the doorway. "We all done here?"

Matt did not turn away until he was certain the fight was out of the guy. "I sure am."

"Right." Vic kicked off his sandals and stepped into the center of the room. "Give me a hand with the real cupcakes, why don't you."

Matt changed into rumpled sweats and took over the newbies. They were still wide-eyed over what they had just seen, and almost too eager. Matt walked them slowly through a stylized fighting routine called a kata, talking them down to relative calm.

Class over, Matt stepped into the changing area and toweled off. The bearded guy still sat where Matt had planted him, tracking Matt's every move. Matt took note and let it go. Tenth Ward attackers came in two sizes. Once they were bested, either they accepted him as one of their own, or they turned feral. This guy could go either way.

Vic obviously felt the same. Instead of ordering the current students off the floor and the next group on, he said, "Everybody find places around the wall."

Matt stood before the mirror and waited out the crush. He knew what was coming. Ordinarily he would have been thrilled. Today, however, he just marked time on fate's inescapable clock.

Vic continued, "This is Matt Kelly. Graduated yesterday from FLETSE, the new training school in Georgia for folks aimed at the high-octane world of ops. As in field operatives."

"A *fed*?" The bearded guy punched the cushion beside him in disgust. "You let a *fed* in here?"

"And before that he graduated from Tenth Ward. Just like you guys." Vic faced Matt and bowed. And attacked.

Some of the kids gasped. No wonder. Vic was a very beefy man and showing his age. But when Vic let loose, his fluidity was a wonder to behold. He feinted and kicked and jumped and kicked twice more before landing. Any of his moves could have been a killing stroke.

Vic allowed himself to unleash because he trusted Matt. Matt responded as Vic required, with equal ferocity.

When Matt had first started coming to the dojo, Vic's sparring partner had been a guy who had served in Vietnam with Vic. Matt had never seen a borderline maniac before then. The vet never said his name. If asked, Vic had always replied, "He's just an old buddy." The vet never spoke. Not a word. His silent glare totally freaked the uptown kids. But they all looked forward to his sporadic visits. This was why a lot of them came, so they could pretend that one day they'd wake up and possess that fanatic ferocity.

Matt had no idea what they said about him when he was away. He liked to pretend the sessions were no big thing, just a way to keep his timing. But he knew what it was like to sit on the sidelines and watch round-eyed as two guys went head-to-head. Like the movies had come to life.

Vic's synapses and muscles were aging. Matt adapted, slowing his own strikes a fraction, redirecting the explosive force of his kicks.

Until Vic hammered him. A kick out of nowhere. Smack on the chest where he had struck the bearded guy. Matt landed hard on the tatami.

When his eyes cleared, Vic was leaning over him. Vic did not ask if Matt was okay. Vic never asked that. Just, "You think maybe playtime is over now?"

Matt lay there until his heart returned to normal. The bearded guy chuckled softly, loving the sight of his foe laid out. But easing up as well. Vic's gaze flickered over to him, a glance that nobody in the room noticed except Matt. Matt, however, understood. The risk that Calvin would be waiting for him in the parking lot with a Sig on full automatic was gone.

Matt rose in stages. Letting his strength fully return. No way could he take a second one of those.

Their dance became edgier. The rage almost real.

Matt let Vic dominate the air. He stayed firmly planted on the ground. His chest ached with each breath. He held to defensive movements, gradually slowing, as though the chest punch was draining him. Which it was. His heart felt on fire.

Vic went up for a second chest kick. Matt made a double block with left knee and elbow, overprotecting his vulnerable point. And exposing himself to another attack in the process, which Vic had obviously expected because the kick was a feint. Vic pivoted and swung his *other* heel in a rotating kick aimed to take Matt out.

Only Matt's block was a feint as well.

He dropped to one hand and knee and swept Vic's other leg out from under him.

Vic tried to flip and roll from his fall. But Matt was there to pin him to the floor. He bladed his hand and chopped the exposed carotid artery. Stopping only when he made contact with sweaty skin.

Vic hammered the tatami with the flat of his hand. Set and match.

They stood. Bowed. Vic turned to the class. "He bettered me. How? Anybody?"

The kids were too shell-shocked to respond.

"Matt's greatest strength is his ability to hide everything about himself. He keeps everything deep down and reads the smallest signals and gestures. He uses them. But only when he's ready. Only when he's fully *charged*. Then he attacks, just lets the secret power rage up. Then it's over, and he goes back to being the bland little cupcake that is all the world ever sees."

Vic paused to breathe hard. His back was to Matt, and he did not see the impact his words were having. This was not praise. Not with Trish waiting. This was a conviction.

Vic went on, "Matt hides his force better than anybody I've ever met. He is like water. He flows around life, but there's nothing to see, nothing to notice, nothing to tell you what you're up against. You think you know him, but you only see the lie, the exterior. Which makes him impossible to read. A perfect opponent. Almost like he has no center at all."

The hospital released Matt for the funeral. Dr. Krishnamurti was reluctant to let Matt go. The doctor was the hospital's spokesperson and had enjoyed a lifetime's publicity in eleven days. Matt had seen him daily on the evening news. Dr. Krishnamurti had talked about Matt as if they were chums. Yes, Matt was doing as well as could be expected. Yes, of course, grief over the loss of his mother slowed the healing process. But Matt's concussion was completely gone. The burn on his temple was healing well and no grafts were planned. And the splinter driven into his thigh like a brick bullet had not severed tendons as first feared. Matt was attending twice-daily physical therapy sessions. Dr. Krishnamurti loved using Matt's first name. As long as the television lights stayed on, the guy yapped.

Dr. Krishnamurti wasn't much older than Matt and was still learning to hide his ego. His need to talk down to the world turned his every word and motion into bad theatrics. The nurses all played mute in his presence. Matt did not cross him until the doctor insisted on personally pushing his wheelchair to the front entrance. Midway across the front hall, Matt braked hard with his good leg and announced, "I'll take it from here."

"Sir, hospital regulations require—"

"Save it." Paul Kelly wore a dark suit and sunglasses and had not uttered a word since embracing his son upstairs. "If my son wants to walk, then he's walking."

The cameras were there beyond the entrance. Their lights turned the glass doors into polished shields. Matt could see nothing save the blinding illumination. He hesitated, but not because of the public attention. Moving through those doors meant accepting the challenge.

"You all right, boy?"

"Fine, sir."

"I can call back the pest with his chair."

"No. I'm good to go."

They passed through the entrance and met the barrage of sound. Police kept the journalists back, but not even the day's purpose could silence them here. The limo driver stood with the rear door open. Matt eased himself in, then slipped over so his father would not need to go around.

Sol Greene, his father's campaign manager and best friend, reached across the front seat and offered his hand. "Can't tell you how sorry I am, Matt."

They had seen one another almost every day. But this particular morning required a stiff formality. "Thanks, Sol."

"How are you feeling?"

"Better."

"She was a wonderful woman, Matt. We all miss her terribly." The day's somber mood settled onto Sol's face in timeworn creases. "You need anything?"

"I'm fine, thanks."

"Hospital food reminds me of stuff you clear out of the disposal. I should know. We've got a few minutes; we could stop—"

Paul Kelly said, "You heard the boy. He's fine."

"I was just asking, Paul."

"I don't want to deal with stops and strangers. Not today."

"Sure, sure, no problem."

"There will be all the food in the world once we get this over and done."

Sol said to the driver, "Let's go."

Matt was dressed in a dark suit and fresh shirt and gray tie. Everything had been brought to his hospital room by Sol Greene. Matt's first inkling of what lay ahead had come three days before. By then he had been more than ready to leave the hospital. The twice-daily face wraps, done to help speed the healing process and reduce the risk of scar tissue, were finally over. His leg wound was closed, the muscle strong enough for him to start using light weights in his physical therapy routine. Then Sol had shown up and asked him to stay. Not his father. Paul Kelly had paid his son perfunctory visits most days, but said little. Communication had never been easy between them. Sol had played his customary role of mediator and asked Matt to hang tight for three more days. No reason had been given because none had been required, which was good. His mother's absence had keened through the hospital corridor, a lament borne on electronic monitors and astringent odors. Matt had simply nodded acceptance and waited to be alone again.

The limo's interior hummed with a repressed energy. Paul Kelly pointed his sunglasses at the side window and idly tapped his fingers on the glass. Sol kept to his somber silence, his body swiveled partway around.

The tension heightened as they approached Mount Vernon Methodist. The street in front of the Peabody Music Academy was cordoned off and filled with press and news vans and satellite dishes and antennae and cameras. The media coverage was immense. SENATORIAL CANDIDATE LOSES WIFE LESS THAN A MONTH BEFORE THE ELECTION. SON EMERGES FROM HOSPITAL TO GO DIRECTLY TO HIS MOTHER'S FUNERAL. NO ARRESTS MADE. Matt could feel the headlines shaping in the air around his head as he emerged from the limo.

The granite church was blackened by two centuries of city soot. The arched entrance doors loomed before them. The church's interior was darkened by a future bereft of Megan Kelly and her talent for giving joy even to her conflicted men. The doorway framed a silent challenge so intense it crimped Matt's chest. Matt gritted his teeth and limped forward beside his father. He had failed her before. He would not fail her now. He would find his mother's killer and bring him down.

Inside, everything bore Sol's trademark professionalism. The press filed into the upstairs gallery. The church downstairs was packed. The choir sang. The pastor spoke. Sol rose and delivered a brief eulogy on behalf of the bereaved. Megan Kelly's numerous friends filled the church and sobbed. Even the pastor, Ian Reeves, a man his father disliked for reasons never expressed, wept from his chair on the dais.

When it was over, Matt rose and motioned one of the pallbearers aside. His body was one huge ache. The press thunked down the back stairs and piled outside for shots of the wounded kid, his scalded face framed by his mother's casket. Matt did his best to shut them out entirely. He walked forward with the grim determination of one whose quest was about to begin.

At the gravesite Matt stood to the right of his father. Though it hurt his leg to remain at attention, he took refuge in stonelike rigidity. The day was heavily overcast. A wintry wind drifted through the gathering. The cemetery was rimmed on two sides by a forest of hickory. Magnolia and dogwoods sprouted in careful abundance along the silent lanes. The heavy gloom heightened their flamboyant autumn colors.

Toward the end, Matt had to hold his father upright. Paul Kelly took it very hard as the pastor, his wife's dearest friend outside the family, closed the Book and took a step back. Matt's father had shown no emotion all day. But his famous control was shattered at the sight of his wife's body being lowered into the grave.

As he started to lead his father away, Matt spotted Trish on the other side of his mother's grave. She had come by the hospital several times. Her visits had been almost as strained as those with his father. As Matt gripped his father and headed back to the waiting limo, he felt anew the constant defeat from every beautiful woman who had ever dared love him.

A groan from his father was all it took to refocus his attention. There was room for only one concern now.

Matt dreaded what was bound to come next.

———

Detective Lucas D'Amico held to the crowd's edge and studied the perimeter. It was a cop's way of attending a funeral. Some perps got their jollies hanging out and seeing the carnage they wreaked on people's lives.

The papers were making a lot of noise over the murderer being from the right-wing fringe. On the surface it made sense. But D'Amico had his doubts. Still, the case was almost two weeks cold and they didn't have a decent lead to their names. Having the papers make noises about a freakoid hiding in the western hills took a lot of heat off the chief's head. So D'Amico kept his doubts to himself and followed the routine.

He watched the kid lead his father back to the line of black limos. Matt Kelly was limping worse now than when he had left the church. The wound on his left temple was healing, but the scab still looked parboiled. Even so, Matt Kelly remained a good-looking kid. He sure turned heads among the gathered women. He carried himself with a soldier's posture, kept his dad upright, and hid his own distress well.

Lucas D'Amico doubted anyone else could see how much it cost the kid to basically carry his old man down the path. D'Amico watched them closely and ditched them both as primary suspects. They hadn't been high on the list to begin with. Lucas D'Amico liked the way the kid looked after his old man, even when it cost him. The fact that two strong men were laid this low said a lot, as far as D'Amico was concerned.

D'Amico's own name had been good for some ribald comment when his own dad had been a cop and the Baltimore underworld had been ruled by two Neapolitan clans. But nobody had mentioned that to Lucas in years. Nowadays Baltimore's crime was high-profile and multiethnic. The Italians were still around, but they had to battle for turf with the Viets and the Haitians and the 'Ricans and the homeboys. Not to mention the gangbangers migrating up from northeast Washington.

The cops had changed as well. Few of the old clans were still on the force. Lucas D'Amico was the only third-generation cop working out of headquarters. When his old man had carried his gold badge into the front line, his best buddies were almost all from cop clans like his own. Irish, a few Polish, the occasional black. Tight. When his old man had caught a bullet, Lucas had supported his mom and been carried himself. It did him good, seeing these two, the old man sobbing hard and the kid limping but still supporting his father's weight.

Camera flashes and television lights framed the gray day. The pair of them leaving the grave site made for great news coverage. Not to mention how the unsolved murder had turned a local race into a national event. Lucas spotted the mayor, three city aldermen, the local Democratic congressman, and the lieutenant governor. A lot of muscle in the power world, watching the departing pair. Lucas studied some of the faces, saw the mix of sympathy and envy. He wondered with a cop's sense of irony which of them might be willing to sacrifice a family member for this sort of coverage.

His attention was caught then by a portly man holding back, watching the two men stagger toward the limo. He remembered the name — Sol Greene, a top political strategist and Kelly's campaign manager. D'Amico and his partner, now laid low by another chest infection, had interviewed the guy twice. Sol Greene wore the sort of slick suit favored by people who bought without looking at the bill. Inside-the-Beltway, Capitol-Hill glossy. But no amount of silk and starch could do anything about the guy himself. Sol Greene was a doughboy long past his sell-by date. Discolored, fleshy, nervous.

Lucas walked over. "Terrible thing."

Sol was so focused on the press and his candidate that he hadn't even noticed Lucas's approach. He glanced over but clearly couldn't make the face.

"Detective D'Amico."

"Oh. Right." Sol resumed his observation of Kelly's slow progress. "I've already talked to the cops."

"Sure. That was my partner and me. He's out with the flu."

"Right." Sol wasn't paying attention. Or he was, and trying hard not to show it. "You need something, call my office, why don't you?"

The guy watched father and son like a director offstage. His work was there on public display now. He couldn't do a thing but sweat — which he was doing. His features gleamed in the steel-gray afternoon. "You okay, Mr. Greene?"

"Do I look okay? The election's less than two weeks away." The portly man rubbed his forehead hard. "You caught the fringe dweller that did this to my candidate?"

"We're working on it."

"Yeah, well, work harder." Sol Greene did everything but snap his fingers. "Excuse me. I got to go speak to the mayor."

"Sure, pal. You do that." But the words were spoken too softly to carry, and only after Sol Greene stepped away.

———

As the mourners gathered, the press placed their house under siege. Sol organized a trestle table packed with food and drinks. The press ate and hung out in the narrow park running down the center of Eutaw Place, interviewing any guest willing to stand still.

Matt observed all this from the living room's front window. He stood at the periphery of the gathering, silent and watchful. Mourners patted him on the shoulder, spoke a few words, shook his hand, and moved on.

Matt spotted Vic Wright standing in the front yard, eating from a paper plate. He was talking with Detective D'Amico. Vic spotted Matt in the window. He gave a quick hand gesture. Vic had no interest in meeting these people. He just wanted Matt to know he was there.

Matt heard the guests behind him quietly discussing the case. Right-wing fringe, they said, the same verdict Matt had heard on the hospital television. Some fanatic sneaked down from the hills, did his worst, and vanished. Remember the Carolina manhunt a couple of years back, the army was brought in, the bomber's picture flashed on the nightly news, and the killer stayed on the loose for nine months? And the Baltimore cops don't even have a name. Matt gave no sign he heard them. He did not like having to use this gathering as a time to plot. But he had to move while he could.

Trish moved up alongside him. "Can I get you anything?"

In reply, Matt took the drink from her hand and set it down on the already crowded coffee table. She looked at him curiously but made no objection as he gripped her elbow and steered her through the crowd. He spotted Jack van Sant, the personal aide to his new boss at State, standing in a corner by himself. Matt's entire quest depended upon having a word with the man. But this had to be done first.

Now that he'd turned toward the room and the people, however, he was open to approach. Midway to the front door, the pastor who had given the benediction lodged himself in Matt's way. Ian Reeves nodded to Trish and asked, "How are you holding up, Matt?"

"Fine, sir."

"You don't look fine. You look distraught." Ian was fleshy and not the least bit handsome. Every part of him, from his lips to his wayward hair to his mud-colored eyes, seemed plucked from nature's Goodwill box and fitted together at random. All but his voice, which could deliver the straightest blow with such care and concern there was no pain. "I shall miss your mother. A very great deal."

The words were the day's simplest soliloquy and the only one that threatened to undo his control. Matt clenched his entire body and managed, "Thanks for what you had to say in church. Though I'm not sure how much I actually took in."

"To be honest, I didn't hear much of it myself." If Ian noticed Matt's tension, he gave no sign. "She was a great inspiration to a lonely guy in an ill-fitting collar. The one I could trust with what needed to remain not just secret, but unsaid."

Matt nodded and slipped around the man. He had to get outside before his resolve splintered and fell with all his unshed regret.

To Matt's relief, both the detective and Vic had departed. Matt led Trish down the front stairs and turned his back to the clustered journalists. "Thank you so much for coming."

Trish wore her long hair swept back from left to right. Matt considered it a California style, one that went with head flipping and feigned indifference. Which was what she did now. "You're sending me away?"

"Everything you said about me, every argument, every demand, they were all correct." The day's pressure was a balloon in his chest and gut. "How am I supposed to care for somebody when I don't even know who I am?"

Her hair was brown and blond, a few shades darker than his own, and her best feature. "Why does it take a tragedy for you to open up?"

He shook his head. He could probably come up with an answer, but the day did not hold enough room. "I have to go."

"Will you call me?"

"Probably not, Trish."

She leaned forward and kissed the unscarred side of his face. "Good-bye, Matt."

He watched her walk away. Then he turned and used the iron

railing to push himself up the stairs. His wounded leg was growing increasingly sore. Just then, however, he did not mind. The pain deafened him to regret's heartfelt moan and helped him focus on what was coming.

Sol Greene met him at the front door. "Your father needs you."

"Where is he?"

"In his office." Sol's worried expression told Matt all he needed to know. "At least, he was."

As Matt crossed the living room to his father's office, Jack van Sant stepped into his path. He had been serving as personal aide to the director of State Department Intelligence for two years, a job Matt had heard referred to as an acid bath.

Van Sant, however, seemed no worse for the wear. He was a former marine and bore the day with a stolid sense of duty. "The ambassador asked me to pass on his sincerest regrets, Matt."

"Thank you for coming, sir."

"No sirs in this game. Jack will do just fine."

"Please give the ambassador my best."

"Roger that. He told me to say you should take as much time as you need; report back when you're ready."

Even though he had plotted it out while still on his back in the hospital, Matt found it hard to shape the words. "That may not be happening."

"Say again?"

"I've been approached by the CIA."

Van Sant blinked slowly. "The ambassador will be sorry to hear that."

"I doubt he knows I exist." A slurred voice erupted from the next room. Sol Greene waved urgently. "If you'll excuse me, I think my father needs a hand."

Matt's father was handsome even when extremely drunk. A bottle of single malt stood on the wet desk blotter. Matt could smell the spilled liquor from the doorway. Beside the bottle stood a replica of Paul Kelly's newest development project, a nine-block section of downtown Baltimore. His business office in Camden Yards had a much larger mock-up in the boardroom. Matt ignored it. He had grown up being surrounded by renditions of his father's latest prize.

Paul Kelly was holding court. "I never planned to enter politics. But Sol claimed I was a natural and Megan thought it'd be fun. Right, Sol?"

"A natural." Sol moved up alongside his candidate but made no attempt to dislodge him from the crowd. Most of the others clustered around Paul Kelly held a glass in their hands. But Paul was the only one drinking. "Megan thought so too."

"'Course she did. What else is she gonna think when our in-house pro gives her the word?" Paul Kelly gave each word very careful work. Pretending he could hide his state from the gathering. "When I sold that company in Colorado, where was it? Can't remember. Isn't that a hoot? Bled for the sucker, lived it night and day for two years, can't remember where . . ."

"Vail, Pop." Matt stepped into the group. "It was your second—"

"Hotel. Sure, I remember. Finally got rid of that nightmare and started talking early retirement. How long ago was that. Six years, right?"

"Eight, Pop." His folks had returned to Baltimore the year Matt had completed undergraduate school and joined the Vail police. And been disowned in all but name by his father.

"What I said. My old buddy Sol was waiting to pounce. State legislature." He had trouble with that last word. "Megan loved the social side of politics. Right from the start. She would've taken Washington by storm, right, Sol?"

"She was made for the role," Sol agreed, very sad.

Paul Kelly hammered back the single malt. When his head lowered, he finally saw his son. The glazed expression tightened. Or perhaps it was just the balloon in Matt's gut. "How old are you, boy?"

"Thirty-one, Pop. Come on, how about—"

"Thirty-one years old. Graduated with honors from Illinois. Duke Law. Clerked for the state supreme court. My kid, the highflier."

Sol stepped in close. Used the voice he reserved for crucial political moments. "Paul, listen, why don't you let Matt help you upstairs. Have a rest."

The entire room watched Matt pry the glass from Paul Kelly's hand.

"I'm not done with that."

"Come on, Pop. Time to roll."

When Paul Kelly looked ready to argue, Sol said, "We're right down to the wire, you hear what I'm saying? Tomorrow you've got to be in top form."

This time Paul Kelly did not object as Matt guided him through the crowd, accompanied by sympathetic murmurs. Somebody patted Matt on his shoulder. Another commented on what a good son he was, what a strength and support to his dad. Especially given everything he had been through himself.

Sol followed them in worried silence. At the foot of the stairs, Matt said, "I can take it from here."

Sol looked worried. "You sure?"

Paul Kelly took a two-handed grip on the railing. "Didn't you know? My son's a cop. He's paid to handle drunks."

In the bedroom Matt continued to play the dutiful son. His mother would have wanted it. "Mind your father," she always said quietly, part admonition and part plea. Matt remained where he was. "Pop, don't you want to lie down?"

Paul Kelly was weaving about, struggling to focus on a room and a world where his wife no longer resided. "Still can't believe she left me like that."

Megan Kelly had truly loved her husband. The fractured relationship between father and son had caused her great pain. Matt watched his father meander toward the closet and heard in his mind the angry words that his father had so often shouted at her, the only times Matt had ever heard raised voices in the house. Whenever his father yelled, "Why do you always take his side?" Megan Kelly always replied in the same soft and forceful way: "Because he's your son."

Paul Kelly made it no farther than the corner cupboard. Matt became filled with the same gut-wrenching tension he had known since childhood, the internal Klaxon that shouted alarm. The cupboard was placed between closet and bathroom. Megan Kelly had packed it with memorabilia. Whoever had set the bomb had first come upstairs and shattered every pane of glass and stolen one item, Paul Kelly's Congressional Medal of Honor. The picture of President Ford pinning the medal to his father's uniform was gone too, but the police had that.

They had found a thumbprint on the frame and taken it in for identification, but had so far come up with nothing. The killer had gone through every room in the house. Stealing one thing, smashing another. Just one item from each room was missing. Matt knew all this because Sol had told him. Sol called the act demented, the Washington heavyweight shivering slightly as he described the mangled cabinet door. The police took it as routine. A lot of killers took trophies.

In Matt's room, the killer had smashed a clock and stolen an award. The clock had been a brass antique timepiece that once had sailed in a British privateer. The award had been for Matt's first full-contact win.

Paul Kelly asked the shattered cabinet, "Why did he steal the medal?"

"I don't know, Pop."

"I always wanted to throw the junk away. But Megan wouldn't let me." Paul Kelly weaved about and stared at his son. "My legacy."

Matt made his face like stone. Here it came.

"My *success* is my legacy. Not even Megan's murder is going to destroy that." He tried to bounce back and forth from one foot to the other. The boxer's stance was how he faced the microphone. It was a trademark move. The political cartoonists were already dressing him in a fighter's robe and gloves. Only now he was scarcely able to keep on his feet. "Know what my only failure is?"

Matt crossed the room. His father tried to shrug off Matt's hand. Matt kept hold and guided him to the bed. "Give me your jacket."

"My *son* had everything going for him. Not like me, clawing my way out of Fells Point with nothing but guts and empty pockets. What does my *son* do? Hides away in some bureaucratic D.C. tombstone." Paul Kelly fell onto the canopied bed. He dropped his tie to the floor. Kicked off his shoes. The thuds seemed timed to his words. "My son." *Clunk.* "The failure."

Matt scooped up the shoes and tie and carried them and the jacket to the walk-in closet. His leg was throbbing.

He froze in the doorway.

His father, oblivious, kept talking. "Couldn't even give him one of my companies to run. Oh no. I knew all along he wasn't man enough to take up the reins."

His mother's side of the closet was completely empty. Someone had come while Matt was still in the hospital and cleaned out all her things. Matt limped inside. A lingering trace of her scent was all that remained. The vacant space glared at him accusingly.

His father stained the shadowy room with his words. "Only reason he's alive today is because he let his own mother get killed."

Matt had long since stopped questioning why his father showed one face to the outside world and concealed another for moments like this. Before, Megan Kelly had always been there to stop him. A few words from her had always been enough.

His father continued tossing verbal daggers. Like he was slowly waking up to the fact that Megan was no longer around to shut him off.

One of Matt's secret gifts was an ability to copy almost anyone's voice. His mother had been the only one to ever know. Others had suspected—teachers, fellow students, a few opponents who had let him slip from dark corners because they thought they heard the law. Matt had never used it against his father. Perhaps there had been an unconscious dread of being discovered and labeled even more a fraud than his father already thought him to be.

Matt pressed the palms of both hands to his temples, clamping down hard enough to push back the pain. He tilted his head slightly and pitched his voice lower.

"Paul? That's enough now. Give it a rest." He used the voice of Uncle Sol, the balm applied to a thousand such episodes from his past. Speaking to the empty side of the closet. Recalling other times when his mother had been absent and Sol had stepped in. "How'd you like the press to hear you?"

Matt hung up the jacket and draped the tie around the hanger. He limped back into the bedroom. "Did you say something, Pop?"

His father lay on his back, staring mutely at the ceiling, blinking slowly. Nothing stopped his father like the threat of public disclosure.

There was a soft knock on the door. Sol Greene stepped inside. "Just thought I'd check and see how Megan's boys are doing."

"Everything's fine," Matt said. "Right, Pop?"

His father continued to study the ceiling in silence.

"I suppose we better let Paul rest, then." Sol Greene let Matt usher him from the room. "Call if you need anything, Paul."

Matt shut the bedroom door and followed Sol down the upstairs hallway. Sol stopped at the head of the stairs and said, "I thought I just heard the strangest thing."

"What's that?"

"Oh, it's nothing. Put it down to an awful day." Sol's face was slack with bitter regret. "Your limp is worse."

Matt patted his arm, liking Sol immensely for the unshed tears. "I'll be fine."

Matt wrenched himself free of the nightmare that had held him under with suffocating force. He rose gasping from his bed and waited for the panic to ease. It had been the same dream as in the hospital, made worse by his mother's funeral and the absence of painkillers. He was blown out of his body by the explosion. He became lost, never to find his way home again. Standing now in the center of his bedroom, Matt willed the sound of wind chimes to fade away.

He showered off the dread and entered a world filled with his mother's memory. The downstairs apartment had been her gift upon his graduation from Duke Law. Eight years earlier, Paul Kelly had sold his Vail hotel and moved back to Baltimore. Matt had felt no tie to his parents' hometown and had no desire to return. He had opted instead to join the local police force, which his father had fought tooth and nail. In the dark hours that came with any job, Matt knew he had selected the profession partly because it made his father's blood boil. What Matt had not expected was how much he had loved the work.

Two and a half years as a Vail cop, however, had convinced Matt he had found the right profession but the wrong job. The work and the people were both too restrictive. The best local cops had no interest in a world beyond the county's boundaries. So he had quit and gone back to school.

By his third year at Duke Law, Megan Kelly had resigned herself to her only son living in harm's way. Not even the year of clerking for a state supreme court justice had altered Matt's focus. Megan Kelly had

redone the ground-floor apartment in a surprisingly masculine manner, with muted colors and walnut wainscoting and Revolutionary War
prints. It was to be a place where her grown young man could return
between postings. A silent message of acceptance. Despite the perpetual loathing her husband might feel for Matt's chosen field.

That morning, narrow daylight greeted Matt as he fixed a solitary
breakfast. The rising sun managed a tight fit between the trees and the
carriage house, illuminating the void where his mother's presence used
to dwell.

Matt took his time dressing. He selected the same dark suit as yesterday, his best. Today he chose a striped shirt and woven silk tie. His
day was carefully mapped out, but the timing was down to others. He
listened to the house overhead awaken and gradually fill. Campaign
staff moved back and forth between the carriage house and upstairs,
careful not to look inside as they passed beside his kitchen window.
Matt could imagine the fumbling as they sought out new routines, ones
where Megan Kelly was no longer there to smooth and hug and smile
and care.

The call he was waiting for came at ten minutes past nine. "Matt,
this is Jack van Sant. Ambassador Walton would like to see you."

"Any time."

"Can you make it down here for eleven? Good. I'll pencil you in."

Matt went upstairs. This required passing the side wall. He had
seen it the previous day, but it had not registered. Today the crowd was
gone, the press chasing somebody else's tragedy. The hole had been
repaired with new brick, but the scar was still evident, as big as the
wound to his heart.

He used his key to let himself in the front door. Dark-suited power
brokers clustered in the living room and the front hall. Matt recognized
a deputy mayor, two aldermen, a banker, and one of Sol's D.C. staffers.
Another group gathered by the office doorway. His mother might be fresh
in the ground, but his father's business and campaign both rolled on.

Muted voices sounded from within his father's office as Sol slipped
through the door and gave the next group his professional hello. Matt
knew Sol was very aware of his presence. Other people were watching
as well. Matt took his time greeting the people he knew and accepting

their quiet condolences. In their faces Matt saw the same barely suppressed excitement he sensed in Sol Greene. These people gave special emphasis to their words. Matt was to make sure to tell his father Paul Kelly could call on them for anything. Matt accepted the words with somber thanks. He read the unspoken as clear as day. He felt the tension vibrating through the handshakes and words and electric gazes.

His father was going to the United States Senate.

The house's main floor was split in two, with a large central hallway joining the halves. To Matt's left was the living room, which opened into his father's office by way of sliding doors. A broad stairway faced the front door. To his right were the dining room and a small den which led to the side entrance. Everyone in the front hall and living room glanced at the door from time to time, but never for very long.

Matt walked down the hall. Behind the stairway and his father's office was the entrance to what had been his mother's study. The shut door stood as silent and forlorn as a wooden tombstone.

Matt entered the kitchen and poured himself a cup of coffee he did not want. He looked out over the carriage house and waited. He did not wait long.

Sol entered and shut the kitchen door behind him. "Can I have a word, Matt?"

"Sure."

"Let's step into the dining room, why don't we."

A long crack ran up the wall connected to the den. Matt turned so that his back was to that wall.

"How are you holding up, Matt?"

"All right. Tired."

"Yeah, I doubt any of us are sleeping all that well. You need a staffer to help with something—drive you around, do shopping—just say the word."

"Thanks, Sol." Sol had played the mediator for as long as Matt could remember. The giver of birthday gifts his father forgot. The man who escorted Megan Kelly at Matt's starring events. The one who helped them pack or unpack or cook or pretend that all was well in their travel-torn existence. "Is that what you wanted to see me about?"

"No." Sol Greene was the same age as Matt's father, fifty-eight, but looked ten years older. Maybe fifteen. And seriously out of shape. Sol's neck spilled down from a lumpish chin. Small ears seemed scarcely separated from his head. His hair was wispy and colorless. "I was wondering how long you were planning on staying around."

Matt gave no sign this was why he had come upstairs. "A few days more. Nobody is in that big a hurry to have me start active duty."

"Could you maybe take some sick leave?"

"I suppose I could."

"There's no good time to ask this. But the pressure, Matt, you wouldn't believe the strain we're working under."

"I hear the latest polls have you eight points up."

"These things can change overnight." Sol gave him a worried look, clearly not finding what he sought in Matt's expression. "You know how much your father wants this to happen."

Matt gave Sol the opening. "And Mom."

Sol expelled a tight sigh. "She would've been perfect. The Washington society queen."

They shared a moment's silent reflection. Then Sol added, "Matt, I know you said you weren't going to do anything for the campaign. And I respected that."

"But things have changed, right, Sol?"

"Matt, he's all alone out there. I can't stand at his side. It won't work. He's alone and he needs . . ."

"Me."

"It'd mean the world to him. I was sort of hoping he'd have said as much when you guys headed upstairs yesterday."

Matt hid his bitterness in his mug. "He was pretty tanked."

"Who could blame him, right?" The appeal was naked in Sol's gaze. And the excitement. *They could win.* "What do you say?"

Matt set his mug on the dining room table. "I want something in return."

Before he finished talking, Sol was already nodding his head. "This could be good for us, Matt."

"It's not about the campaign."

"No, no, of course not." Even so, his eyes scanned ballots not yet counted. "The police are handling it, though. We're getting periodic updates."

"The police don't have a lead to their names. I want to do what I can to keep them focused."

"When have I ever refused you anything? Of course I'll try and set this up."

"No, Sol. What is it you're always telling me? You get paid to win."

He liked that enough to smile. "You say that like a politician."

Matt headed for the door. "If you want me, you'll make this happen."

From the outside, the new *Baltimore Times* Building was a study in bland functionality. The downstairs lobby contained three alert security guards, a bas-relief of H. L. Mencken, and the intense young woman. "Mr. Kelly? Judy Leigh. Thanks for calling."

Judy Leigh was petite, intelligent, direct, and visibly pregnant. She was also frizzy-haired and dark-eyed and looked like she would never willingly waste a single minute. She asked, "Mind telling me how you got my name?"

"I followed your reports from my hospital bed."

"A number of other journalists covered the murder."

"That's right. They did."

She smiled acceptance of his compliment. "While you were still laid up, we were read the riot act by your father's campaign manager."

"Sol Greene."

"He basically told us if anybody came near you, we'd be permanently barred from further access for as long as your father is in politics."

"I'll handle Sol."

"To what end?"

Matt glanced to where a young photographer pretended not to listen.

Judy Leigh said, "Why don't you go set up in the dining room?"

The photographer replied, "I'm good to go right here. The light's—"

She applied more force. "Give us a minute."

When the photographer had sulked off, Matt said, "I'm offering you a permanent exclusive. Call me any time. If I can't respond, I'll tell you."

She made no attempt to mask her eagerness. "In exchange for?"

"One question now. Maybe more later."

She was shaking her head before he finished speaking. "I can't divulge confidential sources, Mr. Kelly."

"Matt."

"Confidences remain confidences for keeps, Mr. Kelly. Everything else is public record."

"Still, that's my request."

"I'll tell you what I can in good conscience and nothing more."

"That will have to do." He glanced at his watch. "I have to go into D.C. If you're free, you can interview me while I drive."

She did not need to think that one over very long. "Do we have time for a couple of photos before we hit the road?"

———

The longer Judy Leigh listened to this kid talk, the more convinced she was that Matt Kelly's greatest struggle was against himself. He could hardly have been more than a few years her junior, but that was how she thought of him. A tall, muscular, soft-spoken kid who desperately needed a mother's comfort.

Judy Leigh suspected she was having a hormonal attack. Her mother had warned her these things could rise up at any moment during her first pregnancy. And when they did, those chemical triggers would totally eradicate the myth that she had control over her body or her mind. Judy Leigh decided there was no other possible reason for this sudden urge to wrap her arms around a total stranger and let him weep the tears he was just begging to shed.

Even though Matt offered a lot less than she wanted, Judy definitely had a story. The day after they lay the lady to rest, the candidate's son speaks of the mother who was murdered on her own doorstep. The unsolved crime of the year, two weeks to the election, a *Baltimore Times* exclusive. But Matt Kelly was not a good interview. His responses were terse, his silences lengthy, his strain constant. A personal question shut him down entirely.

Even so, he made a valiant effort. His voice grated as if he were gargling broken glass. But he kept on. Mile after grueling mile down I-95. About how his parents had grown up Fells Point poor. Harbor town tough. Heavy drinking, brawling, crime ridden. His father's father had been a steelworker in the shipyards. His mother's mother had run a dive known for smugglers and gunfire. Those tidbits alone made the journey worthwhile. No such historical color emerged through Sol Greene's careful sanitization.

When Matt turned west on the 495 Beltway, Judy asked, "What can you tell me about the day?"

It was clear that the question worsened Matt's internal battle. Even so, she felt his loss with such severity she wanted to weep for him. He gave her a few terse sentences about the despicable. Then shut down entirely.

Judy let the silence hold until she felt it was safe to ask, "Describe for me your mother's finest quality."

"Joy." The poor kid didn't even need to think. "She looked at a person and saw only the best."

The way he choked on that last word, she knew he would not give her anything more. She watched him openly, framing what she would write.

There had been problems early in her pregnancy. The doctor had warned that they might not be able to have another child. She hoped she lived to see her baby boy grow up big and strong and make babies of his own. But if he ever had to talk about his own mother after her passing, she would lie content if he spoke of her with such love.

When Matt took the Rosslyn exit, Judy realized with genuine regret that their time was almost at an end. "Okay, Matt Kelly. What did you want to ask me?"

"You broke the story that right-wing fanatics were most likely behind the bomb."

"That's right."

"Where did you get the information?"

"I can't give you names."

"I understand."

"A senior member of the police force spoke to me in confidence. And it was confirmed by someone close to the mayor." Judy's emotions might have been raw and wounded from the drive, but she was still a reporter. She could see that the information gripped him hard. "Why is that important?"

"I'm not going to deal in hypotheticals." Matt Kelly went back to the cold and the steel. Which was remarkable. Matt compartmentalized better than a crime reporter. "If I have something definite, I'll give it to you."

"You're going after your mother's killer?" The thought gave her a double thrill. Stronger than the idea of an ongoing exclusive was the certainty that he was going to make Lexington Market sausage of whoever had targeted that lady.

Matt replied simply, "If I have something, it's yours."

"Okay." She looked around. The Key Bridge was straight ahead, Georgetown just beyond. "Where are you headed?"

"Work. I shouldn't be long."

"You're in intelligence, is that right? CIA?"

"State Department."

It meant nothing to her. Judy pointed at the Metro station sign. "I'll get out here and take the rails back."

"I can drive you if you want to wait."

"Thanks, but if I want to make the morning edition, I need to scoot. Besides, I can write on the way." She offered her hand. "Stay in touch, okay?"

———

Downtown Rosslyn could hardly have been any more faceless or bureaucratic or boring. Rosslyn possessed not a single decent after-hours gathering spot. People who worked in Rosslyn fled across the Key Bridge to Georgetown the first chance they got. The place was a tangle of six-lane streets, parking lots, and hostile high-rises. Workers emerging from the Metro never bothered to look up. The sky was as imprisoned as they were.

State Department Intelligence was housed in the Diplomatic Security Building on North Lynn. International ops occupied the eighteenth and nineteenth floors. National and international threat analysis covered floors four through nine. The Rewards for Justice program, the prize money for information leading to the capture of known terrorists, was on the eleventh. The Embassy Courier Service and the Anti-Terrorism Assistance Program were housed a half-mile away, but their directors all worked out of DSB-1.

Analysis and ops were both divided into military-intelligence type regions. This was hardly surprising, since Ambassador Walton was a former chief of Air Force Intelligence. The regions were not split based on size or population, but threat assessment level: Western Hemisphere Affairs, Africa, Middle East, Southeast Asia, China, and so forth. Just like the military.

DSB-1 was classed as "emergency essential," which was intel-speak for keeping fully trained specialists on duty 24/7. The State Department was known for having no esprit de corps. Most State staffers were viciously proud of their backstabbing skills. The exception was this building, most especially within ops. Ops was never referred to as operations. Ops was ops. This was where the work got done. Regional security officers were a clan unto themselves. They were posted abroad. They acted alone. They were responsible for the security of all American government nonmilitary establishments, including every embassy, in the entire world. Any terrorist threat that might be linked to one of these targets fell within their domain. They handled extremely dangerous assignments. Trust was essential. The same level of trust and camaraderie was true of CIA and defense ops as well. But State had one essential difference that had attracted Matt from the outset.

Size.

Defense devoured 85 percent of the nation's intel budget. And that did not count the quick-strike network farmed out to the Delta Force and Rangers. CIA ops numbered in the thousands or the tens of thousands if in-country locals were included.

State Intel ops was minuscule. The total number of operatives was a highly guarded secret. But they numbered less than five hundred. They were overworked and overstretched and liked it that way. They were known throughout the intel world as highly trained, extremely adaptable, trustworthy, and completely void of jealousy. They did not trade information. They gave it away. This made them unique among America's intel divisions. State ops scorned the intel battle over turf.

They were too small to do anything alone. They were out there, hanging in the wind, hoping for allies. They gave what they had whenever they had it. In return, they asked only that someone be on the other end of the phone when it came down to life or death.

The Diplomatic Security Building's exterior was as nondescript as modern architecture could achieve. Locals might pass the entrance a hundred thousand times and see nothing. No name denoted who worked inside. DSB-1 employees were taught to disengage whenever asked about what they did for a living, or where. The foyer was blank marble. Nobody entered without authorization. A uniformed sentry stood just inside the doors, there to accept all deliveries and field all unauthorized queries. The reception desk was tucked behind a battery of palms, so it was possible to see the bulletproof glass and armed guard and sensors only once a visitor was buzzed through the locked entrance. The employee turnstiles looked normal enough but required both a badge and a numeric code that changed weekly. Between the turnstiles and the elevators was a trophy wall of photographs. The most recent were of agents killed in Afghanistan and Iraq. In keeping with State Intel's low profile, there were no names.

Ambassador Walton ruled State Intel from a fiefdom the size of one city block, a series of carefully guarded offices covering the entire twenty-fourth floor. There was no nickname for either his penthouse or the man himself. He scared people that badly.

After retiring from the air force, Walton served as ambassador to two war-torn Central African states. He held the posts under two different presidents, one from each party. The people who had served under him came in only two sizes. Either they preferred being strapped to the business end of a howitzer to another day on his staff, or they considered him the finest man alive.

Ambassador Walton's personal office was severely functional. The only extravagance was a wall-sized view over the Potomac to the forests and spires of Georgetown University. The man himself was a human bulldog. Bald-headed, big-eared, face tightly scowled, his square teeth made to gnaw bones. A bark to match. "Kelly! Good to see you up and about. How's the leg?"

"Better, sir. Thank you for asking."

"Don't stand there at attention, son. I left our man's army nine years ago. No, the other seat's more comfortable. You want anything, coffee?"

"I'm good to go, sir."

"That'll be all, Jack." When the door clicked, Ambassador Walton demanded, "Now what's this Van Sant tells me about you and the CIA?"

"I'm afraid it's true, sir."

"Haven't you heard, Kelly? They eat their young over in Langley." When Matt did not respond, Walton added, "We're talking, so I assume there's room for discussion."

"I haven't completely made up my mind, sir."

"CIA is notorious for how they treat new recruits. They'll either work you to death or bury you in the subbasement reserved for rookies. You'll be one of a thousand greenies. Take it from me, son. You know the expression 'goat-rope'?"

"That's a new one, sir."

"Picked it up in the Gulf. You tie a herd of goats together, it still doesn't mean they're going where you want. What you're walking into over there, Kelly, is a glorified goat-rope. It's no fun being last in line when somebody's herding goats."

"They've promised me a move straight to the field, sir. Advance training, covert intel, black ops, the works. No time spent in analysis at all."

"Now you listen to me, Kelly. I've read your file and I like what I see. Smarts and combat skills and ambition. That's about as good a combination as I could ask for in somebody who doesn't have a day's experience in the field." Walton rose from his chair and began marching the length of his office. "I'm surrounded here by analyst clones. Ops and analysis are worlds apart. You served with the police, right?"

It was all in his file, but Kelly confirmed it anyway. "Twenty-nine months between university and law school."

"Where was that?"

"Vail. My father was running a hotel. I wanted some time off school and thought I'd give it a try. Loved the work but not the smallness of the job."

"Rule one in this town, Kelly. Wear your medals. An example. Your record says you took the SWAT training at the Denver academy. You came out where in your class?"

"First."

"Same again at FLETSE. Which brings us back to the subject at hand." He stabbed at the floor below his polished broughams. "These analyst clones don't have idea one why my field ops do what they do, where the risks lie, and what the take is. Analyst clones live and breathe the clock. They want reports on every meeting. They want details that don't mean diddly. Know why? Controlling the clock means controlling the man. It has nothing to do with getting the job done. I want a man in that outer office who knows how to spell results. What I want to know is, are you that man?"

Matt scoped out the view and held back. Not yet. But soon.

"You want ops, Kelly? I'll give you ops. But first I want to *train* you. Me. A two-year crash course in how to rule the world. After that, we'll set you up with DS in Paris. You know what we handle from the Paris embassy, son?"

"All of North Africa."

"Right the first time. Not to mention being an independent top gun at the snazziest address in Europe. Place de la Concorde. The mademoiselles will stop by after tea to take a number and stand in line. We'll have to bring you home for periodic blood transfusions."

The man's intensity was as strong as his aftershave. Matt asked, "You'll let me have this in writing?"

Two pale blue marbles gleamed with triumph. "That'll be your first task. Draft the orders for my signature. Two years to the day after you sign on as my adjutant. Do we have a deal?"

"Absolutely. But before I can start, I need help with a personal matter."

"Name it."

"I want to be assigned to the Baltimore field office."

Walton's shock was enough to send him back behind his desk and into his chair. "You'd rather die a slow death in a backwater Homeland Security field office than run with the big dogs? You're not talking sense, Kelly."

"Temporary assignment only. I have three weeks coming, sick and compassionate leave combined. That should do it."

"To what end?"

"They haven't found my mother's killer. A case like this, it'll never be declared cold, not officially. But the local cops are under growing pressure to deliver a suspect. They'll arrest a warm body, run him through the courts. Whatever the verdict, they can then claim they've done their job."

"Know this for a fact, do you?"

"I've seen it happen in Vail, sir."

"You want to make sure they stay honest."

"That's it in a nutshell, sir. I want the right man taken down. And I want to be there when it happens."

Walton pondered that. "I do this, you'll commit to two years with me, five in the field."

"Seven years for three weeks? That's—"

"That's a take it or leave it offer, Kelly." Walton saw the waver and started laying ground fire. "Let's see. Death of a senatorial candidate's wife, we must have an in-house division that could conceivably look into the issue."

"Office of Protective Intelligence Investigation," Matt supplied.

"Done your homework. Good. I like that. So what's your answer, son?"

"I accept, sir."

"That's my man." He hit the speaker button. "Jack, get in here."

"Sir."

"Jack van Sant's the guy you'll be replacing. Have him give you the ten-cent tour."

"If you don't mind, sir, I'd like to get things moving in Baltimore before close of business today."

"No problem with taking the fire to the enemy. Next time you're down is fine." He waved his aide forward. "Jack's office shares the same view as mine. Don't know how much time you'll have to enjoy it. Jack is off in two months to, where is it you're headed?"

"Baghdad, sir. Deputy Chief of Green Zone Security."

"Jack, cut this man some orders. He'll tell you what needs doing."

"Roger that, sir." He offered Matt his hand. "Good to have you on board, Kelly."

"You need anything, Jack is your man. But I want to be kept in the loop. Savvy?"

"Yes sir. Thank you."

"The only thanks I want from you is good work. And one more thing." Walton waved a warning finger. "Everything you've heard about me? It's all true. I'm a take-no-prisoners kind of boss. You do bad work, you'll be out so fast the revolving door will fan the entire twenty-four floors. You do good, you get the gold. We clear?"

"As crystal, sir."

"That is all, Kelly."

Detective Lucas D'Amico's morning started with a typical emergency. There had been a lot of those recently, most due to the fact that his wife was no longer around to help deal with their daughter. June had passed on fifteen months earlier. Lymphoma. An urgent call from head-quarters meant getting his daughter up before she was ready. Katy was twenty-three and the anchor of his world. She had a severe learning disability. Her developmental progress had been arrested at around age five. When everything went well, she was an angelic child. But Katy did not like having her routine disturbed. On days when work compressed their morning routines, Katy tended to have what his late wife called messes. With Katy, messes covered a lot of ground. But Lucas had finally gotten Katy dressed a second time and in the car and deposited at her school.

Ian Reeves, the pastor who ran the center, stepped from his office to greet the pair of them. He accepted Katy's hello-hug with, "Now isn't that grand."

Katy had two voices, an almost-whisper and a train-whistle shriek. Today it was soft and sad. "Katy's been a bad girl."

"I don't believe that for an instant. Not an angel like yourself." He patted her shoulder and guided her into the office. "Go and find Anne. I'm certain I heard her asking for your help."

When his daughter had disappeared, Lucas started in, "I know I'm still overdue for our talk. But things—"

"There's no need to be going on like that. Don't we all know the burdens you've been facing? How are you, old friend?"

"In a hurry."

"Then I'll walk you to your car." Ian waited until they were outside to say, "A place has opened at the home. I thought you should know."

"I don't want to put Katy away."

"That's precisely the reaction I'd be expecting from you. But you're alone now, and the child is a burden. And we're not talking about putting her away anywhere, which you well know. I hope we're friends enough for me to speak frankly."

"I don't know what I'd do without her," D'Amico replied.

"She wouldn't be moving to the other side of the world, Lucas. Just half a block down from here. You could walk over and see her every day of the week." Ian shut the car door and said through the open window, "Katy is alone a great deal more than some might call healthy."

Lucas had been raised within the Sacred Heart community, as tight a Catholic neighborhood as had existed in old Baltimore. Raised there, took communion there, schooled and churched there. But he had been married in the Methodist church on Mount Vernon Square. June had never asked him to convert, but the change had been a natural outcome of loving a woman who was far too good for the likes of him. His mother had thought otherwise and had noisily carried her shame to the grave. Lucas started his car and replied, "I'll think about what you've said."

———

Hannah Bernstein was the first female homicide chief in the city's history. She had been Lucas's boss for six months now. Word had it she might one day become the first female police commissioner. There was a lot of hostility within the department to Bernstein's advancement. Before she was known, she was marked.

Homicide was the most tightly knit team in the force and the worst division for any outsider to stake her territory. The work's finality and risk made for bonds that didn't sit well with outsiders, particularly those using the division to weasel their way higher. But for reasons D'Amico could not fully explain, he suspected Bernstein was something else entirely.

Though D'Amico came from generations of cops, he was not old school. He did not hold with those who were hostile to the idea of

Bernstein simply because she was a cop of the female variety. D'Amico ignored the grousing and did his own checking. He learned Bernstein had fought hard for Homicide and gained the slot against the wishes of both the chief and the mayor. When she arrived, Bernstein proved to be both ambitious and driven. She was abrasive, demanding, and pushed as hard as any male boss Lucas had ever known. Lucas was still not certain what he thought of Major Hannah Bernstein.

He knocked on the chief's door and entered. Bernstein did not look up from the file she had opened on her desk. "Have a seat. No, not there. Plant yourself in the corner."

Lucas pulled a chair over by the window, where he could see both the division chief and whoever was going to be roasted. "Who's on the firing line today?"

She responded with a question of her own. "You see today's paper?"

"No chance."

"They gave the local section's entire front page to an interview with the Kelly kid. The way he talked about his mother made me want to weep." She turned a page in the file. "Until I heard he was paying us a visit."

"Matt Kelly is here?"

"Downstairs." Bernstein slapped over another page. "This had better not be somebody's twisted idea of humor."

"Sorry, Chief. I'm not following."

She continued to peruse the Kelly casebook. "How's Clarence doing?"

Clarence Bledsoe was D'Amico's partner. "Worse. The doctors are talking pneumonia."

"You have actually seen him?"

"Yes, Chief. I visited my partner. He's not shirking."

"Just asking." Bernstein was in her late forties and was very attractive in a sharply angled manner. Her hair was going prematurely gray, but this only added to her allure as far as D'Amico was concerned. She tended to wear business suits of the mix-and-match variety, all of them high quality. Today it was charcoal and navy and tight enough to show the lady spent some serious time in the gym. "How long has Clarence been off, a week?"

"Five days. And he is very sick."

"We're understaffed, as you well know. What does the doctor say?"

"Give it a rest."

She came up for a glare.

"You asked what the doctor said. I'm telling you. Rest."

"Don't get smart with me." She returned her attention to the file. "Either the Kelly husband or wife play around?"

"Not that I've uncovered. Megan Kelly was strong in the Mount Vernon church."

She studied him. "That's where you go, right? Is there a conflict of interest here?"

"She and June were pals. I knew her enough to say hello. End of story." When Bernstein resumed her reading, D'Amico added, "At the funeral I had a word with Vic Wright, runs a full-contact karate joint in Tenth Ward. Used to do patrol with D.C. cops. Vic had a good word for Matt Kelly."

"That means precisely nothing to me. Not this morning." She picked up the phone, punched a number, and said, "Okay. Send the Kelly kid up. And tell Dorcas I'm ready for her."

When she slammed the phone down, D'Amico asked, "Why is Kelly here to see you and not me?"

"The things I have to put up with in this job, you would not believe. I have had calls from the mayor, the chief, and the governor's office. I'm surprised the president of the United States hasn't buzzed me on this little item." At a knock on the door, Bernstein barked, "Inside!"

"Major Bernstein?"

"That's right." She pointed at a spot on the floor directly in front of her desk. Her gaze remained upon the case file. "You already know Detective D'Amico."

Kelly limped slightly as he approached the desk. Lucas found himself straightening slightly. Even in his wounded state, the kid carried a high-octane energy. Tension and something more. Which was remarkable. Because all he showed the world was bland.

Matt Kelly was just as Lucas remembered, only more so. He stood before the desk, parade rest. Up close the burn on his temple was redder, angrier. The way his short blond hair had been shaved away from the burn made his mild expression even more bizarre. His green eyes were unclouded, his chin slightly cleft, his features carved from stone-colored flesh. Whatever Kelly did to stay in shape, he did it a lot.

Bernstein did not offer Kelly a chair. "I'm seeing you because I have been so ordered. But I have no intention of making room within my department for the feds' poster boy."

D'Amico caught the kid's flash of irritation, there and gone so fast it might never have happened. Matt Kelly didn't like any reference to his looks. Which was odd enough for D'Amico to make a mental note.

Bernstein leaned back in her chair. Crossed her arms. Gave him a full-on glare. The kid held up well. He remained at parade rest, staring at a point just above the major's forehead. Ready to wait forever.

The standoff was interrupted by a knock on the door. "Come!"

Dorcas entered. "You wanted to see me, Chief?"

"Matt Kelly, meet Dorcas Schaeffer. Dorcas handles our records from the floor below this one." To Dorcas, "You find him a spot?"

"All set up." Dorcas was attractive in a warm and motherly fashion. Dark red hair tumbled over her shoulders. Fine bones. Well-padded frame. Merry eyes with more than a hint of steel. Dorcas was married to a sergeant in the Western district. But this did not keep her from giving the kid a speculative once-over. "You'll like it down there, Kelly. No phone, no window, everybody ordered to ignore you except me."

Bernstein told Dorcas, "Go see about getting Kelly a temporary pass." When she departed, Bernstein went on, "As far as the outside world is concerned, that corner of Records is now officially part of Homicide. Complain all you like. But that's as close as you're coming to my team."

Matt Kelly maintained a bland calmness. But he also did not give ground. "What was the right-wing extremist claim based on?"

Bernstein turned up the flame. "You're questioning a police investigation?"

"The press received this information from two sources. I know that much. One was a deputy mayor, right? The other a senior officer within the police force."

Bernstein hated anybody taking the offensive in her office. "How *dare* you suggest I should divulge confidential sources in an ongoing investigation!"

"All I want to know is, is this normal procedure? To feed the press such information before a suspect is actually identified?"

She stared at him. D'Amico was intrigued as well. Other than the scarred temple, the kid actually seemed fire resistant. Bernstein demanded, "Who *are* you?"

The kid gave her question no attention whatsoever. "Would the press normally hear such information from two senior sources?"

D'Amico decided it was time to step in. "Nothing is normal about this case. We have a candidate for the United States Senate targeted four weeks before the election."

Matt shook his head. "I don't think so."

D'Amico was intrigued. "Exactly what part of this investigation are you questioning?"

Bernstein liked losing control of the flow even less. "This is not the issue under discussion here!"

Matt Kelly remained not so much calm as Teflon-coated. "I am asking how right-wing extremists got identified. And I am wondering whether my father was the intended victim."

Bernstein leveled her finger across the desk. "You. Out."

"All I want to know is what evidence—"

"Now."

When Matt Kelly had departed, she said to the door, "Do you believe this kid?"

"He was asking some good questions, Chief."

"He's a *fed*."

"Kelly's right. There's no hard evidence to suggest any fanatic was behind it."

She did not give him the argument he half-expected. Instead, "You know how it goes the same as me. We don't have a suspect, so the guys taking public heat choose whichever option suits their purposes and let it slip to their connection with the press."

"Just the same." D'Amico was staring at where Kelly had stood. "Did you see where Kelly graduated first in his class at the Colorado Police Academy?"

Bernstein hesitated in the process of turning the page. "Yes."

"CPA is where we send our TAC team for training." TAC was what the Baltimore police called their SWAT team. "Duke Law with honors. Clerked for a state supreme court justice. And he commanded the color guard at the FLETSE rollout. This kid is something."

"That changes nothing. He's fed, he's a member of the victim's family, and he is officially not welcome." She signed a worksheet and opened her next file. "Your job is to find a way for us to show him the door."

"Chief—"

Bernstein started on another file. "You've got two days."

Matt shared the elevator with a pair of homicide detectives. The cops gave him a smirking inspection, probably checking for new burns. Matt responded with his standard calm and glanced at his watch. Waiting for the chief's summons had put him very late for the day's political event. His father would be livid. Matt pretended not to hear the detectives' quiet laughter as he exited at lobby level. He had to find some way around Bernstein and her banishment.

Dorcas Schaeffer and a female cop stood by the guard's station as he approached. The guard was big-boned and overweight and street-scarred. "This the fed you were telling me about?"

"Matt Kelly."

"Okay, Kelly. Step on that yellow line there so I can take your photo." As Matt moved over, the guard asked Dorcas, "Two weeks do?"

"Bernstein says he won't be around long enough to print and tag."

The female cop stood well back, watching him intently. Jet-black hair and eyes contrasted sharply with pale skin and lips only a shade warmer. Her hair was impatiently short, her beauty balanced with no-nonsense directness. Her nametag read "Morales."

Matt asked, "Do I know you?"

She and Dorcas exchanged glances. "Not exactly."

Dorcas said, "Matt Kelly, Connie Morales."

The guard had an expression from beyond time and a voice to match. "You take a bullet, Kelly?"

"Bomb fragment."

"Shotgun's what put me down here, riding desk. Just another place to count down the days 'til I pull my pin."

Something in the guard's words pinched Connie Morales's face up tight. She said to Matt, "More likely you got hit by part of that brick wall."

Matt swallowed hard. "You were there?"

"Second on the scene." Connie Morales had a Latino's almond eyes and pronounced cheekbones, but her English was mid-Atlantic Anglo. "I'm sorry about your mother."

For the first time that day, Matt had to struggle to maintain his facade. "I need to ask you some questions."

"I don't think so."

The guard broke in, "You were a cop; Dorcas got that right?"

"Two years."

Dorcas asked, "What, you didn't like the hours?"

"I loved everything about police work. From day one I was always headed for something in this field."

A response flickered down deep in Connie Morales's dark gaze. The guard said, "So now you're a fibbie."

"State Department Intelligence."

"Never heard of that one." The guard withdrew the pass from the laminating machine, checked the edges, pulled a neck-cord from a box, and handed both over. "You're good to go, Kelly."

"Here's the deal," Dorcas said. "Chief Bernstein wants you out."

"I'd have thought the Baltimore police department would be happy to have federal support in a case that's growing colder by the day."

The guard actually laughed. "Man, are you ever new."

Dorcas pointed at the ceiling overhead. "Records is on sixth. You're assigned an empty cubicle for as long as you care to park yourself. Wear your pass at all times. And stay out of Homicide."

Before him, the metal detector gaped like the entrance to purgatory. Matt made a process of threading the cord through his pass. "Is there a gym around here?"

The guard replied, "The one upstairs ain't nothing to speak of. Free weights and bad air is all. What you looking for?"

"Leg machines."

"Take a left out the doors and go up two blocks to Education and

Training. ENT used to be out by the Ravens camp. They moved it downtown last year, gave us new space for prints and processing. Gym there's real nice. The TAC officers use it all the time."

"Thanks." Matt saw the rejection in the female cop's gaze, but had to ask anyway. "Could I just talk to you about—"

"Soon as Chief Bernstein gives the okay." Her voice contained a thousand-pound weight, impossible to shift. "Happy to oblige."

———

Matt left the parking lot across from police headquarters and headed for the decrepit waterfront sector known as Harbortown. His car was a BMW 750i, seven years old with less than twelve thousand miles on the clock. When Matt's father had started his campaign for the United States Senate the previous spring, he had asked Matt's mother to get rid of her Beemer and buy something American. This from a man who had just spent three hundred thousand dollars on a campaign bus. Matt knew because his mother had told him. Megan Kelly had given her beloved Beemer to her son. When Matt's father had complained, Megan told him that she had sold it. Which she had: for a dollar.

Domino Sugar was the sole survivor of what once had been a waterfront complex producing goods and money three shifts a day. "Sweet Times," Baltimore had called the 1940s. American Sugar's first refinery had anchored the Patapsco River industrial estate. Farther north had risen Bethlehem Steel's largest mill. The Martin company took that steel and rolled out fourteen fighter planes a day. They both competed for labor with the Baltimore shipyards, which in their heyday employed one hundred and thirty thousand people. Beyond them rose McCormick's drying kilns. Matt's mother used to talk about how the spices woke her every morning the wind blew off the bay. Now Matt drove through a cemetery of lost industrial might.

Domino Sugar was a stubborn monolith surrounded by steel relics and weed-infested shadows. When Matt pulled up, his father was exiting a warehouse as big as an airplane hangar. Paul Kelly shook hands with hard, solid people who punched the clock for a living. Matt stationed himself across the voluminous parking lot next to the campaign entourage and waited.

Paul Kelly walked over, waved to the last departing official, then said around his smile, "This is how you live up to your end of a bargain?"

"I got held up at police headquarters, Pop. I'm sorry."

"We're not in the apologies business. This is about *winning*. You've heard that word before, right?"

Sol hovered by his candidate's side. "Steady, Paul, it's no big deal."

Paul Kelly kept aim on his son. "One event per day. Your terms, not mine or Sol's. Yours. And the event had to be in Baltimore's four counties region. So we line you up for high-profile events, places we expect national coverage. Not only do you show up late, but I'm confronted this morning with press Sol did *not* authorize."

Matt did not bother to hide his surprise. "The paper wrote something?"

Sol looked extremely uncomfortable. "They gave you the entire front page of the local section. You haven't seen it?"

"I figured it was a wash. The reporter didn't take a single note the entire time we talked."

"She probably taped." Sol was not concerned with the mechanics. "Matt, it's important that everything to do with the press go through me."

"What did she write?"

"What . . . It was mostly about your mother. Well written, actually."

"I don't understand. You're giving me a hard time over a good article?"

Paul Kelly closed the distance between himself and his son. "Your mother wanted us to *win*. That's what we're talking about here."

"Paul, come on." Sol tugged futilely on the candidate's sleeve. "We're attracting the wrong sort of attention."

Matt asked softly, "Did one of your cronies in the mayor's office plant the story about right-wing fanatics setting the bomb?"

The skin around the candidate's eyes and mouth tightened to parchment. "We've come back from six points behind to eight ahead. Do you have any idea how important that is?"

"Absolutely, Pop." Matt took slim pleasure in how his voice revealed none of the emotions roiling beneath the surface. "I rank that one notch below finding out who actually killed my mother."

Officer Consuela Morales did not sign out a car because she needed wheels. She took the car because she needed to remind herself she was still a cop. No matter what the sergeant said or the lieutenant thought. At least she was a cop until she handed in her badge. Which, given the world's current state, might well be tomorrow.

The garage's duty officer looked like he wanted to deny her the ride. He knew, of course. All of Division One knew. She had dissed the lieutenant and was a marked target. But her record was too clean for the lieutenant, a prehistoric relic with a bad case of the grabbies, to fire her outright.

So Connie was reduced to taking what she thought of as the AA job route. One day at a time. This on a job she had formerly considered her one and only.

The duty officer refused to meet her eye as he shoved the clipboard through the cage. "Sign at the bottom."

Connie saw the car she'd been assigned and wanted to argue. But she held back. She had become extremely good at stifling rage. She caught the keys he tossed at her and stomped away.

The black Chevy Cavalier was eight years old and universally loathed as the division's worst ride. The car was filthy and normally left to rot in the basement's back slot unless called out for undercover. The duty officer did not glance over as she burned rubber up the ramp and did a four-wheel skid onto the street.

Connie drove through the dismal quarter known as Downtown and headed for the medical examiner's office. Whenever she could, Dorcas Schaeffer gave Connie files to deliver. These days, it was her only official ticket to get outside, at least for a few minutes. Connie handed the files to the ME receptionist, then meandered back uptown. She studied the dilapidated structures and the ruined lives outside the various soup kitchens and dollar shops. Taking her time, growing increasingly bitter as she pretended to be a cop.

Connie pulled into a cop slot in front of the new Education and Training Building. Upstairs, Connie dropped off more case files and logged in three fingerprint requests, all basic non-officer drone work. Anything to keep her outside the division building a little longer. This enforced lethargy was killing her inch by inch. She had joined the force for action. If not action, then at least forward motion. These days, each shift was ten years long.

Dorcas Schaeffer was doing her best to get Connie a transfer. But Connie was a rookie cop with less than a year on the clock. Her allies in Division One were too worried about their own jobs to stick their necks out for a rookie. What a records clerk could do in the face of a lieutenant with a death grudge was anybody's guess.

Connie passed by the gym on her way back to the car. The place was open to all officers but used mostly by the high-octane TAC squads. Baltimore PD did not use the term SWAT. TAC stood for Tactical Unit. TAC included QRT, for Quick Response Team, Baltimore's equivalent of SWAT. TAC also included K-9, bomb squad, mounted police, riot control, and emergency evac. Connie had lusted after an assignment to TAC since day one. TAC also liaised with Homeland Security, the only division to openly flout the commissioner's directive to block out the feds. Connie assumed the ongoing feud between senior officers and the feds was the same male hyper-ego garbage that was basically shutting down her career. It was all the reason she needed to want things to take a different route.

The gym had a waist-high glass wall fronting the hall. ENT clerks called it Steroid Alley for the TAC guys who strutted in loose tank tops and cutoff sweats. Two female clerks walking ahead of Connie stared through the glass and hummed appreciatively at what they saw.

This time of day, the gym was empty save for two overweight recruits training hard for their upcoming physicals. And over to the other side, all by himself, was the federal agent Connie had met that morning.

Matt Kelly worked a leg machine and fought a whole world of pain. His left thigh was wrapped in a white bandage, but the muscle to either side writhed in time to his face as he pumped and released. He worked the one leg with maybe sixty pounds of weight and gasped through each extension. His sweatshirt was drenched almost black. He finished the reps and lay back on the bench, chest pumping.

These days, Connie would have loved to hate all men. When she lay awake at night raging at life's injustice, the temptation bit at her brain with the force of a superheated drill. She did not give in only because of her father, a man she admired above all others. He had pointed out in his mildest voice that the lieutenant would then have won inside as well as out.

Matt Kelly began another set of reps with his damaged leg. Even with his temple burned and mouth gaping and chest heaving, the guy was incredibly handsome. He seemed boy and man in equal measure, with a remarkable air of fragility about his muscled frame. And so clean-cut he squeaked.

Not to mention the newspaper article Dorcas had shown her after Kelly had left, the one mostly about his mother. The article had left Connie wanting to weep, something she hadn't done in years. Not on the outside, anyway.

Connie stood in the hall and debated. The smartest thing would have been to walk on, get in her car, drive back to Division One, and grit her teeth through the rest of the day.

She pushed open the door. "Yo, Kelly."

He swiveled his head on the padded bench. The guy was so blasted from his workout he could not place her. Which she liked, in a slightly wacky way. Connie loathed how men flayed her with their gazes, as though they could claim her through intensity of looks alone. She said, "You drive over from headquarters?"

He gasped, "Walked."

"Go shower down; I'll give you a ride back. Long as you don't ask about what I can't answer." She shut the door and strode down the hall, smiling at nothing. Definitely a bad idea, involving herself in a feud between the homicide chief and a fed. Which was reason enough to go for it.

———

Matt massaged his sore leg because it gave him something to do. The police officer next to him was a beautiful enigma. She seemed friendly but emanated a tension as strong as an electrified fence. "Why won't you talk about the incident?"

"You were a cop. You know the rules. It's against the law to discuss an ongoing police investigation with an outsider."

"I'm not . . ." Matt frowned at a stench rising from the floorboards. "What is that smell?"

"Couldn't tell you. Probably something vile." Connie was driving slow enough to look over. "How's the leg?"

"Better. I think I smell exhaust fumes."

"Could be. This car was born bad and grew worse."

"Why don't you get another one?"

"Gee, Skippy. I never thought of that." She ground the steering wheel between her fists. "So you're a cop who went over to the feds."

"Law school first." They were driving pockmarked streets lined with buildings soot-washed of color. "Does it always take this long to drive to headquarters?"

Even the simplest question twisted her features. "So sorry. I didn't realize you were fired up to get back and ride an empty desk."

"I'm not."

"Then relax." She took a left. Matt was increasingly certain she was driving away from both the waterfront and headquarters. "So what's it like working for the feds?"

"I have no idea. I just finished my training."

"Fresh caught." She turned another corner and doubled back. "Should've known. You have that raw look. Especially on your left temple."

"Cute."

"Was that a smile, Skippy?"

"My name is Matt."

"I know . . ." Connie lifted her radio and listened intently.

To Matt the radio gave off nothing except verbal static. He could understand nothing. "What's going on?"

"Probably nothing," she replied and thumbed the volume control.

A woman's voice rattled the tinny speaker. "One Baker forty-two, respond to base."

Connie said, "Baker is day shift. That's dispatch for Division One, my area. The dispatcher is trying to raise a car that's not—"

"One Baker forty-two, respond."

Connie slowed by lifting her foot off the gas. "Probably snoozing off a long lunch in some alley."

A new sound came from the radio, a fierce electronic alarm.

"Simulcast," Connie said. "Alert tone. Wake the guy up."

Matt asked, "Can you tell me what's going on?"

"I thought you were a cop."

The dispatcher repeated, "One Baker forty-two. Come in."

Matt said, "I was the youngest rookie in a village force. The closest I got to being a real cop was hauling drunks out of après-ski bars. Or sitting behind a desk listening to *other* cops make a drug bust. You can't imagine how that felt."

Connie looked at him, her eyes open wounds. "You'd be surprised."

A new voice came over the radio, a woman but deep enough for a man. "KGA. Where'd you last have Baker forty-two?"

"That's the duty sergeant," Connie said. She braked hard and swerved to the curb. A truck hugging their rear squealed and blasted the horn. Connie seemed not to hear.

Dispatch replied, "Baker forty-two last called in at fifteen-fifteen, doing business checks in the six hundred block of Stiles."

"That's Little Italy," Connie said and keyed her mike. "Dispatch, this is one Baker thirty-six. I'm three minutes out. Over."

Dispatch called, "Any officer in contact with one Baker forty-two?"

When there was no response, Connie said, "Dispatch, this is one Baker thirty-six requesting point. Over."

"Roger that, one Baker thirty-six. Confirm you are point."

"Thirty-six out." Connie gunned the motor and peeled away from the curb. "All *right!*"

"What's happening?"

"I get to be a cop." She fiddled under the seat and brought out the portable light. "Clamp that to the dash."

Matt studied the lovely face, saw pain that did not diminish with her new animation. She drove one-handed, holding the radio with her other as the dispatch repeated her request for one forty-two to come back. "Please, please, don't answer."

"You want him to be in trouble?"

"No, Skippy. I want to be a cop. Just for five minutes."

Dispatch: "One Baker thirty-six, what's your twenty?"

Connie answered, "Turning off Pratt, Dispatch. I'm coming ten-twenty-three. Will advise."

They both heard it at the same instant. To Matt it sounded like banging on a metal door. Realization struck only because Connie ignited. She hammered down the gas pedal so hard her leg locked from hip to ankle. She shouted into her radio, "Shots fired! Shots fired!"

They entered Little Italy at warp nine. The Cavalier was not made for such speeds. It groaned and rocked hard enough to rattle Matt's teeth. Connie clipped a bakery van parked illegally on a blind corner, then skidded through the turn.

And took a direct hit.

The windscreen shattered before Matt even heard the gunfire. The sudden webbing cost Connie her vision. She slammed both feet onto the brakes. Matt heard the second round of gunfire and felt the hood hammered by metallic fists. Then their right-front tire went down. The car veered left, jumped an unseen curb, and crashed through a store-front window.

"Get out! Get out!" Connie smashed open her door, flipped and rolled. Matt dived out his side as another drumroll struck the trunk. They scrambled under the car. "Are you hit?"

"No."

Connie shouted into her radio, "This is one Baker thirty-six, I'm taking fire!"

It sounded to Matt like a dozen voices were all trying to scream through the radio at once. The radio garbled and popped until dispatch shrilled, "This is general twenty-three! Officer taking fire in the vicinity of Pratt and Stiles!"

"Over here, Skippy." To his surprise, Connie was talking softly now. And smiling. She waved him toward the side wall. Matt winced as metallic hail tracked his progress under the car. "You okay?"

"I think—"

Dispatch said, "All officers are advised to keep this frequency free. One Baker thirty-six, report your status."

She looked around and said to Matt, "I am *never* going to live this down." She keyed the radio and reported, "One Baker thirty-six. Dispatch, I'm in the front window of a lingerie shop on Stiles."

Matt's heart thundered so loud it was hard to hear the gunfire. His hands and knees were scarred by glass shards. He was coated in dust and debris. His throat was so dry he couldn't swallow. And the lady was *laughing*.

More bullets hammered the trunk. *Bam-bam-bam*. Matt thought the shots were coming from two different directions. But it might have been twenty.

Only then did he hear the women screaming from the back of the store.

Connie slid forward on her belly, scouted out the shattered front window, then came back and reported, "One Baker thirty-six. Dispatch, I spot two shooters. One is in the front door of Patrino's Bank on the corner of Stiles and Exeter. The other is in the parking lot—" She paused calmly as metal rained down, and then continued, "Shooter two is in the parking lot across Exeter."

"Roger that, one Baker thirty-six. Any sign of the other officer?"

Connie replied, "One Baker thirty-six, we have an officer down. I repeat, officer down. He's huddled in a doorway across from me."

The duty sergeant came over the radio, roaring now. "Where's my backup?"

The shooter was angling now, driving them away from the window. Matt compressed himself more tightly up against the wall. And against Connie. To his right a beheaded mannequin smiled beguilingly. He asked, "Can you give me a backup piece?"

"Negative." She flinched as their space was raked by fire. "You're a civilian ride-along, Skippy. Move back into the store."

"You just said it yourself. You have an officer in trouble." The only reason he stayed calm was the coolness he heard in her voice. "Give me your backup. I'll lay down cover fire."

In response, she yelled out, "Yo, Jamie. You okay?"

A faint voice called back, "Leaking from the shoulder. They clipped my radio."

"Hang in there! Help's on the way."

"I got their car; they're not going anywhere except on foot. I'm keeping them pinned, but I'm running low."

"Right with you." She listened a moment. To Matt the sirens sounded a hundred miles away and crawling. She flipped onto her back, reached down, and unstrapped a lady's-size Remington from her ankle. "This thing is accurate to a distance of about four inches."

"All I'm doing is making noise." Matt checked the rounds. "Just tell me when and where."

Connie was already crawling forward and answered him with ice-bound intensity. "Bank entrance on the corner to your left. On my mark."

He scrambled up until he was pressed in tight between the wall and her. He could smell the fresh soap in her hair. "Roger that."

Connie gathered herself for the sprint. "Jamie! Aim for the driver!"

"Check."

"Now!" She catapulted up and roared across the street.

Matt stuck his head and shoulder out into plain view, intending to confuse the shooters with two suddenly visible targets. The bank was a strictly local affair, an ancient stone low-rise crammed tight between row houses. Matt took aim at the shadows inside the entrance and fired. The police officer was pinned into a shallow doorway across the street and one house back. One glance was enough to know the man was hit. Matt fired according to procedure. *Bam-bam*, pause, *bam-bam*, pause. The would-be robbers ripped through automatic-fire clips. Across the way the wounded police officer fired steadily.

Just as Connie made the road's opposite side, she faltered slightly and tripped over the curb. She fell into the doorway beside the other cop.

"Connie!"

"I'm good." But the sound was weak and the shots were constant, raining down on their doorway. And the sirens did not seem any closer at all.

Matt clicked on an empty chamber. He dropped the gun and scrambled back. He fell out of the window display and yelled, "Where's the rear entrance?"

Four women huddled behind the shattered glass counter, shrieking and looking at him in dusty terror. He started to ask again, then spotted the lace curtains and the doorway beyond. He ran out, booming through the door, blinking in the sudden light. He raced down the back alley, gunfire and sirens echoing in from all sides.

The bank's entrance came into view the same moment he heard Connie scream something. He did not know what she said. The buildings formed a tight cavern that wrecked all sounds. He was afraid he heard pain in the voice. He saw the nozzle-flicker from the shooter in the bank's entrance and kept moving. His entire body was clenched against the bullet he knew was bound to come.

Then he saw the second shooter. The guy was crouched behind a van with two flat tires and a shattered rear window. The guy spotted Matt an instant later. He started to bring his gun up, but in his haste the muzzle got caught by the corner of the van, which was all that saved Matt.

Matt charged forward and rammed the guy. The shooter's gun went skidding off across the parking lot. The man was small and Asian and fast. He slipped under Matt's blow and kicked. Matt saw the incoming strike and twisted enough to take it on his shoulder and not his neck. Even so the blow sent him reeling.

The attacker slipped a knife from his pocket and shouted a challenge Matt did not need to hear. He kept backing away, but the attacker was no longer thinking about anything except rage over a day gone extremely wrong. He feinted and sliced. Matt felt the wind past his face, then reached and slapped the man across the eyes. Another strike, this one slower, and Matt managed to grab the attacker's wrist.

The attacker kicked Matt in the ribs. Matt held on to the knife-wielding wrist, though it was like trying to grip a steel python. He battered the man in the face, trying for the eyes again and failing. The man shouted a curse and ripped his knife-hand free.

Matt backed farther, hoping it was not just adrenaline fear that made the sirens sound closer. The attacker heard them as well, for he shouted once more and made a panic strike. Matt blocked with his arm and went for safety in the air. Even with his injured leg it was the highest leap he had ever made, an airborne attack that had him aiming *down* at the guy's head. He spun in the air as the knife went wide, then slammed into the man with his bad leg. The pain was a white-hot flame from knee to gut.

The attacker stumbled back. Matt landed hard, with no strength for a second leap. He jammed forward into a tangle on top of the attacker, gripped the knife-wrist and punched hard at the throat. He knew the man was doing damage with his free hand but Matt felt nothing. His entire being was focused on the blade scraping against the pavement. Matt held on for dear life.

Then the first cop car came screaming up. Then a second.

Shouting arms reached in and grappled with them both. Matt released his hold only when he was certain the attacker's knife was gripped by other hands.

"Gazelle!" The cop looming over him pointed and shouted, "We got us a gazelle; he's over the rear fence behind Exeter!"

Two cops took off as Connie came limping over. She said to the cops gripping Matt, "Let him go; he's one of ours. Sort of." She stepped in closer and demanded, "What on earth were you thinking?"

"That you'd taken a hit."

"Didn't I tell you I was okay?"

"You sounded hurt." He spotted the stain on her arm. "How are you?"

"It's a scratch, Skippy. Ricochet. Stone." She was holding her forearm with her hand, so she pointed with her chin at his leg. "He get you?"

"No. The old wound opened up again."

"Hang here a second; let me make the preliminary report. Then we'll go get patched up." She grinned at him then, her dark eyes sparking. "Having fun?"

"Are you serious?"

"Absolutely. Catching the bad guys, saving the good ones; this is my idea of a very good day."

Matt and Connie Morales shared a ride to Mercy Hospital. It was, according to Connie, the closest ambo delivery slot to Little Italy. Connie continued to astonish him. She sat up in the stretcher across from his own, rocking easily with the overweight truck as it wailed its siren through the afternoon traffic. She watched everything with happy interest, as though having a rock slice her arm was reason enough to dance.

The ER doctor was totally unfazed by Matt's reopened wound. "The new tear is minor. Your wound is healing clean," he announced. "I'm going to forget about repacking and stapling. Think you can avoid another bout of search and destroy for a few days?"

"Sure." Matt could hear Connie complaining beyond the curtain that she didn't want anything that was going to draw focus from the day's events, and the doctor insisting that he needed to probe the wound. Matt said, "I was expecting punishment detail for bringing this in."

The doctor applied goo and gauze. "This close to the Fells Point projects, we see a lot of cops. This wound is almost closed. You're working the muscles; you're keeping it uncontaminated. Not to mention the fact that you're keeping the streets clean."

"Trying." Matt flushed with unexpected pleasure at being classed as just another cop.

"Then we can't complain, can we. Okay. You're good to go. You need anything for the pain?"

"I'm okay, thanks."

The doctor gave him a brisk emergency-room nod. "Hold off the exercises for a day or so; that should be long enough. You got anything to wear?"

"Just the trousers I came in with."

"They've been tossed. Hang on, I'll get you some scrubs."

A nurse with a top-sergeant's air brought him a pair of light cotton pants and informed him that the other police officer had gone upstairs for a scan. Matt took a seat along the waiting room's back wall. He observed the frenetic flow and let the exhaustion and the adrenaline aftershock ease back a notch. He shut his eyes and saw the gun swivel toward his face. Only this time it came all the way around.

He jerked back to ER reality. He turned on his phone to discover he had seven messages from Judy Leigh at the *Times*, all repeating the same message in steadily rising panic: Call me. He did and gave her a blow-by-blow, handing all the credit to Connie.

The nurse returned to tell Matt the lady cop was asking for him and directed him back to a long, half-empty ward. Connie lay on the covers, her bloodstained shirt cut off at the shoulder. Her forearm was strapped with a bandage so white it looked starched. She grinned at the sight of him. Which was understandable. Matt wore a filthy dress shirt, dark polished loafers, and pale blue drawstring surgeon's pants.

Connie said, "Send in the clowns."

"They dumped my trousers."

"Yeah, they wanted to do the same with my blouse. I told them, a genuine Donna Karan from Filene's Basement? No way. How you doing, Skippy?"

"All right." He settled into the chair by her bed. "Why do you call me that?"

The doctor had obviously given her something for the pain, for her grin was a little loopy. "I don't know. Since when were nicknames supposed to make sense?"

"You had to have a reason."

"You look like such a white-bread wonder boy. The fed who's been raised in some totally safe world. Not a trace of street to his name. Got peanut butter and jelly sandwiches with milk after school. Like that. Skippy."

"I know street."

Her laugh was a full-throat affair, deep and genuine. "Sure you do."

An orderly appeared, pushing a wheelchair. Connie obviously knew the routine well enough not to argue. "You handled yourself well out there; I got to give you that." She offered Matt her arm and let him help her settle. "Push me out of here, will you?"

"Sure." Matt found himself wanting to tell her about Vic and the full-contact dojo. Which was amazing. He had never mentioned his martial arts training to a soul. His mother had found out only because she had followed him one afternoon. His father still did not have a clue. He admitted, "I've never had a nickname."

"That's totally bogus."

"We moved all the time. I had four eighth grades in three different states. I guess I was never in any place long enough to get tagged."

"Yeah, well, I've got a couple you're welcome to." She pointed to the nurses' station. "Hold up here. I've got to sign before they open the gates."

When they pushed through the doors into the ER waiting room, Connie's good mood vanished. "There goes the neighborhood."

"What's the matter?"

"Everything." Connie braked with one foot on the floor. She was unsteady but determined as she pushed herself out of the chair. "Been nice while it lasted."

Matt spotted the homicide detective he had last seen in the lieutenant's office. D'Amico was talking to another man Matt did not recognize. "They're probably here to see me."

"Wish you were right. The guy to your right is Lieutenant Calfo, head of my division. His primary role in life is to make my life miserable."

"That's crazy. You just saved a cop's life."

Connie walked over and said tonelessly, "Lieutenant."

"Who gave you permission to respond to a call?" Calfo was narrow in every aspect of his being—jaw, hair, eyes, and voice. He shook his head in pure disgust. "Of course, given your past record, I should have figured you for such a stupid act. You just handed me your career on a plate. But I guess you know that."

Matt felt an unexpected stirring in the normally empty space between his gut and his rib cage. The space that didn't appear on any medical chart. The one that hummed and vibrated to atmospheric shifts, the way people spoke or looked at him, the subtle changes that nobody else seemed to notice. Matt had a lifetime's experience of suppressing his emotions. Even in an unfamiliar environment where he was both new and too good-looking, or at home with his Jekyll-and-Hyde father. Now he felt himself coming to an uncontrollable boil.

The lieutenant had a cop's experience of fronting down dangerous people. Yet the change in Matt's expression caused him to blink. "You got a problem here?"

"Officer Morales just saved a policeman's life. Get out of her face."

Everybody looked at him. Connie, a passing doctor, the homicide detective, the lieutenant. D'Amico was the first to respond. "Ease up there, Kelly."

"Kelly," the lieutenant repeated. "You're the unauthorized ride-along?"

"You say one more word to Connie," Matt said, "and I'll break your jaw."

For some reason, D'Amico found that reason enough to disguise a laugh with a cough. The lieutenant gave the detective a sour look before asking Matt, "You looking to get arrested?"

"Go right ahead," Matt offered. "I've got an interview lined up with the *Baltimore Times*. I'll be happy to describe how the Baltimore police reward their best officers with reprimands, and let the scum rise to the top."

Connie said, "The lieutenant is just here for my resignation. Same as every day. Isn't that right, sir?"

The sad cast to her features only fanned Matt's rage. He said to the cop, "Crawl back in your hole while you still can. This is your last warning."

The lieutenant looked from one face to another. "Feel free to stop by my office any time, Officer Morales. Long as it's before tomorrow's roll call." He stormed away.

Detective D'Amico watched the other man depart with mild amusement. He said to Connie, "I take it you've told our visiting fed about your little incident."

"Not word one, sir."

D'Amico liked that enough to smile at Matt. "Want to tell me what happened out there?"

Connie replied for him. "We gave our report at the scene, sir."

"I'm sort of responsible for the kid here. Give it to me from how Kelly happened to be in an unmarked police vehicle."

Matt and Connie related the events in turn. D'Amico listened and said nothing. When they were done, he asked, "How were you getting home?"

"Cab, I guess."

"Hang on a second; let me go get my car."

"We can make it fine, sir."

"Take it easy, Officer." D'Amico patted Connie's good arm. "Let me do a little something for one of our own."

For some reason the detective's words creased her face with very real pain. D'Amico pretended not to see. "I'll be right back."

When they were alone, Matt asked, "What incident?"

Connie took a long breath. "You never said you knew the Rabbi."

"He's one of the detectives handling my mother's case. What did you call him?"

"Rabbi. He's extremely religious."

"He's Jewish?"

She looked at him. "With a name like D'Amico? Get real."

"It doesn't make sense."

"Cop nicknames are supposed to be prickly." She gave a professional's pause, then added softly, "Skippy."

"I asked—"

"I know what you asked. I'm trying to decide whether I want to tell you or not."

"Whatever."

"Don't go huffy on me." She sighed. "Lieutenant Calfo's nickname among the female officers is Hands. Do I have to spell it out for you?"

"No."

"When I arrived at Division One, he took me for my first ride-along. Just showing me the Fells Point projects, or so he said. Making me drive so both his hands were free to roam. When I refused to get back in the car with him, he started searching for me in out-of-the-way spots. He'd block my way and make lewd suggestions."

"Why didn't you report him?"

"He's a cop."

"What's that supposed to mean?"

"If you were around for a while, you'd know. Number one, he doesn't do anything where there's a witness. Number two, he's part of the cop world, which is very male and very tight. You bring a fellow officer before IA, EEOC, the union, especially a green recruit like me, you're done."

The agony in her face was such Matt couldn't bring himself to ask what had happened.

She told him anyway. "I had a bad day. My boyfriend and I broke up. Hands caught me coming out of the locker room before roll call. Made his standard offer. I just couldn't take it. So at roll call I stood up. In front of the entire watch, I asked him how he'd feel if somebody harassed his wife like he did me. Or his daughter. Or how he'd like his wife to hear what he'd been saying to me. Because that was *exactly* what would happen if he *ever* spoke like that again. One *word* and I was driving to his house. I had his *number*."

"I'm really sorry—"

"Yeah, well, I don't need your sympathy, Kelly. I'm doing just fine."

"No you're not."

"Sure I am. The lieutenant just said it. All I got to do is stop by his office and I'm on my way. One step from a bright new future." She looked at him then, her dark eyes brimming. "Who needs this grief anyway, right?"

———

The detective drove his Crown Victoria in what Matt considered typical cop fashion. Eyes scanning everything, foot heavy and impatient. D'Amico gunned through potholes like a kid meeting a puddle. He dropped Connie at a town house in Locust Point, an area that could not decide if it was up and coming or sliding into oblivion. He helped her up to the front door, smiled her inside, returned to the car, slipped back behind the wheel, and said to Matt, "So tell me what happened back there in Little Italy."

His leg was hurting him now. Enough that he wished he had accepted the doctor's offer of a painkiller. "We already did."

D'Amico's tone did not change. Even so, he slipped from amiable cop to detective in the space of one sentence. "Pretend I'm somebody who might actually be able to do something for you. If I wanted. Which I'm not at present sure I do."

Matt forced himself straighter in the seat. "What do you want to know?"

"What neither of you said before."

"We told you pretty much everything."

"There's never everything." He scooted around traffic like it wasn't there. Beeped his horn at someone too slow off the light. Took a corner far too fast. If he'd been a civilian, he could have been arrested for careless and reckless. "You'll wake up in the middle of the night and think of something that'll jar you hard as a hammer. I'm asking you to think about it now."

It was there before the detective had finished speaking. "She was so cool."

"Who, Officer Morales?"

"Connie was shouting into the radio. Before. When we heard the shots. She yelled something, I don't remember what. And floored it."

"Did she have the siren on?"

"Just the light. I guess we were too close already for her to bother with the siren."

"I'm not asking to get her into trouble. I just want the full picture. So she didn't have on the siren, and she drove hard down the street."

"We'd already turned off the main thoroughfare. I don't know the name."

"President."

"We heard the shots, she radioed it in, and she jammed down on the accelerator. We did a wheelie around the corner, and *bam*. We got hit."

"They blew out your windscreen."

"Right, like she said. We were running blind."

"And they'd taken out your tire."

"Yeah, we skewed pretty hard after that. That car of hers was terrible."

"That ride definitely won't be missed around the division. So that was when you did the ski jump over the curb."

"Right through the shop window."

"What happened then?"

"She ordered me out of the car. We rolled under and jammed up close to the wall out of firing range. She made sure I was okay, then moved forward for a look-see. Radioed in the shooters' positions and the officer down. Then we planned out the attack." One part of Matt's brain told him why the detective was talking him through it, showing he was right there. The other part, the main part, was reliving the moment again enough for his heart rate to surge. He could feel the glass in his face as he rolled from the car. Smelled the bizarre combination of gunfire and perfume. "She was so totally in control. Absolutely calm. She knew what had to be done and she was ready. She didn't want me to get involved either."

"But you did."

"The officer was trapped across the street and she needed cover fire. We were huddled between the tires and the side wall, taking fire from the guy in the bank door. The other guy we couldn't see." Matt wiped his hands up and down the surgical trousers. The flimsy cotton went a shade darker with his sweat. "It was so fast."

"And loud. A thousand things going off at once, and all that popping."

"She wanted to save the other cop. I knew that was her first concern. But she had to cross the street. And the other police cars were taking forever."

"They always do."

"So I offered to lay down cover. She made me cool enough to think. I don't know how I'd have been if . . ."

D'Amico pulled up in front of the brownstone on Eutaw Place. He just sat there and waited. "What I'm hearing is, Officer Morales is a good cop."

"A great cop." Matt swallowed hard. "Better than me."

D'Amico gave a quiet little huff Matt thought might have been a laugh. Or just quiet approval. "I doubt that."

"Can I ask you something?"

D'Amico shifted in his seat. His eyes were heavy lidded now, revealing a cop's readiness to deny Matt access. But all he said was, "Sure."

"Did you make the right-wing fanatics for culprits in the bombing?"

D'Amico blinked twice, measuring him. "Who is asking?"

"Just me. It's not going anywhere further."

"Then the answer is no. I followed up with every known suspect. Statewide there is only a handful who could handle an explosive device like the one that took out your mother. They and their bat-wing followers. Everything checked out." He gave it a second's pause, then, "Mind telling me why you don't make them for this?"

"They've never been foes. Oh, they made noises. Mom talked about them sometimes. But there was never a sense of real threat. Never a warning of any kind, you know, 'Don't come to our hills or you'll go home in a box.' Nothing."

"You did homegrown terrorist training in your ops school?"

"A lot."

"So you know what you're talking about." D'Amico gripped the steering wheel, twisting his hands back and forth. "First time I heard the reporters spouting off, the whole thing sounded pat. Like what happened with the race issue down south thirty years ago. Any crime goes unanswered, we dump it on that side of town."

Matt knew that was all he would get that day. "Thanks."

"No problem." D'Amico waited until Matt climbed from the car to ask, "Aren't you going to ask me about a transfer from your cubicle in Records?"

"Would it do any good?"

"Couldn't say for certain. But you got some bonus points coming your way, saving a cop's life."

Matt settled back into the car. "What are you not telling me?"

"Around Baltimore police headquarters, a federal tag is worse than a rap sheet. There are people who will do anything to keep you out of the game room. But today might change things. Not for feds in general. That'd take a shift in the earth's axis. For you. If, say, you could bring us something the feds aren't giving up, Chief Bernstein might be convinced to reconsider." D'Amico smiled and added, "Skippy."

Matt awoke to sweats and vague dreams of gunfire and lingering crystal chimes. The doctor's orders kept him from running at dawn, nor did he much feel like it. He could hear his father moving around upstairs, talking through the day with Sol and a couple of other early risers. Matt ate standing by the kitchen sink, then left the house.

The Federal Building rose above a six-floor parking lot, across Lombard from the federal courthouse. Homeland Security occupied one entire floor, marked upon entry by nothing save a security cop on permanent bored detail. Matt showed his credentials, got checked off the duty list, and waited in the special agent in charge's front office. His father's latest project dominated the west-facing view. Some of Downtown's decrepit office blocks had been empty for more than a decade and stared back in sullen hopelessness. Matt hardly saw them. He was no clearer on what direction to take than he had been the previous evening. Nor could he say why the homicide detective unsettled him like he did. Lucas D'Amico's quiet manner covered a multitude of layers, all of them subtly threatening. Matt was still thinking about the cop when the SAC arrived a few minutes after eight.

Bryan Bannister, the special agent in charge, was as ironed and starched as his navy suit and white button-down shirt. Crisp, direct, hard-edged, not a fraction of wasted seconds to his psyche. "Very sorry for your loss, Kelly."

"Thank you, sir."

Bannister pulled a file from the wire basket and seated himself, already deep into his rapid scan of the contents. "The directive assigning you temporarily to this office arrived yesterday. But it doesn't indicate the priority level."

Matt might have been new to the force, but he knew enough agency doublespeak to reply in kind. "I'm the only one tasked to collect on it, sir. It's way down everybody's list but mine."

"So State has the lead on collecting here."

"Yes sir."

"You have point."

"Correct, sir."

The agent said nothing because he didn't need to. Matt knew exactly what the man was thinking. The SAC's role had changed enormously since 9/11. This place was still on the books as an FBI field office. But Homeland Security now demanded that all resources be available to other intelligence agencies. Bannister was not asking because he was concerned about helping Matt get his job done. The agent wanted to cover his position.

Bannister asked, "We're on flank?"

"I doubt, sir, that there will be any need for further agency involvement."

The office was standard field-office grim—bland desk, squeaky chair, fake-wood shelves, obligatory family photos, trophy wall, and mountains of papers and forms. The SAC made notes in the margin of the office directive and slipped it into his out tray. "You're new to fieldwork, I take it."

"Green as they come, sir."

"You heard of stovepiping, Kelly?"

"Yes sir."

Bannister explained anyway. "Pre-9/11, intelligence work was all tightly controlled. Information went up the in-house chain of command; orders came back the same way. There was no crossover at all. Agencies didn't talk to one another. If you were caught talking to another intel division, it meant your career."

"The law of the iron rice bowl," Matt agreed. "Every agency was out to protect its own funds and turf."

"You've got it. But today, now, we're facing a totally different world." Bannister pointed at the filed orders. "Case in point. Here you are, a State Intel agent, sitting in a regional FBI office, wanting to liaise with Baltimore police on an unsolved murder."

Matt responded to the unasked question. "I used up all my in-house markers to get this assignment, sir."

"Still, you got to admit, it's interesting. A green officer being assigned to such a highly sensitive case. Not to mention the fact that just prior to your walking through this door, I received a flash cable from home office, directing me to offer all possible support to this case. That's a lot of pull for an agent fresh out of academy."

"Ambassador Walton wants me as his new adjutant. I agreed to take the job. But I asked for this assignment first. I'm not out for headlines here, sir. I just don't want the police to find some body they can squeeze to fit the perp sheet."

"So this is about revenge."

"Justice," Matt corrected. "I want the guy who did this. Your office is welcome to all the credit."

The SAC nodded approval. "I've heard State Intel doesn't include backstabbing and spotlight-grabbing in its training routine. Nice to see that it's true."

"Sir, I need to ask a favor." Matt ran through an abbreviated version of the previous day. "I've been assigned a desk in Siberia. The detective said I might be able to work more closely with them if I could bring something to the table."

"A Baltimore cop told you that?"

"He seemed to suggest that the feds might be holding back."

Bannister studied him for a long moment. "Sit down, Kelly."

"Thank you, sir."

"I've been in this job for six months. I've met with the local police a grand total of once. It was at a dinner with the mayor. We had prime rib. I sat three chairs down from the new commissioner. He refused to shake my hand." He picked up his phone and punched in a number. "Bring in the armory file."

Matt asked, "They have refused the FBI's assistance on this case?"

"Point-blank. The Baltimore police department is a mess. Some very good officers are hamstrung by politics. Baltimore has one of the highest murder rates in the United States. They've got gangs; they've got drugs; they've got neighborhoods I wouldn't enter without SWAT. They need a shake-up at police headquarters. They need a strong-arm boss who will come in and clean house." He accepted a manila folder from a young woman in a navy suit and continued, "You didn't hear any of that from me."

"No sir."

"Eight months ago, we had a break-in at the National Guard Armory. You know the one?"

"On Martin Luther King and Preston."

"A neo-Nazi crew got away with a truckload of automatic weapons, decommissioned claymores, and C-4. That's our turf."

"Theft from federal property," Matt supplied.

"Right. My predecessor set up a sting. Got some information. Traded that for more. We brought in some agents from Delaware. Worked it for two months. Made a dawn sweep on nine different locations. All but one of our arrests took place inside Baltimore city limits. Know how my predecessor liaised with the Baltimore police?"

"No sir."

"He didn't tell them diddly. Not a single word. The police commissioner found out on the morning news. Didn't go down well. The commissioner—not this one, the one before—he went on television and blasted us proper. My predecessor responded with a leak to the local press. About how a police dispatcher was the live-in girlfriend of the neo-Nazi leader behind the heist. How she bought the break-in team enough time to get away by alerting her man. Which led to the last commissioner's resignation. His deputy is now the top man. He's still friends with the one we got canned. You getting the picture?"

"Loud and clear."

"Two nights after the new commissioner was sworn in, one of our agents came off duty and was arrested a block from here. Failed taillights. Found drug paraphernalia in an evidence bag. How it got in the foot well of the backseat I am not even going to comment on. My agent spent the night in the drunk pen. The press went into a feeding frenzy. Our agent was cleared but found himself reassigned to Fresno. And that, Kelly, is the last time we've had official contact with the Baltimore police." He shoved the file across his otherwise-clean desk. "But there's been a change at the top over here in our office. I'm willing to take a chance. Just one."

Matt reached for the file. "Thank you, sir."

"There's information in there that could burn us, Kelly. You sure you can trust this detective?"

"I think so, sir."

"You let him know that if they use this against us, if any of it ever goes public, they've just made a new enemy."

"You got it, sir."

"One more thing. There's a consultant living out by Gunpowder Falls State Park. He's former British military, does bomb work for Homeland Security. Name is Allen Pecard. I've liaised with him on several cases. He's good, Kelly. Before you return to the police, I'd strongly advise you to go have a word with this man."

"I'll leave now."

"Pecard's address is on the first page. I'll call and give him a heads-up." He dismissed Matt with a wave. "You'd best make one thing perfectly clear to those folks in police headquarters. I'm in this saddle for five years. If they see this as a chance to burn the bureau, I've got a long time to get even. Make sure they understand that before you hand anything over."

———

Matt headed north on the Jones Falls Highway, driving hard. He skirted Lutherville and entered the borderlands around Gunpowder Falls. Baltimore's octopus reach could still be seen. On both sides of the road, rolling farmlands were being carved into subdivisions. He spotted a mailbox made from an ancient cannon and turned down a graveled lane.

Allen Pecard's home was surrounded by heavy woodlands. Matt caught the fresh smell of newly cut lumber as he climbed from the car. An old barn was gradually being reshaped into a garage with a large office or guest apartment overhead. The house was as old as the barn, a farm cottage redone in slow and exacting stages. The front porch was a masterpiece of pegged maple and hand-turned banisters. A varnished swing creaked in the chill breeze. Matt rang the doorbell. A second time. A third.

He was about to leave when an older man in blue denim coveralls and a muddy T-shirt ambled around the side of the house carrying a shovel. He had the stooped quality of someone long used to heavy labor, grown old before his time. "Help you?"

"Is Mr. Pecard here?"

"Might be. I believe I seen him round here somewhere."

"Can . . ." Matt stopped because the man had turned and shuffled out of sight.

Matt came off the porch and followed. But instead of leading Matt to Pecard, the old man made his way to the back of the cleared yard. He dropped into a hole he was digging and asked, "What you be wanting Pecard for anyway?"

"I'd say that was between me and the man."

"The *man*." He dropped his head and began digging. "Come to see the *man*."

Matt searched the yard for a sign of someone else. The hole was surrounded by raw earth and wood chips and a trio of muddy stumps recently plucked from the earth. Between them and the house was a lawn tended with military precision, a painted-stone border, and a hedge of blooming shrubs. On the hole's other side the forest closed in tight, ready to reclaim its territory as soon as the digger's back was turned.

"You be another of them fellows up from Washington? Wanting the *man* to solve your problems for you?"

Matt returned his attention to the digger. "What kinds of people come to talk with Pecard?"

"Oh, folks like you, I 'spect. Got themselves guns but no shooters, crimes and no answers."

Matt glanced at his watch. "If Mr. Pecard isn't available—"

"Else they got bombs with strange habits." He pitched another load of red earth. "Like they blowed out one wall of a house and left all the china in the next room just standing there, neat as you please."

Matt stared at the sweaty back. "Who did you say you were?"

The man straightened. In so doing, he became a second man. Someone else entirely. Intent and focused and ten years younger. And scornful in a clipped British manner. "You saw only what you wanted to see, Mr. Kelly. You judged me by my clothes and my stoop and my speech. You didn't look any closer. You ticked me off your list and stopped paying attention."

Matt was too dumbstruck to speak.

Pecard resumed his digging, shifting the earth with ease. "If I had been your mother's assassin, Mr. Kelly, I could have killed you twice."

Matt managed, "Guilty."

Pecard gestured at a second shovel half-hidden in the tall grass. "Perhaps you'd care to give me a hand."

Matt had little choice. He slipped off his tie and shirt and reached for the shovel. His injured leg complained bitterly as he landed in the soft dirt. The hole was a sharp-edged rectangle about eight feet long and chest-deep. "Bannister called you?"

"That is not the question." The man's precise speech was doubly jarring, given the initial mask he had shown and his current sweat-stained state. "You came out here with only one issue that matters. The rest is mere noise."

Pecard went silent on him. Matt dug and searched and came up with nothing he felt was solid enough to ask. He worked with his back to Pecard. Images from the blast seeped through the surrounding earth. Once more he walked along the side wall. Again he saw the blurred image of someone who might have slipped from around the house across the street. But the image was the same as always, diffused and dreamlike. Matt attacked the earth, his fractured memories, the pain in his thigh. He should *remember* more. But he could not. Just the way the man moved, or might have. Like a shadow. Melded into the trees and the shrubs at the rear of their neighbor's house. There but not there.

Matt pushed the image away. Noise, Pecard called it. Matt knew the man digging at his back would not speak again until Matt asked the right question. Which meant looking at the one single solitary point only Pecard could answer. He ran back through the report Bannister had given him.

He jammed his shovel into the earth. "The FBI report says you claim the blast was caused by a decommissioned claymore. One of several stolen from the National Guard Armory."

"Are you telling or asking?"

"The way the file read, you figured this out without a lab." His leg was complaining fiercely now that he had stopped. Matt clambered from the hole while he still could. Seated upon the lip, he asked, "How?"

"First give me the why, Mr. Kelly." Pecard stood a trace under Matt's height. His T-shirt was matted to a lifetime warrior's frame. He possessed no body fat whatsoever. Just sinew and muscle and sunburned hide. "Obviously I am cleared by Homeland Security. Why ever would I choose to work without proper laboratory analysis to confirm my findings?"

Matt could not decide whether he liked the man's testing. "The previous SAC claimed publicly that all the claymores had been accounted for. If you used their lab, there would be a paper trail. The former SAC would have been publicly shamed. This way, he owes Bannister big-time. Assuming Bannister told his predecessor what you discovered."

"I can assure you of that. Life in your nation's capital is all about debts and favors, Mr. Kelly." The red clay sucked noisily as Pecard pried out another shovelful. "Even a rank beginner such as yourself should be aware of this."

"So how—"

"Decommissioning a claymore is quite simple. All one must do is remove the explosive core. The mine itself is too tough to deconstruct." Pecard tossed out his shovel and clambered up the side. "Imagine, if you will, a thick plastic pie with a hole in the middle. The charge and the mine are both shaped to aim the blast with pinpoint accuracy. It must do so in order to achieve its stated objective, which is to take out a tank."

"The blast made a twelve-foot hole in the house and didn't damage anything else."

"Which meant your assailant placed his signature device upon a reinforced base." Pecard fished a water bottle from the grass and offered it to Matt.

Matt waved away the bottle. "How did you identify it as a claymore?"

Pecard drank deep. When he wiped his mouth, he left a muddy smear across the lower half of his face. "Claymores are fired by a special high-octane explosive. Virtually impossible to locate on the open market. Your homegrown user will replace the charge with C-4. That's strong enough to blow, but not strong enough to demolish. Bannister had one of his men track outside the police perimeter. They identified yellow plastic shards from a tree across the street. The claymore's yellow plastic exterior is turned to dust by the normal charge, but hard enough to resist total destruction with C-4."

The man's hair was military stubble against a raw-earth scalp. A scar ran up the right side of his neck and wrapped under his ear. The eyes were as clear as sunlit glass. It was impossible to imagine this as the broken-down, shuffling old man he had seen before. "How did you fool me? I mean, before."

"I suggest you focus, Mr. Kelly. We are discussing the bomb that killed your mother." Pecard rose to his feet and started toward the house. "Your next task is to identify the question which the local police have been unable to formulate properly. When you do, phone me. And not before."

Pecard pried off his boots, dropped his coveralls in a heap, and then called back, "If you fail to accomplish this in twenty-four hours, Mr. Kelly, don't bother phoning at all."

———

Matt returned home to shower and change clothes. He pulled behind the house, where he had parked with his mother. He cut the motor and sat listening to the voices barking inside his head. Doing what Pecard said. Separating the noise from the one critical point, the next step. The clue on which he needed to take aim.

He got out of the car and walked around the corner. Retracing his steps from the moments preceding the blast. Matt did his best to ignore the confusion and the guilt and the pain. Walking and looking and asking himself what he did not see. He studied the freshly repaired wall, the new bricks brighter in color, the new door sparkling in the autumn sunlight. Then he turned and looked at his father's face staring down from the side of the carriage house, twelve and a half feet tall.

And it hit him.

Matt pulled Pecard's number from the FBI analysis sheet. When the man came on the line, Matt said, "The things that were stolen and the things that were damaged. One from each room."

Pecard gave a moment's hesitation in response, all the reward Matt figured he would ever get from this guy. "Yes?"

"So the bomb was not the killer's only message." Moving forward with confidence from having gotten the first part right. "He spent a lot of time going through the house. Leaving us a message. We need to find out what that message was."

There was another longish pause, then, "I want to see the bomb fragments the police gathered. You will find them in their evidence lockup. I should imagine that access is severely restricted."

"I don't know—"

"Make it happen, Mr. Kelly. I will meet you there at five."

When Officer Consuela Morales had finished her trainee period at
Western and discovered she was assigned to Division One, her
feet did not touch earth for a week. Nowadays, though, going to work
meant shouldering a hundred-ton load. She was reduced to looking
back in fondness on her early days as a cop—all six months of them.
Knowing that was probably all she would ever have.

Division One fronted Baltimore Street and occupied space reclaimed
from the notorious Block. The Block was Baltimore's badland, a strip of
sleaze and organized crime and semilegal prostitution and clubs that spe-
cialized in degradation. There was still a Block, shaved down to a half-
dozen clubs along a fifty-yard strip of grime and jaded lust. But with the
Division One police station as their new neighbor and cop cars patrolling
its length every few minutes, the Block was effectively neutered.

Division One handled crime from Fells Point to the Harbor
District and Cherry Hills. But what made Division One even more
appealing to Connie was the tunnel. An elevated concrete platform ran
from Division One to headquarters, which fronted Fayette and City
Hall. The tunnel was her passage to the big time. TAC. Violent
Crimes. The Organized Crime Unit. And the pinnacle of city police
work, Homicide. All standing just fifty meters away, beyond two sets of
heavy steel doors. Beckoning. Waiting. There for her to claim.

Connie pulled her SUV into the fenced-in lot and went through
her windup. She unlocked the carry-case and slipped on her belt, gun,
collapsible baton, Taser, and radio. As if she was actually going to go be

a cop. Going through the morning motions had once been an adrenaline rush. Now the last five minutes to roll call stretched out in a tortur-
ous stupor.

"Hey, Morales. How's the arm?"

She faced one of the cops from the previous day's incident. "I'm
good to go, Brodski."

"I stopped by the hospital on the way over. They're sending Jamie
home tomorrow. Day after at the latest."

"That's great news."

"Yeah, the bullet missed the bone and sailed clean through. He'll
be on light duty for a couple of months, but they think he'll be okay."

She didn't mean to, but the words came out bitter. "Jamie would
die pulling desk."

The other cop had the decency to wince. "Tell me."

Every shift had one officer assigned desk duty. That officer handled
the phone and foot traffic and a lot of mindless paperwork. Every lost
poodle, angry neighbor, mishandled garbage bag, and nonviolent
squabble landed there. The desk was normally handled by an officer
assigned light duty, or an older officer approaching retirement, or someone being hauled before IA whose powers of arrest had been withdrawn.

Connie had pulled desk every day since her public run-in with the
lieutenant. It was killing her.

Brodski said, "Jamie asked me to say thanks."

"Hey, just doing my job. It felt pretty good too."

Brodski shifted his feet. "I've been hanging out here waiting for
you. Word is, me and Miles are up for a medal."

Miles was the other cop who chased down the gazelle. "That's
great, Brodski." Then the reason for his hangdog expression struck
hard. "You have got to be kidding me."

"Technically, you weren't on patrol duty. So you can't be rewarded
for handling a crime you weren't supposed to be called out on."

She flung her shoulder bag onto the ground. "That's it. I'm done."

"Just hold on a second, okay? I've been waiting for you because
Miles and me, we told the lieutenant we wouldn't take the medal. It
was your call. You're the one who saved Jamie's life."

Acid bit the back of her eyeballs. "Take the medal."

"No, Connie, it's not—"

"Tell Miles. How often do the good guys win?" She stooped over for her bag. Straightening took forever. She felt a million years old. "You both should take it and run."

"What's going down in here, it ain't right. I just want you to know. Most of the other guys are feeling really low about it, you know."

"Thanks, Brodski. But I'm all done here. Hands has finally beat me."

"You can't quit on us. You're a good cop."

She hustled for the entrance and slammed through the doors and said to nobody in particular, "Yeah. I am, aren't I."

"Are what?"

It took a moment to realize she was facing the homicide detective from yesterday. "You want a piece of me too, Rabbi?"

The guy had a surprisingly gentle smile. "Protocol says you need a little more time on the job to be using my nickname."

"Yeah, well, on some other day I might care." She tried to shoulder by. "If you'll excuse me, I'm late for roll call."

"I've already cleared you with the sergeant," D'Amico replied. "You and I need to have a word."

She was about to object when Lieutenant Calfo stormed out of the duty room. He fisted a crumpled sheet in D'Amico's face. "What is this?"

D'Amico did not back up. "Read it and weep, Hands."

The lieutenant flushed. "You got no right, calling me that."

"Hey, I'd love to stand here all day, talking about an officer's *rights*." D'Amico placed soft emphasis on the last word. "But we've got homicides to solve."

The lieutenant was so angry that the hand gripping the papers trembled. "You know what the other officers think of Morales? She's the division's number one hump."

There was little worse a cop could be called by a fellow officer. A hump was cop-speak for an officer who fell apart under stress. They let fear take control. They fumbled their weapon or discharged it badly. They imperiled everyone around them. To have a hump arrive on backup was worse than facing the danger alone.

D'Amico replied, "Interesting word to use for somebody who saved an officer's life yesterday, Hands."

"Connie Morales wasn't authorized to be out at all." The lieutenant was shouting now. "That girl is *trouble*."

D'Amico remained calmly unscathed. "Yeah, well, I'd say this *officer* is my problem now." D'Amico took Connie by the arm and steered
her around. "Get out of my face, Hands."

Connie let D'Amico lead her past the duty room because she was
too numb to object. The entrance was full of astonished faces. A tall
black officer, Miles, gave her a grin and a thumbs-up.

The lieutenant realized he was the object of an entire squad's attention. "You're promoting her because she's disrespectful?"

"I'm just trying to further a good cop's career, Hands." D'Amico
pushed through the doors leading to the tunnel. "That's a critical
responsibility for every senior officer, remember?"

———

They were in the elevator. Riding to the seventh. Connie realized the
detective had said something to her. "Excuse me?"

"Your name. Morales," D'Amico repeated. "Is that Latino?"

"My folks were both born in this country. My father's family is
Colombian." She felt so weak she wanted to lean against the wall. But
she wouldn't. Not on her life. "My mom's folks are from Buenos Aires."

D'Amico gravely accepted the information. "Me, I'm your typical
Baltimore mongrel. Father half Neapolitan, half Pugliese. Mother pure
Polish. But at least they were all Catholic. Then I went and married a
black Irish, a Protestant. Mother carried the shame to her grave. This is
our floor."

He ushered her out and past the case board. "You've been here
before, right?"

"Sure. The standard rookie tour." She couldn't take a thing in. "I
hooked up with another group so I could go through twice."

"Right. So you know we work on two shifts, not the three of patrol.
Nobody checks you in and out. If you're not pulling your weight, the
lieutenant will let you know. Everybody working homicide is basically
expected to live and sleep their job."

She was mortally ashamed to feel a burning trace down one cheek.

The hand that wiped the wet away was shaking so hard she almost missed her face.

D'Amico pretended not to notice. "The division chief is Major Bernstein. That's her office behind the glass doors there. She ought to be a captain. But the city administration did away with that rank. Captains were civil service, which meant they could only be promoted up through the ranks. The city wanted to make all division chiefs political appointees, which most senior officers consider political garbage. But they didn't ask our opinion. Bernstein is one of these new deputy majors. Around here we call them mini-majors. Just don't ever let the chief hear you say that."

Connie clutched her satchel to her chest in order to have something to do with her hands. She was getting struck by waves that left her wanting to break down and sob, then it would pass, and they'd be another ten feet or so through their stroll down the bull pen's central aisle. Blanking out for a second or two, then coming back around.

"The lieutenants and sergeants have their offices around those two walls." Detectives who staffed the cubicles glanced up, scored her with tight cop looks, nodded to D'Amico, and went back to whatever they were doing. "Admin, evidence, and interview rooms behind those doors. Cold case and redrum on the other side of the elevators. Redrum is murder spelled backward. It's our word for cases tied to serious drug busts, the ones we share with Organized Crime and ATF, DEA, FBI. Or we would, if we were on speaking terms. Which we're not. You know about that, right?"

"I've heard." She could scarcely manage a whisper.

"This way." He led her into a narrow hallway branching off the bull pen. Four cubicles, half the size of those occupied by detectives, fronted the corridor. "Soon as I clear it with the major, this will be your new home. She's at a meeting with the deputy commissioner. I got the lieutenant to sign off in her absence, so we're provisionally cool." He gently nudged her into the cubicle. "This section is known as Homicide Ops. It's responsible for chasing down evidence, contacting the labs, coordinating with TAC on a bust, basically anything the detective you're assigned to work with needs doing."

She just stared at him. Like the utterly green rookie she was. Speechless.

"You'll also work with problem witnesses. We get a lot of those. People who're scared or threatened and don't want to show up for trial. And you'll be passed over to Organized Crime sometimes, particularly on kidnapping and extortion cases."

D'Amico settled himself comfortably against the side wall. He might as well have been discussing the weather. "Don't think this is an automatic pass to the first team, Morales. TAC detectives are considered Homicide's farm team. Any who want to apply would get first pass whenever a slot opens here. But you do your job and make your mark, people are going to notice. If I were you, I'd start on the detective exam soon as you've got in the time."

She wanted to throw her arms around his neck. Instead, she spoke with a voice that was two octaves lower than normal. "I owe you, Rabbi. Big-time."

D'Amico gave an easy shrug. "What say you take a while, get yourself settled in. Soon as the major arrives and gives us the green light, we'll go fight us some crime."

When Matt entered headquarters, the officer at the front desk greeted him with, "Yo, Kelly. How's the leg?"

"Okay, thanks."

"That was some move you made, going after an armed robber with your bare fists." The guy had an astonishingly ugly grin, all yellow teeth and caverns. "Bet it gives you the sweats, now that it's over."

It probably would, if only Matt could separate that from his nightmares over the blast. "I must've jerked awake a dozen times last night."

"Tell me 'bout it." He picked up the phone. "D'Amico says I was to call ahead. But you can go straight on up."

"Thanks."

As Matt passed through the metal detector, the cop added, "Looks to me like there's some changes coming down."

"What do you mean?"

"Go upstairs; have a look for yourself; tell me I'm not right."

D'Amico met him at the elevator, accepted the FBI report, and led Matt back to his cubicle. The detective pulled a second chair from across the hall, told Matt to have a seat, and gave the pages a careful read. He sat and pulled at his lip for a second. "This is good and not good."

"I don't understand."

"Don't get me wrong. The information here is vital. But the timing—"

A voice called out, "D'Amico!"

"Back here."

"You wanted to know when the chief arrived."

"Be there in ten."

"Roger that."

The detective waved the pages at Matt. "Is this everything?"

"No." Matt told him about the meeting with Pecard, and what he had learned. D'Amico studied him a moment longer. "That was a good move, going out to see the guy personally."

"Bannister suggested it."

"You ever work a homicide while you were with Vail PD?"

"Follow-up only. Biggest bust I made was a kid stealing skis."

He nodded slowly. "I got to tell you, this is the first solid evidence we've seen in a while."

"Pecard wants to come in and take a look at the bomb's remains this afternoon."

"Does he now." D'Amico crossed his arms. "He tell you what was going down between the feds and Baltimore police?"

"Bannister did that."

"Bannister's the new SAC over at Homeland?"

"Yes."

D'Amico rose to his feet. "I'll need to run this by the chief. Come on, let me show you around."

The bull pen was split down the middle by a solid wall of elevators and interview chambers. Major Bernstein's office, her two aides, and the senior lieutenant occupied one outer wall. Sergeants and admin staff flanked two other walls. The final exterior side contained interview and holding chambers and a conference room.

The odor within Homicide was as pungent as it was subtle, an electric mix of old cordite and gun oil and sweat and tension. D'Amico walked him by the active cases board and explained how it was broken down. "The cases written in blue mean a cop was involved in the shooting. Those investigations we share with IA."

Matt fingered a tiny pin stuck into the board beside one name and asked, "What's this for?"

D'Amico's voice didn't change a notch as he replied, "It means an officer was shot and killed."

Matt tracked down the seven rows, representing the sergeants and their active caseloads. There were a lot of empty pinholes in the plastic board.

Their tour over, D'Amico pointed him into a chair by the chief's outer office. "Wait here."

The shouting started about two minutes later.

———

The homicide chief's office was separated from the detective bull pen by a cheap wall of Plexiglas. The mobile wall had been somebody's lousy idea for saving money and preserving future flexibility. Matt sat with his back to the wall and overlooked the bull pen. Heads appeared now and then over the partitions, glancing his way, smirking the message that it was better him than them. Matt could not tell what Bernstein was saying. But the chief's rage vibrated the wall.

"Hello, Skippy." Connie leaned against the wall next to him. "Here to watch me crash and burn?"

Matt replied, "What's going on in there isn't about you."

"I wish that were true." She winced at the next verbal barrage. "You're looking at the quickest homicide career in history. Here and gone in three hours. Just the same, I wanted to say thanks for backing me up yesterday at the hospital. You don't know what that meant."

"Enough to have you stop calling me Skippy?"

"Maybe not that much."

"How about dinner sometime?"

The response came with the easy speed of constant practice. "That's probably not a good idea."

"No. I suppose you're right."

She almost managed a smile. "A fighter you're not."

"Don't be so sure." He had a thousand reasons for letting it go, especially all the pretty faces in his past. Even so. "My father is invited to the owner's skybox for the football game Sunday. I can bring somebody if I want."

"A lot of girls would love nothing better than an afternoon in the Ring of Power. That's what they call the skybox level. But my place in life is two decks down."

"You're a Ravens fan?"

"Season tickets, baby. Go birds."

D'Amico opened the door. "Okay, Kelly. Inside."

Connie rose with Matt and asked, "Is it time for me to go pack, Rabbi?"

"Not just yet." He motioned Matt forward. "Let's go."

Two assistants, one male and one female, manned computer stations in the chief's outer office. They offered Matt amused sympathy as Bernstein barked through her open door, "Front and center, Kelly. You too, D'Amico."

D'Amico slipped into one of the two chairs fronting the chief's desk. "I wasn't going anywhere."

Bernstein said to Matt, "Sit."

"I'd rather stand, ma'am."

"Did I offer you a choice in the matter? No, I did not." She used thumb and forefinger to lift the pages he had brought. "You want to tell me what I'm looking at here?"

"Confidential FBI files, chief."

"I can read. I'm talking about the felony this suggests. As in withholding evidence vital to a homicide case."

D'Amico spoke up then. "The SAC would probably say he passed it over at our first request."

She glared at the detective. "Did I ask for your help?"

"No, Chief."

"I'll thank you to stay mute until I do."

D'Amico laced his fingers across his chest. "Sure thing."

"We are two weeks into an unsolved homicide! Why wasn't I alerted to this analysis before now?"

Matt took his cue from the placid detective seated next to him. "My guess is, the SAC probably didn't have any more reason to trust you than you do him."

Her glare was hot enough to bore holes. "I'm ordered not to shoot rookie federal agents in my own office. But I might make an exception in your case."

D'Amico coughed. Bernstein snarled, "Are you giving me smart?"

"No, Chief. Not me." D'Amico coughed a second time. "Just bad chicken livers."

"I'm told they need another information officer down in the front foyer. You keep that up, you'll see how much I love slapping down officers who think they can give me smart in my own office." She re-aimed at Matt. "I thought I could rely on you to follow orders, Kelly. That's what you fibbies are known for, right? Taking handsome classes, being first in the chin-up competition, and following the rulebook?"

"Chief, I—"

"You were ordered to stay downstairs in Records. So what do you do but sneak into an unmarked patrol car and take a drive with an officer on Division One desk detail. Suddenly this same officer goes haring off on a call she should *never* have answered with a federal ride-along in the car." Bernstein's voice rose in stages. "She then drives this unauthorized ride-along into a free-fire zone! Does that sound *sane* to you?"

"That is absolutely not true."

"Oh, really. Which part?"

"Ma'am, Officer Morales saved a cop's life out there."

"And might have cost us a fibbie's life in the process. Which isn't a bad trade, I'll give you that much." She shifted papers on her desk to give her hands something to mangle. "Do you have any idea the storm that would have generated? No. Of course you don't. Because if you had, you'd be downstairs in your safe little cubicle waiting out your time."

"Officer Morales is an extremely good cop."

"So now I'm expected to take the word of a green fibbie on which of our cops is stand-up." Bernstein's expression tightened further. "Morales is a woman on her way out. And you've just moved up her departure date."

"That is such a total waste."

"Furthermore, I have a written protest from Lieutenant Calfo in Division One accusing you of abusive and threatening language at a crime scene. He is requesting that I discipline you, Kelly."

"That's not how it was at all, Chief. To begin with, we were at the hospital."

She slammed an open hand down on the sheet. "How and where a lieutenant chooses to address a new recruit is no concern of a rank outsider!"

D'Amico coughed again. Harder this time. Suddenly Bernstein

couldn't decide whom to burn with her gaze. "I'm inclined to take this matter up with the DA's office."

D'Amico shook his head. "Bad idea, boss."

"Oh, is that so. Explain to me why I shouldn't have this punk ushered off the premises."

D'Amico pointed out, "He's brought us vital data we didn't have."

"Correction. Poster boy here waltzes in with a bomb-blast analysis we should have had *two weeks ago*."

"Skippy's right, Chief. From their end, it's we didn't ask, so they didn't tell."

She showed angry astonishment. "You can't possibly be giving this punk a *nickname*."

Matt marveled at his internal state. He had a lifetime's experience of dealing with unfair rage. If forced to fight, he would. Otherwise, he deflected until his first chance to flee. He had been raised on a constant fare of leaving. But his internal response was always the same, a clenching down. He had a prey's ability to read signs and prepare for sudden flight.

But not today.

He sat while the major blustered and remained untouched. The only outrage he felt was over Connie. He interrupted, "Officer Morales is an extremely good police officer, and the lieutenant was wrong to get in her face."

"Pay attention, Kelly. It's your execution we're talking about here."

D'Amico held to his perpetually steady tone. "The SAC has taken a serious risk here, Chief. He's basically handed another fibbie's career to us on a plate. Which suggests to me he's impressed enough with Kelly here to trust him. And us."

"Let me reinterpret that for you." Bernstein's mouth was so tight her lips had disappeared. "Unauthorized federal agents entered *my crime scene*, and they did so without my permission! They *stole evidence*. They found information crucial to an unsolved murder. And they withheld it!"

D'Amico merely said to Matt, "The Homeland Security agent collected shards from a tree, right?"

"Yes."

D'Amico told the chief, "There are no trees inside the tape between the blast site and the side wall."

"What, you went back and checked this out?"

"I don't need to. Using plastic fragments collected from a tree beyond our crime scene, their bomb analyst confirmed the blast was caused by a decommissioned claymore."

Bernstein said, "We're actually talking about one of the stolen claymores the fibbies claimed were all recovered months ago?"

Matt confirmed, "The information in that file suggests their declaration was incorrect."

"You mean to tell me the feds actually admitted being wrong about something?"

"The way the SAC put it," Matt replied, "was that if you let this get out, he has five years to get his revenge."

This time D'Amico laughed out loud. "Give us a minute alone in here, Kelly."

He stood and said, "Chief, Officer Morales—"

"I heard you the first time. Door."

———

When they were alone, Major Bernstein said, "You're planning something."

"I don't like the feds any more than you do," D'Amico replied. "But we're chasing our tails here."

"You want to bring the kid into this investigation?" Hannah Bernstein shook her head in disgust. "I can't believe I'm hearing you tell me that."

"Yesterday, without a weapon, he took down an armed assailant. In the process he helped save a cop's life. When I drove him back from the hospital yesterday, I asked him to replay the scene. You know what he talked most about? How Morales steadied him. Nothing about his own heroics."

"So he's had his macho gene removed. So what." But Bernstein was listening carefully.

"So when I dropped him off, I said if he could come up with some solid goods, I'd try and get him a spot in the investigation."

"That's so far over the line that you're talking to me from the next state."

"I don't think so, Chief. And you got to admit, he's brought in the first new lead we've had in two weeks."

She mulled that over. D'Amico added, "I like him."

"That's not what we're discussing here."

"I'm still without a partner. What's the harm?"

"I can't believe you're actually siding with him on this."

"While we're at it, we also need to talk about Officer Morales."

Bernstein appeared to have been expecting this but still replied, "That's Division One's problem."

"Morales is getting a very bad rap from Hands. You know his rep with women on the force."

"Wait, I remember now." Bernstein leaned back in her chair. "Morales. Sure. She's the one who dissed Hands at roll call."

"Knowing this guy," D'Amico replied, "he probably deserved a lot worse."

"So she's got a beef. Why is this our problem?"

"Hands is gunning for her, Chief. I've asked around. Morales has the makings of a very good cop. She was the other half of yesterday's lifesaving team."

"You're seriously suggesting we should give a rookie a chance in Homicide?"

"We have two open slots in support staff. She's dying a slow death at the Division One desk. I want her doing real police work."

"Is this a favor you're asking, Rabbi?"

"Call it what you want." D'Amico rose from his chair, knowing he had won. "Thanks, Chief."

She let him reach the door before asking, "Do you know what you're doing?"

He paused with his hand on the knob. "Are we talking about the Kelly kid or Officer Morales?"

But Bernstein was already making notes in the margin of her next case file. "You better be sure you know, is all I'm saying."

D'Amico found the pair of them standing in Ops' narrow hallway. Connie watched his approach, so anxious she aged a dozen years. D'Amico told her, "We're good to go, Morales."

Connie asked in a very small voice, "Are you sure?"

"Major Bernstein has given us the green light." D'Amico felt her need, young and so hungry she was ready to weep over the chance just to do her job. "You better be good, all the trouble you're causing me."

She said solemnly, "Just aim and pull the trigger, Rabbi. I'm gone."

"For starters, I'd prefer it if you used my name."

Matt Kelly asked, "Does that work for me too?"

"We'll see." D'Amico pointed him into the next cubicle. "This is your new home for the duration. I've stuck my neck out for you, Kelly. I want professionalism and results and speed. We clear?"

"Absolutely."

"Right. Go see the duty sergeant. Tell him I've okayed a pass for you and the fibbie to our evidence room. What's the analyst's name again?"

"Allen Pecard. But he's an outside consultant."

"Inside, outside, he's still fed." D'Amico turned to Connie. "The guys who pulled the armory job are in the federal wing of the Baltimore pen. Find out their names. Dorcas will help you with that. Do a background search. See if there's a wife or kid or something we can use as a lever."

"Roger that."

"Anything else?" D'Amico noticed Matt's hesitation. "You got something?"

"I'm worried about shaping the words and having them sound as stupid as they feel rocking around in my head."

"Let me be the judge of that." D'Amico led them back to his cubicle and pointed Matt into the only chair. He waited while Connie pulled one from across the aisle, then said, "Know the measure of a good cop? One who can trust his gut. I'm not asking you for facts."

Matt took a breath. "I don't think my dad was the target."

"You said that before." D'Amico settled himself on the corner of his desk. "Explain."

"Dad is never home that time of day. *Never.*"

D'Amico looked at the closed file on his desk. He had read the data often enough to scan through the cover. "Your parents left the house together at 6:45 on the morning in question. They attended a breakfast in Annapolis. A photo op in Odenton. Lunch in Glen Burnie. All political events. Your dad took his campaign bus to Cambridge. That's some ride he's got, by the way. Your mom taxied to Lexington Market. You met her there. You drove home . . ."

Matt halted D'Amico's calm procession of events with, "If the attacker knew their routine enough to set the charge on the side door, he'd know their movements."

"Most bombers are not rocket scientists. They'd count it a success to hit the right house."

"But this charge was *shaped*. The rest of the house was left intact. Pecard called that a signature device."

"Yeah, that's the word our bomb guys used too." He turned to Connie and explained, "A signature device is one intended to leave a message."

Matt went on, "Signature suggests intelligence and planning."

D'Amico shrugged a maybe. "There was no timer attached to the device."

"I didn't see that in the report."

"They don't put down what's absent. Only what they find. No timer. So the guy sets the charge to a wire or something else and he strikes the wrong target. This is not the work of a highly intelligent foe."

"Maybe."

"If you got something else, now's the time." When Matt hesitated, D'Amico went on, "It's not my habit to ridicule."

"I have this image I can't . . ." The words sounded congealed inside his throat. "I could have dreamed it. I still have a lot of strange impressions from that time."

"Being that close to death will do it to you. So you have this image from the blast."

"From before."

"How do you want to check it out?"

"I was thinking maybe I should talk with Connie and the first officer on the scene."

"Officer Brodski," Connie supplied. "He's stand-up. Very aggressive cop. Loves to be first out."

"Okay. So why don't you two get with Brodski, let the kid here run through what he might or might not have seen. See if it sparks something." D'Amico pushed himself off the wall. "Soon as you're done there, Morales, find us a lever with one of the armory gang."

———

When Brodski was seated in the interview room across the metal table from them, the first thing he said was, "Do I need legal rep?"

Connie was genuinely shocked. "Do I look like Internal Affairs to you?"

"All I know is, one day you're dragging around here like the division goat."

"Which I was."

"The next, you're over in headquarters and Lieutenant Calfo is the one acting nervous."

"Hands is scared? Of me?"

"I'd give that a big affirmative."

Connie's day just grew a whole lot brighter. Which was good. Because Matt had gone very distant on her. No surprise there. Discussing the incident had her remembering what it had been like, approaching where his mother lay by the shattered brick wall. And she was *never* going to tell him about that. "This is Agent Matt Kelly."

"You got your own fibbie detail? Way to go, Morales." Brodski was a beefy guy going prematurely bald. He crossed his arms, straining the shoulders and arms of his uniform. "Wait a sec. You're the Kelly kid. Sure, I remember you."

Connie said to Matt, "You're up."

Matt still could not bring himself to look at her directly. "I'd like to ask you both a few questions."

Brodski broke in. "Are we taping?"

"Come on, get a grip. We're just three cops here trying to solve a homicide."

"You just said he's not a cop."

The interview rooms were all the same. Concrete floor, white-washed walls, wire-mesh window in steel door, high ceiling, glaring fluorescents, one-way glass set in one wall. Connie leaned on the narrow table. "Take a good look, Brodski. Does he look like trouble to you?"

"I don't know. I've never talked to a fed."

"Believe me. We're after answers, not trouble." She glanced over. Matt was doing his best to hide his unease and failing. She said quietly, "It's okay, Matt."

The wound came to his gaze. "Nothing is right about that day. Not now, not ever."

"Still, we've got to try, right?"

Brodski was watching the exchange with a cop's awareness. Seeing a lot more than Connie would have liked to show her former Div One officers. But it was too late for that now. She said to Matt, "Ask us your questions."

"Could you please just walk me through that afternoon?"

Brodski didn't respond until Connie gave him the nod. "Lemme think. I was first on scene. You know that already. There was a lot going on. I didn't get backup for, oh, must've been close to twenty minutes."

Connie said, "I was listening to the radio traffic on desk. Brodski was sweating and the dispatch was calling all over the place, going outside division and still couldn't find a free officer. So I sneaked out, grabbed a set of wheels, and went to help."

"Right," Brodski continued. "At first, I thought you were both toast.

I mean, you should've seen the house. And a couple of cars were smoking out beyond the wall—"

"Three," Connie corrected. "Two SUVs and a minivan. The ones high enough to catch it over the wall."

"Whatever. The wall around the door was blown all over the street. Windows in the house across the way were all gone. I could hear your neighbors screaming. I was walking past where you were lying. Then I saw you move. I couldn't believe it."

Connie saw the impact this was having on him. "You all right there, Matt?"

He just raised his hand. *Don't ask.* "Then what?"

"I got my emergency kit out of the trunk and went to work on you. Your mother—"

"Skip that part," Connie ordered sharply.

"Connie showed up while I was doing CPR on you. It probably wasn't necessary, but I didn't know if there had been any internal damage, and it's standard ops in those situations. The ambo showed up right after. They hauled you off to, where was it?"

"Maryland General."

"Sure. Then the fire truck arrived while we were setting up the perimeter tape. Two of the board and I decided not to wait for the fire marshal; he was stuck on some accident site. We were concerned there might be somebody inside. Connie took perimeter and we went for a look. But the house was empty." Brodski shook his head at the memory. "Man, that was one eerie scene."

When Matt remained silent, Connie asked, "What do you mean?"

"You saw the outside, right? The blast carved a fifteen-foot hole. I mean, the side door was *gone.* But beyond that one room, the house was immaculate. We found this one crystal vase standing on the kitchen counter, like it was waiting for flowers. The bomb crew said they'd heard about this sort of thing but never seen one before. I forget what they called it."

"Signature," Matt said slowly. "This is probably going to sound insane. So I'm apologizing in advance."

Brodski shot Connie a look. "Hey, I'm a Baltimore cop. I *live* insane."

"Memories from right before the blast are still fuzzy." Matt talked to the empty notebook opened on the table before him. "But I've got this image in my head that won't go away. I might have seen a guy come from behind me. In my head he takes aim at me with a gun. But he's there and gone so fast . . ."

Connie felt enough of his tension to grind down her response. "Let's just stop with the hesitation, okay?"

Matt gave her an unfocused look, like he was trying to recall who she was.

"Just start at the beginning and walk us through it."

"Right." Matt went back to examining the table's scratched metal surface. The scar on his temple glistened an angry red. "I parked the car in the rear alley. Mom headed for the side door while I took groceries out of the trunk. She was maybe fifty feet ahead of me. More. Then the guy appeared. I think."

"Where from?"

"The house across the street has a hedge. He just appeared and disappeared. His arms were out together like a pro taking aim. Then he vanished."

"What did you do?"

Matt was sweating now. "My gun was in the trunk with my clothes. I couldn't decide whether I'd actually seen anything; it was all out of the side of my vision. I told my mother to go inside. Then I leaned over to set down the bags. Then the world exploded."

Brodski spoke then. "Bending down saved your life."

"Yeah." Matt took no pleasure from the fact. "The doctors said the same thing."

"Okay. Here's what I want you to do." Connie shut the file and slid it toward the center of the table. "Close your eyes. Go back to the moment that guy stepped out."

"Might have stepped out."

"I've already told you. Forget the maybe. Right now, he was there. Okay. Are you there too?"

"Yes."

Connie came in tight. "Bring him around in front of you. You're a pro. Tell me what you see."

Brodski was watching her. Not him. Studying her hard. Until Matt said, "He was tall."

"Taller than you?"

"About the same height."

"Okay. Call it six feet plus. Was he Anglo, African-American, what?"

"White." More definite now.

Connie couldn't help it. Real detective work. At last. She sighed with a pleasure as real as fear.

Brodski was into it now as well. "Anything about what he was wearing?"

A silence, then, "A sports jacket. Not like a suit. A team jacket. Different-colored sleeves from the body. And a cap."

Brodski leaned back. Studied the ceiling lights for a long time. Long enough for Connie to ask, "What?"

Brodski said to the ceiling, "Yankees."

Matt opened his eyes. Just stared at him.

Connie said, "I don't remember that."

"Sure. I saw the guy. Anglo. Bulked up like he was seriously into weights or something. And older, right?"

Matt's wounded expression had only deepened. "I don't remember."

Brodski dropped his chin. "Sure. A Yankees cap and jacket. Standing back from the perimeter tape. He was there."

Connie asked, "Why didn't you note it in the report?"

"What was to report? He was one of the first guys to show up; that's why I remember him. By the time you got there and the ambo took Kelly here away, we had, what, a couple of dozen people out there making noise."

"More," Connie said, watching Matt and worrying over what she saw in his face. Wishing she understood why finding out he'd been right could hurt him so bad.

"Yeah, but him I remember. Standing off by himself. Just standing and watching until the ambo arrived. Sure."

"Think you remember enough to give us a composite?"

"No problem." Brodski rose from the table. "We all done here?"

"I guess so. Matt?"

"Yes." He stood and offered his hand. "Thank you."

"Hey, I'm real sorry about your loss." To Connie, only half joking, "You're sure you're not IA?"

"Yeah, I'm sure." Connie grinned. "But be a pal and don't tell Hands, okay?"

"He'd freak if he thought this meeting was about him."

Connie gathered up the files and steered Matt toward the door. "That's right. He would."

Matt followed Connie down the tunnel and back into headquarters. He knew she was waiting for him to speak. Her sense of worry emanated as strong as musk. But he was unable to respond. Reliving the scene had left him nauseous. But that was not the only reason Matt remained silent. If the man had existed, then his other half-remembered image took a giant step closer to reality. The memory of the blast lifting him off the ground was mixed now with the nightmare he had endured every night since almost dying. This second image was crystal clear. For a blinding explosion of time, he had been outside himself. He had watched himself lying upon the pavement. He had seen his mother's crumpled form. But he could not go to her. She had looked disheveled, which for his mother was unthinkable. Her skirt was up around her thighs. Her hair was flung over her face. The earring was missing from the ear he could see. Matt knew she was dead. Then the image ended, leaving only the smoky burn of guilt over not having kept her safe. One brief flash of viewing himself outside himself. The next thing he knew, he was in the ambulance with two medics working on him and looking very worried.

Matt tried hard to keep from recalling the image or dream or what-ever it was. But it flashed into his vision at the most appalling of times. Like now. Standing beside Connie, waiting for the elevator, feeling the sweat dribble down his spine.

They stepped into the elevator and the doors closed. Moving blankets covered three walls, a roomy coffin for two. Connie gave him the same pinched look she had shown D'Amico upstairs. "You okay, Matt?"

"Am I Matt now?"

"Whatever." Her worry was genuinely touching. "We're still pals, right?"

He pretended to scratch his forehead, removing the damp. "Absolutely."

"You sure?"

"We will be," Matt replied. Her concern was enough to banish the unsolved mystery. For now. "If you let me take you to dinner."

She raised her head, said to the ceiling, "Did I ever walk into that one."

"Is that a yes?"

"Come by my seats at the game Sunday," she said. "We'll negotiate."

"Oh. Is that what it's called these days?"

Which was why, when the doors opened and they found D'Amico waiting for them, they were both smiling. Connie covered it with, "Success."

"Give it to me."

D'Amico studied them both as Connie described what they had learned from Brodski. "So we got us a clue. Way to go, team. Morales, talk to the sergeant, arrange the sketch artist while Brodski's still in recall mode. Then get on the prisoners."

"Roger that."

"Look for anything that might get a guy who's a pro at staying silent to talk." To Matt, "It's time we met your bomb guy."

As the elevator doors shut on them, Connie cut Matt a look and said, "Go birds."

D'Amico asked, "Am I missing something?"

"Football."

"Never caught that bug." He handed Matt a file. "Two copies of your mother's case, one for you, one for the fibbie. This has been highly sanitized. If your tame fed complains, tough. I got to tell you, I'm reluctant to give him this much."

Matt felt the paper vibrate in his grip, an angry buzzing that shook him to his bones.

The elevator opened on the ground floor and D'Amico started for the front doors. "Ask a thousand cops and you'll get one answer. A fed comes at you with a mouthful of howdy and a handful of gimme."

"I'm a fed," Matt said.

"Which is the only reason I'm trusting you with those files. The operative word here is *you*. Personal. Not this joker. Now tell me what you know about him."

"Almost nothing. Allen Pecard is a Brit. He's served as outside consultant to the fibbies. Bannister says he's worked several cases with him and rates him very highly." Matt recalled the initial contact. "He strikes me as a pro."

D'Amico punched through the front doors and headed for Pratt Street. "I'll go this one round, then he's all yours."

———

Pecard was waiting for them outside the ENT. He had traded his work-stained dungarees for a jacket of herringbone twill and black gabardine slacks. Gray-and-white pinstriped shirt. Muted silk tie. Gold collar pin. Black lace-ups so well shined they reflected the afternoon sun. Pecard was a polished English gentleman with the features of a feral beast and the neck scar to match. His clear gaze gave nothing and took in all.

Matt watched as the two men, a homicide cop and a semiretired federal bomb expert, shook hands. They eyed each other like enemy warriors brought to the peace table. D'Amico said, "Evidence is on the second floor."

"Lead on, Detective."

They rode upstairs in silence. The evidence lockup shared the windowless floor with temporary holding cells. The lockup clerks had the pasty look of voluntary prisoners. D'Amico signed them in, pointed to a counter surrounded by stools, and said, "Wait here."

Matt watched him follow the clerk into a second room, this one framed by reinforced lockers. The clerk used keys chained to her waist to open one at the end. D'Amico pulled out a cardboard box and carried it over. He set it on the counter and said, "All yours."

Pecard glanced at the hovering clerk. "Do you mind?"

"The clerk stays," D'Amico replied. "Standard ops whenever an outsider views evidence in a live file."

Pecard shrugged his indifference and slipped a pouch from his jacket pocket. From the pouch came a starched white towel, tweezers, high-powered pencil light, magnifying glass, surgical gloves, and a jeweler's loupe. He slipped on the tight-fitting gloves, opened the box, and disappeared.

Matt forced himself to watch as Pecard sorted through the blackened and twisted elements of a sick puzzle. D'Amico apparently noticed his queasiness. Very little escaped the detective's attention. He kept shooting Matt glances, but did not speak.

Pecard's taut features suggested an elemental nature, one that did not permit the luxury of spare flesh or wasted motion. His hands were big-boned and his fingers splayed, the kind of grip that could one-hand a basketball. Yet he handled the charred remains with an artist's delicacy.

Finally he set down the tweezers and dropped the loupe into his palm and declared, "Mr. Kelly was correct. The target was the woman."

"Oh, really."

"There's no timer, you see."

"We noticed that."

"And no trigger for a wire."

"It could have been vaporized," D'Amico replied. "We're talking about a very powerful bomb, remember?"

Pecard picked up a blackened filament. "This is what's left of your ignition source, Detective."

D'Amico leaned in closer. "Looks like a wire to me."

"It's meant to." The frazzled strand was connected to a base smaller than Matt's thumbnail. "But do you see this flat piece here?"

"Where the trip wire was connected to the wall." But D'Amico sounded less certain now.

"We perform a remarkable duty at the Aberdeen testing grounds, Detective. Every time your authorities get wind of a new explosive device, homegrown or high-tech, charge or delivery method, our task is the same." Pecard twisted the charcoal wire and strand back and forth between his thumb and forefinger. "We work up a dozen or so copies, using all the elements we know they used, whoever 'they' are. Then we blow it up. Over and over and over. Then we inspect the results."

Pecard held the wire before D'Amico's face. "This is an antenna. The base here is a connection point to the receiver. Your ignition source was the most widely owned digital receiver on earth."

Matt said, "A cell phone."

"Very good."

The memory slapped him across the face. "Just as she reached the door—"

"She being your mother?"

"Yes. Her phone rang." Matt stared at the wire dangling from Pecard's fingers. "But it wasn't her phone, was it."

D'Amico said, "We'll need to verify this."

"You do that, Detective." Pecard's gaze remained on Matt. "What would you say is the next step in this investigation, Agent Kelly?"

It was the first time in Matt's life anyone had ever called him that. The jolt was strong enough to pull him back into the room. "Find out who started the rumor about right-wingers going after my father. And why."

Pecard might have smiled. "I believe my work here is concluded."

But D'Amico remained between Pecard and the door. "Help us out here. Explain to me why you're doing this."

"Your question says quite a lot about the current state of things, when one officer of the law must ask another why he's willing to assist with an unsolved murder."

D'Amico crossed his arms and waited.

"Bryan Bannister and I go back a very long way. You know who he is?"

"SAC of the Homeland regional office."

"Bryan asked me to check out the site. He knows enough about explosives to worry that his predecessor might have made a seriously false claim about the armory heist."

"So Bannister expected us to discover this sooner or later," D'Amico interpreted. "Now he's hoping if you help us out, we might toss him a bone and keep it quiet. How am I doing?"

Pecard gave a shrug that could have meant anything.

"Kelly showing up when he did must have been like the answer to a prayer."

"I wouldn't go that far," Pecard said. "If it hadn't been Agent Kelly, another avenue would have been located. Sooner or later."

D'Amico stepped aside. "You can go now."

Pecard said to Matt, "You have the file for me?" He accepted the folder, said, "Stay in touch, Agent Kelly."

By the time Matt returned to his basement apartment, his leg felt like a receptacle for all the day's stress. He took his time stretching, then showered, and then stretched again. Then he made his calls. He had no concern that the two people he needed to reach might already have quit work for the weekend.

Sol Greene, for one, never stopped this close to election day. Sol had two phones and a pager. The phone listed on his business card always responded with a message. The other phone was guaranteed to draw him from the grave.

When Sol answered, Matt heard a band and some big booming voice, not his father's. Then, "What?"

"It's Matt."

"You got to speak up, kid. We still on for tomorrow?"

The message had been waiting for him as soon as he keyed on the phone. "Nine-thirty, WTBF."

"Be there a few minutes early; they'll want to do your makeup. This is big, Matt. You and your dad are going national."

"Sol, I need an introduction."

"What? Sorry, the noise is unbelievable."

"I want to speak with Rolf Zelbert." Zelbert was the dental surgeon from Annapolis. His father's adversary for the Senate.

"Does this have something to do with the police thing?"

"The investigation. Yes. I just need to ask him a couple of questions—"

"Matt, we're nine days away from winning!"

"And I'm investigating my mother's murder."

"There's no way Zelbert is going to tell you a thing about those fanatics. It's not in his best interest!"

"I don't think right-wing extremists were behind this, Sol. And I *know* they weren't after Dad."

"What?"

"We just got confirmation. Mom was the target all along."

"I can't . . ." Sol was drowned out by a thunderous round of applause.

When the noise dropped, Matt said, "I've seen the evidence. Mom was targeted and we've got to learn why."

"Matt, can't this wait just nine days?"

Matt held the phone, weighing responses. "She was your friend, Sol."

"I'm just asking for a little time. Nine days. It's already been what, two weeks?"

Another booming voice proclaimed Paul Kelly for United States Senate, then Sol shouted against the crowd's roar, "Your father's coming on, Matt. We'll talk tomorrow."

———

Jack van Sant answered with, "Agent Kelly, excellent. You're on my list. This call's saved me a dime."

"Something the matter?"

"Negative. The ambassador wanted to confirm the reports were true. You brought down an armed assailant bare-handed and saved a cop's life?"

"Actually, sir, I was unofficial backup. Another officer—"

"Remember the ambassador's number one rule, Kelly. Wear your medals."

"Then I guess it's all true, sir."

"Good work. Nothing pleases the ambassador more than being proven right. For my side, I'm glad to be handing off to another specialist born to ops."

"I need a favor." Matt ran through what they had learned thus far. "We're no closer to identifying a suspect."

"Thirty-six hours into a cold case, I'd say you're rolling."

"The FBI's bomb specialist called this a signature device. I was wondering if you could check and see if any other murders have been committed using decommissioned claymores."

"Consider it done."

"There's no rush."

"Rule two, Kelly. In this town, it's either urgent or it's buried. Back to you soonest."

———

Matt microwaved a ready-made dinner he bought in weekly installments from the Whole Foods market. A healthy bachelor's answer to a fast-food world. As he sat down to eat, the standard evening crowd thumped through the upstairs front door. Matt ate, read the paper, and watched television.

Waited.

Eventually the front door began opening and shutting. Matt turned off the television and listened to a final voice. His apartment was well insulated. But upstairs was floored in pegged heart-of-pine, more than a century old, which his mother had painstakingly restored. She had declared it a crime to cover such artwork with carpet. Matt's father walked heavy and talked loud, particularly when he was in his politicking mode, which these days was Paul Kelly's only forward gear. Matt waited for the front door to *thunk* a final time. Sol's footsteps rounded the house and headed for the carport. The house upstairs went quiet.

Matt came out of the apartment and watched the faceless headlights speed away. He went around to the front door and used his key. "Pop?"

"In the back." The kitchen lights glared upon the ruddy waxed floors. The central hallway was ribbed by bas-relief pillars a shade darker than the floorboards. He glanced into the living room, his mother's favorite chamber. The main floor's only carpet was in there, an antique Isfahan one tone warmer than blood. His mother had brought it home and spent hours congratulating herself for finding a rug that brought out the subtle richness of the wood. Matt tried to push away the memories as he asked, "How was your day?"

Paul Kelly took a cut-crystal tumbler from the cabinet and filled it with ice. He uncapped a blue bottle of Italian sparkling water. Poured the glass full. Downed it. Sighed. "I've been dreaming of this all afternoon. Standing in my own kitchen. Alone. Drinking this water I yelled at your mom over buying. You remember?"

"Four dollars a liter for water."

"This is the last bottle. I count things like that. It's probably a bad sign. Like beneath the television makeup and the power ties I'm coming apart inside."

"I'll buy us a case of the water tomorrow, Pop."

Paul Kelly refilled his glass. "You don't have any idea what I'm talking about, do you?"

Matt slipped into his protective mode, calm and faceless.

His father drank the second glass more slowly. Gauging his son over the rim. He sighed. "This a courtesy call?"

"No, Pop. Something happened today."

"Sol told me you phoned. I told him whatever it was, it could wait."

"The investigation has turned up something you need to know about." Matt gave his father the ninety-second version.

Paul Kelly heard his son out to the end. A first when it came to anything tied to Matt's profession. "They were after Megan? You're sure?"

A band of tension Matt had been unable to acknowledge until that moment unclenched his chest. "This could be a very important development."

Paul Kelly shut his eyes and rolled the chilled crystal against his forehead. "I suppose I should thank you for letting me hear this from you."

Matt knew enough not to ask his father for contact with the opposition candidate. That would have to come from some other source. "You're welcome, Pop."

"Well, this old soldier's off to bed. Sol is coming for me at five. He told you about the television gig?"

"I'll be there."

Paul Kelly waited until his son was in the hallway to add, "What I said about you not understanding, that wasn't . . ."

Matt halted and turned back. Paul Kelly had planted both his hands upon the kitchen counter. He looked down at the glass resting between them, his back bowed from the weight of the past few days. "And how I spoke to you after the funeral. That was way out of line."

Paul Kelly straightened. He smoothed his tie down the front of his shirt. Lifted the glass. Stared at it. Then set it down again. "Sure, I was drunk. But that doesn't excuse what I said."

So many responses came to mind, they lodged in Matt's throat. He swallowed against the rough-edged slab and reflected on how it felt to hear his father apologize without Megan Kelly urging him on. How there were so many other times, episodes beyond count, when his father's cutting edge had sliced deep. But Matt's years of training kept him silent. He was so good at holding back that he could not speak at all, even when all he really wanted to say was thanks.

Paul Kelly started down the hall. As he passed Matt, he touched him on the shoulder. A light gesture, easy to ignore. "Good night, son."

Matt stood and listened to his father's heavy tread up the stairs. Rubbing at the spot on his shoulder. Wishing he had found a way to return the gesture.

The nightmare woke Matt a couple of hours before his body was ready. As tired as he was, Matt knew he would sleep no more. The recent shooting and yesterday's discussion with Connie formed a cauldron of toxic thoughts. His dream contained a rawer edge than usual, ending with him being blown repeatedly across a line of parked cars. Watching it happen from outside his body. Everything etched in helpless detail. Matt rose from his bed, the crystal chimes taking forever to fade.

He went for a predawn run. The hour before sunrise was Baltimore's quietest. No siren sliced the star-flecked night. Martin Luther King Boulevard was empty of Escalades with sound systems like compressed gunfire. Matt ran down the middle lane, taking a route he had laid out in high school. In those days he'd run to Fort McHenry and back, a ten-mile push. Today his thigh sent warning signals as he entered his father's newest development project. Matt leaned against a nineteen-story relic of boarded windows and soot-blackened stone, stretching slowly. The dream's tendrils found him again, their reach greater than his ability to flee. He propped his leg on the building's front step, bent over his thigh, and saw himself fly free of his body while crystals chimed a softly lurid tune.

His grandmother, his father's mother, had been Matt's only connection to a Fells Point heritage. All his other forebears were long gone. In his very early years, Matt had found comfort in the old lady and her porch swing. She had always been there when the family returned to Baltimore, treating his absences as little more than a breath in length. They both knew it was myth, but for a young kid jerked around so much he could lay claim to no home at all, a grandmother's illusion seemed better than any reality. They had often sat on her back porch for whole afternoons. Matt read to her from a collection of religious books she kept there just for him, enclosed in a world whose boundaries were neighbors' fences and a flower garden and wind and the chimes. When Matt was twelve, she had died, as silent in passage as in life. Three weeks later he had entered Vic Wright's dojo and found a different means of dealing with a disjointed life. The chimes were so distant a memory he had no idea what had happened to them, or why they would become woven into a nightmare so vivid it veiled his waking vision.

When his leg was ready, he ran home. The day strengthened to reveal a weather-beaten gray sky. Matt waved to the campaign staffers sharing coffee and war stories in front of the carriage house. Sol's car was already parked out back.

Matt showered and made coffee and reopened the sanitized case file. He waited until seven o'clock to place the call. Pecard's phone rang and rang. Matt hung up and tried his mobile.

Pecard answered on the first ring. "What do you have for me, Agent Kelly?"

"According to the police file, all the items either stolen or broken were trophies," Matt said. "The bomber entered three rooms. Unless one person ransacked the house while the other armed the device."

"Most bombers are total loners. Didn't the detective tell you anything?"

Matt heard the front doorbell overhead, then the soft rumble of his father's voice and a burst of laughter. "The bomber took my first karate trophy. My mother's study was harder to check because a lot of the stuff along the wall connected to the back hall got shattered. But the report says one silver tennis cup was missing. And another was wrenched apart. My dad lost his army medal, and the trophy cabinet was all torn up."

"What does that suggest?"

Matt heard the front door overhead close. Voices and footsteps clattered around the house, heading for the cars out back. "What if the only trophy of importance here was my dad's medal? What if the other stuff was just taken for emphasis?"

"You are forgetting something."

Matt shifted slightly so that he could track his father and Sol. As they rounded the corner and entered the carport, Sol hesitated and glanced back. Staring hard at the spot where Matt assumed he was hidden. Matt said, "The fingerprint."

"One thumbprint, left where it would be found in each of the three rooms. I would class that as part of the bomber's signature. Wouldn't you?"

"But the file says they ran it through the federal system and came up with nothing."

"One moment." There was the sound of the phone being muffled. Then, "Do you know the Vietnam Memorial?"

"No."

"A serious lapse. Cherry Point, above the harbor. I'll expect you there in twenty minutes."

"I'm supposed to be at a television studio for my dad at nine-thirty."

"Then you had best hurry." Pecard hung up.

———

Lucas was deep into his weekend routine when the telephone rang. When he thought back on it later, the moment had a sharply defined edge. "D'Amico."

"Lucas, this is Hannah Bernstein."

To his recollection, he had never heard the chief say her own first name. Or, for that matter, speak in such a hesitant manner. "Yes, Chief."

"I hate bothering you on your weekend off."

"I was just making pancakes for Katy and myself. You should come over."

She had the decency to pretend at a laugh, even tried for a little small talk. "Katy is your daughter, correct? Is that who I hear singing?"

"Yes, that's my darling girl." Katy was bent over a coloring book, working hard to stay inside the borders, singing a song about butterflies and rainbows. Just like any five-year-old.

"Aw, look. Maybe I . . ."

"Hang on a second." He pushed the receiver into the sweatshirt over his pounding heart. He had a sensation of the morning tightening down. He had known the feeling a thousand times before. Every time he entered a bust, an arrest, a parked car with darkened windows and an overamped sound system, an apartment building with gunfire and screams. But never in his kitchen on a gray Saturday morning. He made sure his voice was calm before he said to Katy, "Honey, can you be a big girl and turn the pancakes over in a second?"

"Okay, Daddy."

"Thank you, sweetie." He carried the phone into the living room, letting the swinging door shut behind him. "Okay. Let's have it."

"That's just it. I may be raising alarms over nothing at all. This whole thing stinks."

"Hannah, calm down. Is it okay if I call you that?"

"Eight-fifteen on a Saturday morning, you kidding? I'd be expecting a lot worse names than that."

"Hannah, just tell me what you know. Then we'll take it from there. Together. How does that sound?"

She expelled some of the tension. It carried across the wires. Through the air. Entered via his eardrum. Lodged in his gut. "Seven-thirty this morning, I get a call from the deputy commissioner. My principal ally in the hierarchy. Only now he's cold as steel. Wants me downtown. Mayor's office. Nine-thirty."

"Is this normal?"

"Not the order, not the timing, not the tone."

"Did he say why?"

"He gave me nothing. I made a couple of calls. Either nobody knows or they're too worried about their own hides to talk."

D'Amico lived in the house his own parents had bought back when the mills were rolling and the town's working stiffs walked proud. His front windows overlooked Eastern Avenue and Patterson Park. When he was a kid, on hot summer nights all the families along this stretch carried their bedding across the street and slept in the park. Watching the stars, the adults chatting while the kids raced around until they collapsed. Good times. Now the park was gang territory, the laughter replaced with terror.

"Are you there?"

D'Amico refocused on the here and now. "You think this has to do with the Kelly murder?"

"I've been racking my brain. We're not working another politically sensitive case." She breathed out another shard of tension. "This is crazy. I shouldn't have bothered you."

"No, no." D'Amico knew his gut well enough to listen when it screamed. Like now. "This is real, Hannah."

A pause. "You think?"

"We're finally making progress. Why? Because the kid and the feds have delivered. Somebody has gotten wind, and they're worried. Which means the culprit could be mixed up in the campaign." D'Amico's pacing drew Katy through the connecting doorway. He told her, "Go back inside, honey."

"The pancakes are getting cold."

"You shouldn't have waited."

"But they're not so good if you don't do the butter for me."

"Not now, Katy. Please."

Hannah said, "I'm really sorry about this, Lucas."

"You were right to call."

"How do you think I should play it?"

He liked her being strong enough to admit when she needed help. "They'd find it harder to railroad you if you didn't go in there alone. I'll meet you at headquarters in fifteen minutes."

———

The Vietnam Memorial stood above Middle Branch Park, overlooking the rowing club, the Cherry Hill Marina, and the Patapsco River. Matt rose from the car and stared out over the steel-gray waters to the Harbor Hospital and the *Times's* production center. As he climbed the pebble-stone walk spiraling up the hill, a silver Lincoln LS pulled from the lot. Matt tracked the car's progress until it took the bridge's entrance ramp and sped back toward the city.

At the crest, the POW-MIA flag flew at permanent half-mast between the American and the Maryland flags. The memorial itself was a circular granite wall, a sweeping tombstone listing all of Maryland's lost. Pecard sat on the wall, staring out over the empty gray day.

Matt asked, "Was that Bryan Bannister I just saw drive away?"

Pecard did not look up. "The first man listed here to my right died in '59. Just having a look while the French desperately sought to rid themselves of the entire mess. The last casualty perished in your final tragic push to escape."

It was the most emotion Matt had ever heard Pecard express. "Why would a Brit care about our war in Vietnam?"

"Because I was there, Agent Kelly. Nine sordid months, as counted by outside time."

"Bannister too?"

"He and I worked a case together."

Matt did not know what to say. To his right the harbor cranes stood in rusty salute, while bridge traffic drummed the constant refrain of people too busy to remember.

Pecard rose to his feet, came to attention, and snapped off a salute of his own. "Rest well, brothers."

The still day made for a somber backdrop as they headed down the hill. Pecard did not speak again until he unlocked his car, an immaculate Jeep Grand Cherokee. "You need to be somewhere; did I understand that correctly?"

"WTBF. My dad wants me for a television interview."

Pecard slid the case file out of the way. "Why don't I drive you over? We can talk on the way."

Pecard took the harbor ramp onto the I-95 bridge, then asked, "Why do you imagine they couldn't get a match on your print?"

"The bomber wasn't in the database." When Pecard shook his head, he added, "Either he's never committed a major crime or he's never gone through a government vetting. That seems pretty straightforward."

"Sorry. I don't buy that."

"And I don't see an alternative."

"Think about what you said on the phone. Prizes. Trophies. Used to emphasize your father's stolen medal."

Matt glanced at the file on the console between them. He knew the

data by rote. He studied Pecard. The man had resumed his stone vis-
age, a tightly enclosed coffin of flesh for whatever emotions he chose
not to share. "You're saying the fingerprint is part of the message. But if
there's no ID—"

"You're not looking in the right place."

"Say again?"

"People who are dead, Agent Kelly. Some felons' records are kept
for a time, along with military MIA cases and missing persons.
Otherwise, so far as the federal databanks are concerned, once a person
is declared legally dead, the individual might as well never have lived."

Headquarters on his day off. One of the vows D'Amico had made to himself when June died was to keep his free time for Katy. But there was nothing he could do about this. Hannah Bernstein was not a time waster. Not of her people, nor of herself.

The sky was the color of a fire long dead. The autumn day was void of wind. The stillness heightened his unease. Upstairs was scarcely any better. Hannah's office door was open. She was seated behind her desk. Crowder, the duty lieutenant, stood to one side so he could see both the squad room and Bernstein. Crowder was African-American, a thirty-year vet with a gaze of pure iron. The kind of man who didn't leave an open door to his back even on his own home turf.

Bernstein started in, "Lucas, I can't tell you—"

"My gut tells me you were right to call."

"Your gut," Crowder repeated. "You need a packet of salts, I believe I got some in my desk drawer."

"Funny."

"I wasn't trying to be."

"Boys. Be nice."

Crowder was a perfect pain to everybody within reach. Which was why he would never make it into the ranks of political appointees. D'Amico said, "I'm thinking Crowder should come with us too."

"No, thank you," the lieutenant replied. "I got me some real police work to do."

"They see us as a team," D'Amico went on, "maybe they'll rethink their strategy."

"I have trouble not shooting out a window in the mayor's office every time I park my car," Crowder said. "You folks go have yourselves a time without me."

"No, no," Bernstein said. "Lucas is right."

Crowder's features pinched down until the furrows ran from his nose to his ears. He said to D'Amico, "I advise you never to stand a watch with me again."

D'Amico said, "Maybe we could bring the sergeant as well."

Crowder said, "Now I *know* you're asking for it."

"Good idea." Bernstein said to Crowder, "Go ask the gentleman to join us."

Crowder shook his head. "Lucas, here I used to think you were smart."

When they were alone, Bernstein said, "We're going to look like a bunch of ducks in Saturday suits, waddling across the street."

"When we get in there," D'Amico said, "let's you and me find a reason to disagree."

"Give them the good cop, bad cop thing?"

"Nothing obvious," D'Amico said. "Just offer them a reason to think maybe they can call one and exclude the other."

Bernstein rose from her chair at the sound of two men complaining in the hallway outside her office. "You ever think of going for an admin slot?"

"Sorry. I don't have the talent."

She smiled. Touched his arm. "Is that what they call it these days?"

———

The NBC affiliate station was a charmless redbrick building. A trio of towers served as lawn ornaments. The station's letters and a rainbow peacock took the place of windows. Inside, Matt found an empty reception area and the sound of distant shouting. He checked his watch, then glanced at Pecard. They had less than ten minutes to airtime.

Footsteps pattered down a concrete hallway. A woman raced into view, demanded breathlessly, "Kelly Junior?"

"Yes."

"Where have you been? We're going national and you need makeup . . . Sandra!"

"Right behind you, hon."

"This is the son. You've got to do something about that scar."

"No can do, sweetie." The second woman was taller than Matt, rail thin, and unflappable. "New York wants it big and glaring."

"Whatever. I've got to go tell . . ." Her words trailed off down the hall.

"This way." When Pecard started to follow them, she asked, "And you are?"

Matt replied, "With me."

"Whatever." She hustled Matt down a narrow hall. "Everybody's supposed to sign in and show ID, but an al-Qaeda brigade could waltz through here today and nobody'd notice."

Sandra seated Matt in a cramped overlit room, tucked a napkin into his collar, and went to work. Up close she smelled of cigarettes and a lot of hard years. Two minutes later an older man, balding and portly, bounced off the doorway. He glared at Matt and said, "He's late."

Sandra did not look up. "He's fine."

"New York wants to know if you can accent his scar."

"I suppose I could dab it with Mercurochrome and abrade it with sandpaper. The kid might complain, though. I know I would."

It was unlikely the guy heard her. He moved in closer and whined, "His scar's on the wrong side."

"Excuse me?"

"Great. Now we've got to shift the candidate." He raced off.

Matt asked, "Why do they talk like I'm not here?"

"Hon, you and your dad stopped being people the instant the national morning show took you on. Shut your eyes."

Matt held his breath while Sandra shellacked him with hair spray. When she was done, he said, "I don't like attention being called to my scar."

She liked that a lot. "Sugar, be glad New York didn't ask for floppy ears and a bunny suit."

A man's voice called in falsetto strain, "Sixty seconds!"

"We're done." Sandra patted his shoulder. "Go get 'em, tiger."

Matt entered a doorway with an unlit On Air sign overhead. Sol Greene halted his conversation and came over. "Where have you been?"

"Following up on a lead."

When worried, Sol Greene took on a fretful air that aged and emasculated. He patted his forehead, touched the knot of his tie, sighed, straightened his lapels, and said, "Matt, we're friends, right? I've always thought of you as the son I never had. Your being late to these gigs is not having a good effect on your father. Could you please—"

"Kelly Junior!" The portly man now wore a headset. His bald head glistened. "Can you move a little faster, please."

The studio was a concrete cavern filled with wires, lights, machines, and portable walls. The set was blindingly lit. Matt was led to a half-moon table with two swivel chairs and a padded neon blue backdrop. His father was talking into his cell phone as Matt stepped onto the stage.

The producer told him, "Take this chair. Wait, put this battery pack into your back pocket. Unbutton your jacket, clip this mike to your tie. No, a little lower, please."

His father shut his phone and asked, "You felt like making an entrance?"

"Sol told me nine-thirty."

"Correction. Sol gave you airtime." His father sipped from a studio mug. Eight days of campaigning left, and Paul Kelly was living on coffee and energy drinks. "Sol doesn't make amateurish mistakes. Unlike my son and his single-minded determination to go against the grain."

"Okay, Kelly Senior, your sound checks. Kelly Junior, speak in a normal tone."

"This investigation is vital. You of all people—"

"That's good. Okay, we're live in ten, nine, eight . . ."

There were two interviewers, both female. Their faces occupied two monitors set so Matt and his father looked straight into a camera. All three cameras were remotes, operated from the control room positioned high over the exit. The camera's rubber wheels hissed softly as they moved about the studio. Matt felt a total sense of disconnection to the interview. His father came on with the camera's red eye, a real pro, able to set everything aside and perform. Matt retreated behind his mask and stewed. When the announcers asked him something, he wasn't sure what they had said. He answered tersely enough for his father to turn and give him that smile. The one he had known since childhood. The one that mocked him for not measuring up.

The studio's dark reaches swallowed everything and gave nothing back. The only other people in the studio were two shadows. Portly and erratic for Sol Greene. Tall and still for Pecard.

Finally one of the announcers segued into the closing. Matt could not say which one, or how long they had been on. "Paul Kelly, Democratic candidate for the United States Senate. Thank you for joining us this morning, Mr. Kelly."

"Thank you for having me."

The red light on the close-up camera died. The producer announced from his glass cage, "We're off-air, folks. Thank you. Weather, you're up in forty."

Paul Kelly fiddled impatiently with his tie-mike. "Get this thing off me."

Sol rushed over. "We're due in Annapolis in less than an hour."

"Can I at least wipe this cake off my face?"

"Do it on the bus, Paul." Sol gave Matt a final worried look as he shepherded the candidate toward the exit.

Matt dropped his mike and battery pack on the table and hurried after them. Pecard fell in beside him. The television people ignored them entirely, already tense over the next ninety-second storm.

Outside they were enveloped by a colorless day. The still air smelled of highway fumes and coming friction. He followed his father to the bus. Pecard stepped up beside him. When Matt remained silent, he said, "Mr. Kelly, we need to ask you something."

"Not now," Sol replied.

"Sir, this cannot wait."

Paul Kelly stopped beside his picture on the campaign bus. He smirked at his son. "Who's your English pal?"

Matt studied his father from an incomplete distance, the moment joined to a lifetime of others. Pecard replied, "Allen Pecard, sir. Affiliated with the FBI."

"Affiliated doesn't mean a thing to me." His father continued to address Matt. Too caught up in a treadmill of his own making to notice that his son no longer ran alongside. "Either this man is FBI or he's not."

"Not," Pecard said.

"Great. So I'm being confronted by a boy who's not a cop and a Brit who's not FBI. Wait. Is there a detective in sight? No, there is not." He started for the bus door. "The police must think you're on to something really important here."

"Sir, we need to ask you about the battle where you won the Medal of Honor."

Sol Greene clambered onto the bus. "Paul, we are seriously late!"

"We believe we've uncovered what could very well turn out to be a crucial lead." Allen Pecard pulled a battered notebook from his back pocket. "Would you happen to remember what day—"

"What, so you and this *other* no-account can invade my day with this drivel?" The pancake makeup lay like orange stucco on Paul Kelly's rage as he stormed onto the bus. "Why aren't we moving?"

———

Pecard watched the bus drive away with what might have been a smile. "I believe we might class that as a debt in my favor."

"We got nothing out of that except my dad is going to cook from now to next year."

"On the contrary. This time your father is angry with me. From my initial observations, I believe that makes a distinct difference." Pecard resembled a feisty tom with a distinctly polished air, one who counted any battle where he was left standing as a satisfactory exchange. "Shall we be off?"

Pecard led him back to the Grand Cherokee and headed for Cherry Point. "What do you suppose happened back there?"

"We caught my father on a bad day. Can we talk about something else?"

"Most certainly. Would you care to comment on the silent statue you resembled in that little exchange?"

"How I handle my father is not anyone else's business."

"You did not *handle* your father, Agent Kelly." Pecard granted Matt a chance to argue, then, "You are headed for ops, are you not?"

"Eventually."

"Successful field agents discover their natural abilities and hone them. Their lives depend upon this. You have a knack for reading the subtlest signs in people. It is recognized by those closest to you as one of your most remarkable traits. That and your facility to merge with whichever shadow is closest."

Matt swiveled in his seat. "Who have you been talking to?"

"Let's move beyond that." Pecard was so quietly focused he made a lie of his smile. "Your problem is, you let others shape your response. You adapt according to what somebody else wants you to be."

His heart rate accelerated until it matched the tires drumming across the Inner Harbor bridge. "My problem, is that what you said?"

"What I said, Agent Kelly, was *move on*. It's time you start learning to *manipulate* events." Pecard took the off-ramp but did not head back to the memorial. Instead, he pulled into the marina parking lot and halted in front of the restaurant. "Why do you think I pushed your father? Because I'm looking to see his reaction, and that of his handler."

"Sol Greene."

"The police have obviously written them both off as suspects. But the police also have an unsolved murder. So I arrive on the scene. A rank outsider. And I manipulate the situation and observe their responses." Pecard reached across the seat and poked Matt in the ribs. "Something you should be doing."

"Back off."

Pecard kept poking Matt's chest in time to each word. "You could learn a great deal if you would simply stop permitting others to dominate your responses, and control matters yourself."

Matt grabbed for the hand. And missed. And discovered Pecard was grinning at him.

"Do you see?"

Matt opened his door. Stepped onto the pavement. Stared back inside the car. Filled with an urge to crawl back inside the car and pop this guy. Hard.

Pecard's eyes tightened slightly. It might have been another smile. He was finding genuine pleasure in pushing Matt to the edge. "Here's a thought, Agent Kelly. The next time you confront your old man, try being the controller. Instead of the clown."

As they headed from police headquarters to City Hall, D'Amico walked a couple of steps behind the chief. He liked the view more than a little. She was a strong, tough woman, not so much softened by her femininity as spiced. Her gray hair was cut full to oval-frame her face. Steel gaze to match the hair. Suit a shade darker. Black turtleneck and stockings and heels. D'Amico knew from office scuttlebutt that she had lost her husband to a stroke and been single for more than a decade. The lady was trying to be stone-cold in front of her troops, ready for the battle ahead, but there was nothing she could do about her walk. The lieutenant caught D'Amico smiling over the view and shook his head in amazement. D'Amico didn't mind. It'd been a long time since he'd enjoyed anything this much.

City Hall was a marble and brass tomb on weekends. They took the elevator to the third floor. The power hallway mocked them with echoes and the smell of old wax. Bernstein knocked on the deputy mayor's polished door.

The next door opened. "In here."

They filed into what had formerly been the aldermen's meeting chamber. Nowadays it was reserved for official meet and greets. D'Amico had seen it any number of times on television, been inside twice for awards ceremonies. The room was all gilt and polish, twenty-foot windows, domed ceiling, gold drapes, bronze chandeliers. Six of them.

The deputy police commissioner frowned. "This was supposed to be a confidential meeting."

"You didn't say anything about private," Bernstein said, then turned and told her troops, "Sit."

"We want to speak with you alone."

"There is nothing I care to hide from my division."

Two men faced them, the deputy mayor and the deputy police commissioner. Both were holdovers from the last administration. The deputy commissioner was a long-term Baltimore politico, squat and muscular with toneless eyes. The deputy mayor was taller, leaner, more handsome, but cut from the same political mold. The commissioner said, "They're yours only so long as we say so."

"Is that why we're here?" Bernstein looked from one face to the other. "You've decided to fire me?"

"That depends on the next three minutes."

"Now, now, there's no need for threats." The deputy mayor had wavy hair and a polished gleam. "We're all friends here, right, Major Bernstein?"

"I'm still trying to figure out why I've been called downtown on my day off to get rousted."

"The Kelly case," the commissioner said. "We want you to stay on target."

"I thought that's what I was doing."

"Then you thought wrong. The proper line of inquiry has been clear since the outset. Right-wing fanatics are behind the attempt on the senator's life."

"A couple of corrections are needed to that statement." Bernstein gave as good as she got. "A homicide investigation has to remain open-minded. Tunnel vision is the most common reason investigations go wrong. We have to go in the direction the leads take us."

The commissioner thunked the table between them. "Focus, Bernstein. That's how you solve the case. Everything points toward right-wingers being behind this."

"Do you have evidence I'm not aware of? Because what I've seen recently isn't all that cut and dried."

"This is the way it has to be," the deputy mayor said. "For the next nine days."

"You're telling me to stonewall a murder investigation until after the election?"

D'Amico took that as his cue. "Chief, we're not just talking a week here. Once Kelly is elected, they'll shut us down."

The two men seated across from them both gave D'Amico the slow burn. But his boss did not even glance over. "Thank you, Detective."

The deputy mayor continued to take aim at D'Amico as he said, "We have a lieutenant in Division One who assures us he can make this happen."

"Last time I checked, homicide cases are handled by homicide cops."

"They are if we say they are." This from the commissioner. "We're thinking this case is so vital to the city's good name we need to assign a special task force. With a fresh pair of eyes."

D'Amico's ire was real now. "It's Hands, isn't it. Calfo has agreed to be your tame puppy."

"I resent that slur against a good officer almost as much as I resent hearing your voice at all, Detective."

"Back off, D'Amico," Bernstein said. She continued to the pair, "Evidence we've uncovered over the past couple of days points us to the armory job. Remember that little incident, gentlemen?"

The two men gave her nothing. They didn't need to. The press had publicly fried them both over that one.

"We've finally got a chance to return the favor. If we're right, you can give the fibbies a black eye that'll shine all the way to the Hoover Building."

There was a moment's silence before the deputy mayor replied, "Come see us after the election."

Bernstein clamped down on whatever else it was she wanted to say. She lifted her troops with a motion of her head.

"Chief, one more thing."

"Sir?"

"The Kelly kid. He's off the case as of now."

Bernstein said, "We put him on because your office called me and specifically ordered I make room for him."

"That was then." The deputy mayor directed his words to the spot Bernstein had just vacated. "Get rid of the kid."

"Kelly has proven to be useful to our efforts, sir."

The commissioner swiveled in his chair. "You're telling me your division can't solve a simple homicide on its own?"

"Sir, there is nothing simple—"

"Don't argue with me, Major. Just do it."

———

They took the stairs because their chief was too hot to stand and wait for the elevator. Bernstein's anger carried her half a flight ahead of her men.

D'Amico caught up with his boss as they were crossing the street. "You weren't going to give them what the kid gave us from the FBI, were you?"

"Don't talk silly."

"No, I didn't think so." He found his grin popping out again. "You were great in there, Hannah."

But she was still working off a full head of steam. Her heels came down like she wanted to stab her way through the concrete. Or a pair of stuffed shirts. "I want you to put everything else aside. Focus exclusively on this case. And be fast. I don't know how long we'll have before they shut me down."

"You're sure about this? This could cost you your job."

She responded by turning to the lieutenant and saying, "Reassign all D'Amico's other cases. He's going full-time on Kelly for as long as we can keep the lid on."

Crowder could do pained better than anybody D'Amico knew. "Do I have a choice in the matter?"

"Absolutely. You can do it, or we'll stand here and argue, and then you'll do it."

"Chief, we are seriously overstretched."

"Crowder, this is happening."

The lieutenant gave D'Amico a world-class scowl. "Man, I'm buying you a corned-beef sandwich with a rat in it."

But D'Amico was busy watching Hannah Bernstein carry her ire toward the parking lot. "That is one incredible lady."

"Here's some free advice, D'Amico." Crowder walked away. "You seriously need to get out more."

Saturday was officially Judy Leigh's day off. But her boss was a woman and a mother, a rarity in the newspaper industry. Sarah was dealing with twin teenagers now, which left her less than positively inclined toward motherhood. But she gave Judy a lot of leeway when it came to office hours.

Which made Sarah's greeting when Judy showed up late Saturday afternoon more than a little odd. "You're here."

"And?"

"I didn't expect to see you today."

Judy Leigh's desk was by the newsroom's north wall, separated from the worst of the deadline clamor by a pillar and the jutting corner of the managing editor's office. "The baby's learning to tango. I thought I'd clear up some of the backwork, get my mind off this fifty-pound jumping bean I'm lugging around."

Usually Sarah came back with something cute. As in, you think it's bad now, wait 'til the little dumpling gives you lip at midnight and the words are slurred because of a new tongue stud she forgot to ask your permission about. Like that. Sarah's twin blond teenagers were known around the newsroom as Bandit One and Bandit Two.

Sarah just said, "Today's not so good."

"Excuse me?"

"We have a problem. I was hoping to clear it up before—"

The elevator doors opened. A portly man in a billion-dollar suit walked out, followed by the newspaper's publisher.

Sarah sighed. "Too late."

Judy had never seen the guy before. But she knew him. His portrait hung in the upstairs boardroom. And the downstairs lobby. And the publisher's office. Harry O. Weller. Chairman of Lex Industries. Owner of the *Times* and thirty-seven other papers around the globe.

Weller was as polished as an ugly man could manage. His face looked waxed and buffed. Judy could see her reflection in what hair Weller had left. He moved in close enough for her to smell a spicy mix of aftershave and hair oil. She would have laughed out loud except for the man's gaze. "This the woman?"

"Harry Weller, Judy Leigh." Sarah's voice had gone toneless.

"I thought you said she was out of town."

"I managed to track her down."

"You. Listen up. The kid." Harry Weller was a legend. Not a good legend, mind. But a legend just the same. The son of a Chicago junkyard dealer who had fought his way to the top of the nation's newsprint. The few reporters who had met Weller suggested the junkyard owner might have made a mistake and raised his dog instead. Weller snapped his fingers. "What's his name."

The newspaper publisher was normally a pompous force in his own right. It was only now that Judy comprehended his nickname among senior editors, which was "Native Bearer." He adjusted his spectacles and replied, "Matt Kelly, Mr. Weller."

"Right. You. As of now, the Kelly kid is off your list."

Judy was too astonished to speak. And those eyes. She saw her future splinter and fall apart just meeting the man's gaze.

Sarah, however, was made of sterner stuff. "Matt Kelly is at the center of—"

"Far as you're concerned, the kid is history. His story is finished. You focus on something else. Or leave. Both of you. Pack up and get out. I want your decision now."

The reporter and her editor looked at each other.

"That's what I thought." He wheeled about and said to the publisher, "Get out of my way."

"Sorry, Mr. Weller."

When they were alone and Judy could speak again, she said,

"This is the first time in a week my baby isn't moving. She's frozen up solid."

"We need to do a weekend piece," Sarah replied. "Does owning thirty-eight newspapers make you a lizard, or is it only a lizard that can crawl that high?"

"Am I fired? I couldn't tell."

"The Native Bearer didn't hand out pink slips, so I guess we've both still got desks."

"What do you want me to do?"

"I'd tell you that I'll handle Weller, but you know I'd be lying." Sarah leaned against the pillar. "Do your job. Double-source all material. I'll assign you a few puff pieces as cover. If anybody asks, they'll be your current assignments."

"You want me to find out why Weller is so concerned about Matt Kelly."

Sarah's expression carried a three-alarm warning. "Very. Very. Quietly."

Lucas entered church hand in hand with his daughter. He was used to people staring and hated it just the same. Not for himself. Katy was slow, not numb. She was extremely sensitive to what others thought, which was one reason she remained so quiet. But it was hard for such a large woman to hide.

Rev. Ian Reeves watched them take their seats midway up on the left. Lucas felt his friend's words pressing down upon what was otherwise a splendid autumn day.

On their way over that morning Katy had announced that tomorrow she would begin helping out at the home. She treated it as the most natural thing in the world. It was only after careful questioning that Lucas learned she already worked there on occasion. The two houses, one a hospice and the other for special-needs adults, were separated by a garden that Katy loved to tend. Another surprise. He settled into his seat and tried without success to push aside the sense of his own life, not Katy's, being stolen from him.

He bowed over the pew in front of him. Sometimes he could find a special sense of clarity in these moments. But not today. He missed his wife terribly. June had a way of cutting through his selfish excuses and looking at the core of issues. But he was alone now and could not see beyond his desire to hold on to what was already gone.

———

Matt sat across the central aisle from the detective. Connie had mentioned that the guy was religious. Still, it was jarring to see the man responsible for the investigation into his mother's death enter his mother's church.

A young woman sat beside D'Amico. She was dressed in a dark sweater and long black skirt. The clothes only heightened her lumpish appearance. She was broader than the detective and was crowned by uncontrollable dark hair pinned back with a pair of pink plastic bows. She sat staring forward, not looking at anyone.

Matt dropped his gaze back to his hands. Now that he was here, he wished he had not come. He had awakened that morning to the same jarring nightmare and spent much of the early hours staring out the back window and sipping his coffee. His leg had felt stiff from the previous day's sprint, so he had decided not to run. He could not go to the dojo. He had no campaign commitment until the afternoon game. He had nothing to do except stand by the window and drink his coffee and miss the way things once had been. Finally Matt had dressed and left the apartment without even trying to explain the action to himself, hoping in a wordless swirl of dead emotional leaves that something of Megan Kelly might still be here, in this place she had cherished. Where he had said his final farewell.

After the service, Matt remained seated as the detective led his daughter to the side entrance. Only then did he rise and take aim for where Ian Reeves stood by the rear door.

The pastor greeted him with, "Matt, I thought I recognized you there. How are you, man?"

"I was wondering if I might have a word."

"Of course." Ian Reeves pointed to the corner beside the shelf of handouts. "Step over there and give me a minute. I'll be right with you."

Matt stood and watched the pastor offer each departing parishioner ten seconds of undivided attention. The man had a politician's ability to give single-minded focus to one person at a time. As soon as the last lady had tugged at Ian's sleeve, he turned and said to Matt, "Follow me."

Matt was led to a stone-lined chamber beside the altar. Ian joked with the elders counting the morning's donations as he slipped off his robes. He pulled a gray sweater over his head and led Matt into the pastor's study. "What can I do for you?"

"I need an introduction to Rolf Zelbert." Matt's mother had often mentioned the pastor's Republican affiliation, which Matt assumed was the reason his father disliked Ian. Paul Kelly's world was cleanly divided between obstacles and those who could help him gain the next prize.

"No problem. Rolf is in town today, as a matter of fact."

The blank check caught him unawares. "Don't you want to know why?"

"Is it any of my business?"

"It is if you want it to be."

"Matt, I'm a plain-speaking kind of guy. Your mother's absence leaves a hole in my world. If offering you a helping hand draws her a fraction closer, then I'm having a good day."

Matt rubbed the lower half of his face, trying to conceal the sudden emotion. "I miss her too."

"Which is why I feel so much closer to her when you're around." Ian reached for the cell phone on his desk. "You want to pay back the favor, stop by for a visit. There's a great deal of her in you. More than you realize. It'd do my old heart good to see more of you."

———

The Republican candidate for the United States Senate was a small man with skin the color of a permanent tan, dark eyes, and the aquiline features of a Persian or Armenian or aristocratic Spaniard. Matt found him in the studio of a local NPR station. His campaign manager was a big-boned woman in black with a long silk scarf splashing color around her neck and down one side. She wore thick-framed oval glasses and a worried look. "You're Paul Kelly's son?"

"Yes."

"And you're FBI?"

He offered his ID. "State Department Intelligence."

She examined it carefully. "I didn't know there was such a thing."

"A lot of people don't."

"But I'm not a lot of people. I've worked inside the Beltway for twelve years. I've managed eleven national campaigns and won eight of them."

"I'm not here to cause trouble."

"A rival's wife is murdered and the press suggests backers of my candidate are behind it. The son shows up eight days before the election, wanting to interview my candidate. He represents an intelligence division I've never heard of." She turned her attention back to the glass barrier. "How could this possibly not be trouble?"

They stood in the darkened control room. The sound through the overhead monitor was so muted Matt could not hear what was being said. But the two people on the other side of the glass did not pretend at friendliness. Matt leaned forward and tapped the producer on the shoulder. When she lifted one earpiece, Matt asked, "Could I hear what they're saying?"

Wordlessly the technician offered him a pair of headphones. Matt fitted them on.

"—Gun control?"

"Last time I checked," the candidate retorted, "Megan Kelly was killed by a bomb."

The interviewer was young and earnest and very intelligent. She was dressed in a T-shirt and peasant's skirt. Rolf Zelbert, in sharp contrast, wore a salt-and-pepper jacket that matched his hair and mustache. He was tightly groomed. Equally articulate. And angry.

"But clearly Mrs. Kelly's tragic death raises all sorts of questions about—"

"Crime in general. I couldn't agree more. Pouring billions of dollars into renovating downtown Baltimore is no answer if people are afraid to move here. This city is America's murder capital and assault capital and armed robbery capital. Federal agents claim its harbor is the principal East Coast entry port for hard drugs. This has got to change. If the local authorities are too busy fighting battles over how to spend federal grant money, we will have to find another way."

The young woman sought to steer the interview in another direction. "Would you care to comment about the accusation that right-wing fanatics were behind Mrs. Kelly's murder?"

"That is not the issue. What you should be asking is, why does the press insist on wasting my time with such a ludicrous accusation?"

"The police don't think it's ludicrous."

"These same Baltimore police who have let crime in their city grow completely out of control? Baltimore has fewer cops on the street per capita, and more politically appointed chiefs, than any other American city. *That* is the problem."

"We were talking about right-wing fanatics, Dr. Zelbert."

"*You* were talking. *I* was talking about this city. Baltimore spends insane amounts on social programs that prop up a population who are terrified to leave their homes. They effectively bribe property developers to rebuild areas that gangs have turned into combat zones. Cronyism is rampant. The federally funded social net has become a substitute for decent jobs. Why? Because companies wouldn't dream of setting up in this place."

Matt took off his headphones and said to the campaign manager, "Thank you for your time."

"That's it? That's all you wanted?"

"I've heard enough."

"My candidate had nothing to do with your mother's death."

"I know that now."

She gave him the stare. The one his mother had always laughed over. The Washington insider's glare, fashioned by years of hearing one thing and needing to understand another. "Wait. I've got it now. You're a drone. They sent you over to flash your badge and sniff around."

"My father doesn't know I'm here."

"Who's talking about your father? Sure. It all makes sense now." She was nodding now. "Well, you tell Sol he got in a good hit below the belt. But my man isn't bleeding. You go ask Sol if he saw the polls this morning. We're up two points."

Matt knew there was nothing to be gained from arguing. "Thank you for your time."

"Eight days. You go tell Sol that." She turned back to the glass. "Eight days is an eternity in this game."

Sunday afternoon, the waterfront was awash in the home-team colors of blue and black. Kids as young as six weeks bore Ravens wings tattooed on cheeks, palms, and foreheads. They came ready to yell. Ready to win. The Cowboys were in town, and even the weather rooted for Baltimore.

In bygone days, the city had only one stadium, but that had been good enough for the Colts and the Orioles. Then the Colts had slipped away in the middle of the night and taken the last shards of city pride with them. But Baltimore was a city born to struggle and to win. New stadiums were built. A new team found. New fans ignited. Baltimore came back from the grave. Again.

Connie met Dorcas at Gino's, their pregame spot when they weren't invited to somebody's tailgate heaven. There had once been a dozen or so Gino's around town, owned by Gino Marchetti, a former Colts player and hometown hero. More than half had been fire-bombed after the Colts had fled to Indianapolis. The last remaining Gino's had no relation to the player, was located across from the new Orioles stadium, and served the world's finest hamburgers and beer-batter fries. Three ceiling-mounted televisions blared the pregame broadcast. Dorcas was always on a post-kid diet and Connie almost never ate anything that had a nodding acquaintance with grease. But this was game day. And on game day, none of the house rules applied.

They took their orders to the plastic chairs set illegally along the sidewalk. The tables would have been ticketed as a traffic hazard if half the clientele weren't cops.

Connie turned her face to the October sun and sighed with pleasure. "If I could find a man who was half as good as a home game, I'd be lost forever."

"Speaking of men, is Matt Kelly wearing well?"

"Don't talk with your mouth full."

"I take that as an affirmative."

"Matt is fed. Feds come and go. Today Baltimore, tomorrow Kabul." Connie stabbed fries into the ketchup. "If I'd wanted a leave-home guy, I'd have gone for a marine."

Dorcas smiled around her burger. "Sounds to me like you got a bad case of the shivers."

"Now I know you're crazy."

"Girl, this is me you're talking to. Just saying Kelly's name gives you the tummy quivers. Tell me I'm wrong."

Connie squinted into the sun. "He's here."

"At today's game?"

"He's in the owner's box. With his dad."

"And you came with me? You *are* crazy."

"I'm not ready for a family meet. Besides which, home games are as close to a tradition as anything in my life."

Dorcas snorted but said no more. They dumped their trash and joined the hordes. They took the Camden Yards passage running alongside the new Orioles stadium. The dual-stadium development was a rare monument to good taste and civic pride. The baseball stadium and outbuildings were all done in the same Church Street brick as the renovated waterfront warehouses. The result was an arena that looked as if it had been there since Revolutionary War soldiers rooted for the home team, or so the locals liked to claim.

The crowd was thick and boisterous enough to leave them feeling isolated. Dorcas asked as they walked, "How's it going with those names I gave you?"

Those names, as in the neo-Nazis doing time for the National Guard heist. "I'm still working on them. This is my only time off this weekend."

"So what's the big crunch?"

"I can't tell you."

Dorcas stared at her. "That is so cool."

"Yeah, it's something, all right." Connie grinned. "You're looking at a real cop doing real cop work for a change."

"So how do you like working with Lucas?"

"He's an all-around great guy."

"Yeah, he's that, all right."

"You talked to him about me, didn't you?"

"You mind?"

"Do I look like I mind?"

"Then yeah, I did." But Dorcas didn't smile. "Lucas saved my marriage."

"Get out."

"We hit a rough patch. Lucas helped. A lot."

"What'd he do?"

"What does he ever? Sat Carl down. Got him to talk. You know how tough that is?"

"I know." Dorcas's husband treated words like money he couldn't afford to spend, looking at things he didn't want to buy.

"Two solid hours, my big silent man blabbed away. Then he sat me down and listened to me. Then he had us listen to each other. Got us going to a couples class at his church."

"When was this?"

"Before you joined up. Right after Lucas lost his wife. That was why he got to us. You know, showed us just what was waiting on the other side of that door." Dorcas was sad now. "Poor guy. You know about his daughter?"

"I don't hardly know him at all."

"He's got this kid, Katy. We're talking seriously slow, you get me? But sweet as an angel. I see her around church sometimes. Lucas is trying so hard, but after losing his wife, the whole deal is just dragging him down. Sometimes I think he's too trapped to see it."

Connie pulled her friend to one side of the crush. "Okay. Enough. You know what today is, right?"

"Yeah, yeah."

"Tell me."

"The Ravens' ticket to the play-offs."

"And what are we here to do?"

Dorcas answered like a sullen teenager. "Rumble."

"Right. So let's leave the world out here where it belongs." She grabbed her friend by the arm, handed her ticket to the attendant, ratcheted through the turnstile, and said, "Any more of that long face and I eat your hot dog."

Connie and Dorcas shared a passion that Dorcas's husband considered seriously twisted. They headed up the ramp to their season ticket seats on the forty-yard line. When they emerged into the sunlight, they stopped as always and took a deep breath. Popcorn and chicken fingers and beer and cheese fries and adrenaline. The end-zone screens greeted them with "Get Ready to Rumble." Connie hooted in reply. Tradition.

On home-game Sunday, Connie was no longer a cop with serious career troubles. She wasn't lonely. She wasn't wondering about her home and bills and a future that had looked too bleak for far too long. She was surrounded by seventy-two thousand of her very closest buddies, walking the stairs with a twin sister dressed in matching R. Lewis T-shirts. They were already dancing to Hendrix and P. Diddy before they found their seats. An old man with beer and onions on his breath shouted, "You two put them cheerleaders down front in the trash!" And today, of all days, it was a compliment worthy of a smile.

———

Jerry Freid had worn every nerd's nickname since he started school. Long before geeks existed, Freid had been sidelined and forgotten. Pencil boy. All bones and bottle-bottom glasses. Well, Jerry Freid had finally taken his revenge on the world. In a sweet and singular way.

He actually was a wizard with numbers. If computers had come in twenty years earlier, Jerry might have been the geek making the covers of magazines. As it was, Jerry Freid had grown up a skinny little gnome who loved dark corners, spying, and slipping in the secret dagger. There was no question in Jerry's mind. He would have made the perfect hacker.

He unlocked the Bromo-Seltzer Tower's front door. The foyer was a perfect square, lined in art-deco bronze and floored in marble tile. The entire tower was only eighty feet to a side, which was incredible, since the tower stood taller than the Ravens stadium. Jerry could hear the nutcases screaming their heads off a quarter mile away even with the door shut. The tower had been built in the thirties as an advertisement ploy. Back then, Bromo-Seltzer was the world's best-selling fizz. The tower made national news. Now it was just another of Baltimore's many follies. Nineteen brick stories high, and one office wide. Topped by an absurd concrete crown. Jerry Freid had loved the place at first sight.

He inspected himself in the lobby's mercury-backed mirror. He knew what the world saw. A ferret in a bow tie. Only now Jerry was powerful enough not to care. People were a commodity Jerry Freid could take or leave. After all, friends were only a credit card away.

Especially now that Freid had what everybody wanted.

The brass-cage elevator clanked and rattled as it climbed to his office on the eleventh floor. The city was always going on about turning the whole tower into another of their artsy centers. They'd already done it to a dozen or so places around the city, old warehouses refitted as lofts and handed over for pennies. The artists and film people crowded the new bars and cafés and filled the air with their snotty talk. He hated them all. They were just geeks in fashion black. Nobody had offered Jerry Freid a helping hand when the Hamden bullies were pounding him into the dust. Let the artists fight their own way to the top.

It had started as a small-time thrill. Buy some guns. Read the books. Learn how to file off the numbers. Refit a semi so it became fully automatic, and thus illegal. Then it got bigger. Forge federal licenses so he could buy some heavy stuff. By then he was getting known. Not as Jerry Freid. Never as Jerry. As the man people knew by the box number. By the quality. By the price. Gradually he moved into the stratosphere of illegal weapons. Things only a handful of dealers around the country held and moved. Guns that went for a hundred thousand a pop. More.

The buyers still came, though. A different sort from before. Buyers who valued faceless and nameless and covert intelligence. Because most of the guys in the illegal gun trade made doorknobs look clever. But Jerry was dealing with the top-drawer clients now. They came and they paid his asking price and they vanished. They dealt in ciphered messages and encrypted e-mails and suitcases of unmarked bills.

His office was along the front of the building. Which meant as he unlocked and opened his door, the stadium's noise washed over him. But Jerry didn't notice. Because the client was there waiting for him. Standing by his front window. Assembling the merchandise.

The merchandise that was supposedly hidden behind the false wall in his other office. The office nobody knew about. "What are you *doing*?"

The man did not even turn around. "You're late."

"I'm not and you know it! I always get here before my clients!"

"That's what I mean." The client inspected the grooves in the barrel and screwed it to the stock. "You've always been an hour ahead of time. Today it's only forty minutes. I hope you're not slipping, Jerr. I can't afford that in my people."

"I'm not your anything, and get your hands off that!"

"Why should I, Jerr? We're friends, right? Friends shouldn't have secrets." The man pulled the scope from its padding. "I asked for a Zeiss."

"I couldn't get one in the time you gave me. This isn't stuff I can pull off a Radio Shack shelf."

The client wore an outfit that had gone out of style with the Cold War. A houndstooth jacket and matching turtleneck sweater. Gray flannel trousers. Polished lace-ups. A tweed trilby covered a salt-and-pepper wig. Sunglasses and a bushy mustache hid the rest of his face. Bizarre sort of accent, not one thing or another. Jerry Freid had been handling this particular client for a while and had never clearly seen his face. Jerry had a lot of extremely weird clients. But this one was seriously dirty. That was how Jerry thought of them, the ones who came in with mayhem on their minds and insanity in their gazes. Jerry always went home after a meeting with the dirties and scrubbed himself down with volcanic soap. But he also loved it. Because these were the ones who left him with the worms, the electric beasts who crawled through his gut for days and days. He was close to the edge with the dirties. These were the ones who went out and exacted revenge for Jerry against the world.

"Then I suppose this scope will have to do, won't it." The client slipped the bolt action from the specially fitted padding that lined the black gun case. He motioned at Jerry's desk. "Final payment."

Jerry slit the manila envelope and counted out the hundreds. Then he noticed the sack at the client's feet. "What's in that?"

"Have a look, Jerr. You'll like this."

But Jerry didn't like it at all. The yellow cases glared up at him. "I don't understand."

"Sure you do. Six months back, I shopped you some information, remember? I said you could plan the deal, take whatever you wanted. The only payment I requested was the claymores. All of them. Come on, Jerr. It wasn't that long ago. You've got to remember what you told me."

The client had a gravedigger's voice. A soft whisper of sound, toneless and empty. A harbinger of death, as cold as the black nights when Jerry woke from half-remembered nightmares and heard the client speaking to him. "I gave you plenty. I figured one, two, it wouldn't—"

"We had a deal, Jerr. You say something else, it means you're lying now and then both. I know when you're lying and I don't like it. You got greedy, Jerr. It's a disease that's infecting the whole world, don't you agree?"

He could feel the sweat gather at the base of his skull and slip down the entire length of his spine, a river of dread. "I wasn't going to sell them around here. I knew one buyer away from here. A *long* way."

"The truth. Good. But the problem is, you've still done what you said you wouldn't." The client shook his head sorrowfully. "And now your greed has got you in a world of trouble."

Jerry would have slipped to his knees except for the desk he landed on when his legs gave out. "I know who you are."

"How many of the mines have you sold on, Jerr?"

"Five. A mob connection in Jersey." Another swallow, trying to hold down the gorge. "Did you hear what I said? I had you followed. I know—"

"And these three are all you have left?"

"Yes. I swear." He watched the client slip one of the silicone-coated rounds into the chamber. "Your name is Allen Pecard. I've got everything written down in a safe place. If I go missing, the information comes out."

The gun's snout looked large enough to swallow Jerry whole. But what frightened Jerry Freid even more was watching the client slip a silenced pistol from beneath his jacket. "This time I believe you."

Matt felt like he was choking in the owner's box and its air-conditioned bonhomie. He accepted handshakes and backslaps from ruddy-faced drinkers who wanted the powers to see them being nice to the candidate's son. He smiled his way around comments he scarcely heard. The owner's tame photographer entered the box. The men jostled and joshed one another as they were shifted for game-day photos. When Matt was positioned next to his dad, he asked, "Where's Sol?"

"Back in D.C. taking care of paperwork." His father spoke around a professional smile. "The man hates football."

The lieutenant governor was flush-faced and weaving slightly. "Who's that, Paul?"

"My campaign manager. Sol Greene."

"Can't be much of a manager, he hates this." He sloshed his drink in a staining arc across the carpet. "Call my office, I'll turn you on to some-body who'll trade his youngest child to be up here in the winner's skybox."

Paul Kelly waited until the photographer moved away to lose his smile. "Sol Greene is the top man in his profession. And my best friend to boot."

Matt excused himself and walked up the broad carpeted steps to the buffet table. He picked up a plate but took nothing. He waited until attention had turned toward the two men, one drunk and the other tetchy, and tried to recall a time when his father had defended him with such conviction.

Matt slipped out the door and took the elevator down one floor. A security jock checked his pass, then went back to scanning the crowd. Matt found the arena entrance that matched Connie's seat number and entered the sunlight.

The day was football perfect, something that had escaped Matt until that very moment. He glanced down at the field. The Ravens played like they were meant to. To his left were the meager stands set aside for the visiting fans. Which meant neighboring season-ticket holders were the most ferocious Ravens supporters of all. They were up on their feet now, cheering a Ravens first down, waving in unison as the chains were moved into field-goal range.

Then he saw her. The other fans seated themselves, but two women remained on their feet, dancing to country rock and entertaining an army of supporters they did not even see. Matt had to agree, Reba McEntire had never sounded so good.

The song ended with the next play, but the women remained reluctant to stop their private boogie. Matt took another step, moving to where he could see her face. The afternoon sun turned Connie golden. He had never seen anyone so fiercely joyful. When she screamed her pleasure over a successful play, Matt felt an answering hunger at his very core.

———

The crowd greeted the shooter with a humongous roar. Or so he liked to think.

The building he had selected was half a block from the Bromo tower. He had stopped by earlier, worked the door lock, inspected his perch, and made plans for his emergency withdrawal. That was one of the critical points separating novices from experienced soldiers. Always have a back door identified and within reach. Always.

The building's power was off. The place smelled of grimy memories and futile dreams. He took the cracked marble stairs up to the roof, thirty-seven stories. Back in the twenties when this building was erected, thirty-seven stories would have made it one of the highest buildings south of New York. Now it was a wasted hulk, another victim of Baltimore's gritty decline. He was breathing hard by the time he pushed through the rusted rooftop door. The flooring here was unstable, but the new developers had thoughtfully laid out a metal track for safe passage. The reason was blazingly clear. This was the highest of the buildings in Baltimore's latest development. A billboard clung to the ledge, supported by sparkling new steel claws. It was tilted slightly out and down, so anyone driving along the harbor thoroughfare or seated in the waterfront stadiums would look over and see happy people making beautiful homes in exclusive new Downtown.

His breathing was back down to normal by the time he'd set up the tripod and locked it into place. He used his silenced pistol to punch a hole through the billboard's plywood back, not large, just enough space for his weapon and the top-mounted scope.

He knew the building was tall enough because he had sighted it from the stadium two days back. The stadium had been full of staff getting ready for today's game. It had been easy enough to slip inside. He had worn white worker's coveralls, just one more faceless deliveryman. Security was supposed to be on high alert, checking everybody in proper 9/11 style. But their bosses were cutting deals over in Camden Yards and they were just hourly wage clones, instantly replaceable with another desperate middle-aged mortgage-bound debt-ridden high-school dropout. He had traded howdies with two sullen guards and waltzed right in. Ten minutes later he was back out again, knowing the right box because a deli-laden clerk had told him.

And there it was, coming into vision through his sight. He had always preferred Zeiss because that was what he had trained on. But the computerized Trijicon ACOG—for Advanced Combat Optical Gunsight— scope was brilliant. Its field of vision was clear from the edges right down to the core. He could not see inside the owner's box, of course. But the reflective glass meant nothing. He knew what he wanted. Havoc was his upon demand.

Then he spotted the kid.

Matt Kelly sprang out as clear as day, one thousand and fifteen yards away and still instantly recognizable, the scope was that good. He altered the rifle's stand slightly, bringing the scope's center to bear upon Matt Kelly. His finger tightened upon the trigger. There was no reason to shoot him. But the effect would be equally powerful. And it would do away with an unexpected threat.

The Kelly kid continued down the stairs, then stopped in the full afternoon sunlight, looking down at something else. The game, perhaps. Watching with an intensity the shooter could feel from his perch. As though a match that would find its way to the bottom of tomorrow's birdcage held life-or-death importance. The shooter smiled tightly. This kid deserved to die.

He flipped the bolt, drawing a round into the chamber.

———

The Ravens were ahead by a lot more than the scoreboard indicated. Rushing, first downs, passing, defensive punches, the works. Connie was surrounded by conversations that started or ended with, this was the Ravens' year.

Dorcas said, "Looks like I need to start saving. Super Bowl tickets don't come cheap."

Connie was finding it harder and harder to stop her touchdown boogie. "All the way, baby."

"Speaking of which, you've got an admirer. No, don't turn around. It's wonder boy."

"Matt?"

"Do you know of another?" Dorcas hid her next glance behind a sip of her Coke. "The way he's watching you, I'm thinking love."

"Don't talk stupid."

"And don't you let him down too hard. If you're certain that's the way you want to play it."

The flutter in Connie's gut blinded her to the final play and the halftime gun. "I don't see any alternative."

"He's handsome, he's smart, he's rich, he's connected."

"He's a fed. We talked about that, remember?"

"This may come as a shock. But there aren't a whole lot of perfect men out there, just waiting to peel you a grape." Dorcas had a way of looking at Connie sometimes, like she went from friend to ancient wise-woman all in one breath. "You want to grow old with fifteen cats for company, that's your business."

"What, if I let this one go I'm doomed to seclusion?"

"Now you're the one talking silly." She set down her cup. "I'll go join the longest line in Baltimore and give Skippy my seat. That is, unless you strongly object."

Connie remained silent.

"That's what I thought."

Matt was slow in approaching. The shy little-boy look on his face disarmed her completely. Her normal acid greeting for strays just faded away. Instead she said, "Matt, hey, you're just in time for the world's most seriously lame halftime show."

He smiled then, and it twisted something inside her. When he seated himself, they were so close their shoulders and arms touched. "I like hearing you use my name."

"Nicknames are for the office," she said, then added for soft emphasis, "Matt."

"Is Connie your real name?"

"Consuela. Taken from my mom. She died when I was a baby." Matt stared at her with such intensity she could feel the look down deep, and she both loved it and wanted to run off screaming. Which was absurd, of course. There was still another half to play. "What color are your eyes, Matt?"

"They shift."

"That's good. For a second I thought I was hallucinating."

"You're not. They run through shades of green."

"With some gold in there for good measure. They're nice."

"Thanks. My last girlfriend said they were as shifty as the rest of me."

"She sounds like a real cow."

He broke contact then. Turned and stared out over the field, saying, "I don't know why I said that."

"That's what I'm supposed to be telling you. I shouldn't have called your flame a cow, Matt."

"I never talk about myself like that."

"Never?"

He shook his head, not seeing the band taking shape in front of them. "No."

"Must be awful lonely in there."

He turned back, testing his words, measuring them carefully. "I came down to ask if you'd have dinner with me."

"I told you in the office." But her voice shivered slightly with the strain of not screaming an affirmative. "I'm thinking that's not a good idea, Matt."

"No, probably not." The field got another blind inspection. "My last mistake said I was locked up tighter than the M&T bank vault."

"Are you?"

A very slow nod. "Probably."

She probably would have handed out her standard rejection, had Dorcas's admonition not been hanging there in the brilliant autumn afternoon. "So when do you want to get together?"

The little-boy look was back in his eyes again. "You mean it?"

"Hey, I've got a perfect record at choosing the wrong men." But she was still smiling. Even when the band started up. "See what I mean?"

"What?"

"The band. Aren't they awful?"

He was reluctant now to look away from her. Which was, when she took a moment to think about it, pretty cool indeed. "You're right. They're bad."

"Next month we've got the annual Thanksgiving parade. Say you'll come with me."

Something in his manner said the smile he gave her was a very rare event. "Consider me booked."

"There are high schools in Baltimore who make the national finals every year. We're talking so many awards they don't even list them anymore. These kids couldn't afford instruments if the state didn't pay for them. But they *live* to perform." She gestured at the field. "What do we have out here, but lame white guys who couldn't keep time with an atomic clock. Shoot these guys, bring in the high schools; that's my advice. *Then* you'd see some energy worth watching."

"You really love this, don't you."

"What, football?" She laughed without reason, which was just not her. But the sun was setting over a winning game, and she was seated next to a guy who left her hands clammy. "If I ever left Baltimore, it'd only be for a town where the team has Super Bowl potential. Sort of gives shape to my calendar, if you know what I mean."

"Not really. But I'm willing to learn." He spied Dorcas waving from the stairs. "Your sidekick is back. How about dinner tomorrow night?"

"See you at seven." She smiled him away, said to the air where he had once been, "Matt."

Dorcas greeted Connie with, "You better be glad I'm seriously in love with old what's-his-name. Otherwise, I'd be wrestling you to the ground over that one."

Connie did not reply. The band was finally gone and Bonnie Raitt was singing about how she needed her man like oxygen. It sort of said it all.

The two of them hooted and danced their team through two more touchdowns and a true football stomping. The division crown was theirs, the Super Bowl a date on Baltimore's calendar. A game and an afternoon so fine it kept the frequent fliers in their seats to the end. Except for the ones who felt the need to dance their way through the final play with this pair.

Then the screams started.

———

Matt stayed through to the bitter end because his father did. And because if he leaned up close to the glass, he could catch occasional glimpses of the redhead and the brunette two tiers below his perch. The ones who wore the Ravens T-shirts and the ridiculous glass beads around their necks. The ones who, every time they rose to their feet and danced, a thousand faces turned and grinned and nodded to the beat.

After the game ended, Matt stepped to the back of the room and entered the grind of final handshakes. His father and the Ravens owner traded smiles and jokes about who was going to pay for what come Super Bowl time. Then the glass imploded.

Everybody was either outside in the hallway waiting for the elevator, or milling about the final power play by the buffet table. Which meant the heavy glass shards sliced into carpet and not people. Even so, the golden mirror sparkles sprayed back across them all. Then everybody was screaming and shouting all at once.

A giant's fist punched the wall behind and above Matt. "Down!"

But the owner was a man used to ruling. He didn't crumple for anybody.

Paul Kelly took half a heartbeat to scout around, as though seeking Sol's guidance on how to handle this.

Matt leaped and took them both down, one in each hand. That same instant another shot punched the back wall. No sound except a distant echo, it could have been a bomb or a cannon or even a jet-sized backfire. Far, far away. What Matt could hear clearly was a *crump* each time another giant segment of concrete was hammered to dust.

This higher tier of boxes was taken by native rock stars and the pros for their families, both past and present. Security was tight on this level, where the smallest box went for two hundred and fifty thou plus drinks and food. The muscle guys in overtight jackets came running, shouting into their wrists and waving an arsenal. The owner tried to rise up and crawl forward. But the shots were coming closer. Matt flattened the man with one determined arm, holding his father's face in the carpet with his other.

There was a measured pace to the shots. Three, maybe four seconds between each one. Steady and cruelly deliberate. The air was clouded with blasted concrete and seared with the smell of charcoaled wallpaper. Another *crump*, then more screams and yells and shouts and thundering footsteps. *Crump. Crump. Crump.*

———

Normally after a game the pedestrian walkway fronting Camden Yards was congealed like human glue. The passage was the most direct way back to downtown and the light-rail station. After a win, people stopped for the sideshows and the hawkers and the tailgate parties that spilled out of the lots and went on all night. After a loss, the atmosphere was funereal and progress even slower. Today, however, Matt raced down the walk surrounded by a cluster of twenty or so law enforcement types. Running with him were off-duty cops doing uniform crowd control for the game. Traffic cops in biker boots and leather. Stadium security in fire-engine-red jackets. And Connie. All shouting at the top of their lungs. A lot of them waving guns overhead. The crowd on Camden Passage did a human tidal version of the Red Sea.

Sirens whooped in from all sides. The biker cops and the security guys who ran with radios still wired into earpieces all shouted in unison, "Lombard and Paca!"

They arrived with the first three patrol cars. Guns sprouted, people shouted, hands waved. A uniformed cop setting up a periphery spotted Matt. "You! Back off!"

Connie stepped between them. "He's with me."

"And you are?"

"Morales. Homicide." She flashed her badge. "What do you have?"

"Guy in the university science labs two blocks over called it in. Somebody was up top firing off a cannon. We're waiting on a warrant."

Matt offered, "That's my dad's building."

Connie gripped his arm and bulled forward. She aimed for a senior officer on the building's stairs, talking into a cell phone. "Lieutenant! This is the building's owner!"

The guy flipped his phone shut. "We got your permission to hunt down a possible sniper?"

A voice called, "Chopper is inbound!"

"Go for it," Matt said. "But I don't have a key."

"Long as we have your permission." The officer raised his voice. "Police only!"

They rammed through the front door. Inside was a decrepit lobby of cracked marble and faded gilt. The electricity was off. "Bring us some light!"

While they waited for lights to be brought from the cop cars, Connie crouched by the stairs rising between two sets of brass-lined elevators. "Dust has been disturbed!"

The officer bent down beside her. "Listen up! Keep to the inside rail! You! Go get your camera and kit. Photograph and measure the shoe prints."

Matt offered, "I'll do it, sir."

"You're the owner, right?"

"Owner's son." He showed his ID. "I'm also a federal agent. And I can't handle forty flights."

Connie said, "He's taken one in the leg."

"It's all yours." The officer raised his voice. "Take the stairs single file!"

Matt accepted the Polaroid from a young officer and listened to the footsteps thunder away overhead. He completed his shots and measurements just as Connie returned with the first contingent. "The shooter's long gone. They're searching the floors."

"Probably futile." Matt pointed to an indentation in the dust. "These tracks are headed up, but these go down. Same boots."

"That's why you didn't go up?"

"My leg already hurts from the run." He folded up the camera. "Let's go outside."

A brilliant autumn sunset was framed by other hulks sprouting billboards with paintings of idyllic condos and happy, successful people. Matt leaned against the wall and described for her the attack.

"So your father was the target of another hit."

"A shooter with professional sniper's gear," Matt replied. "He waits until the game is over."

"So?"

"Think about it. If he wanted to take Pop down, he'd do it when there was a big play and everybody would be crammed up against the glass. This wasn't a hit, Connie. This was a message."

"Saying what?"

Cops began appearing in the doorway. Matt pushed himself off the wall. "That's exactly what I intend to find out."

Matt returned home and prepared a solitary meal. He tried to call Sol and his father and got their recorded messages. Not even Sol's emergency line was active. He watched the local news as he ate. The coverage was all about the Ravens win and the attack. The gun was displayed, a statement in and of itself. Matt stopped with his fork poised and listened to the newscaster's excited description. A large-caliber professional sniper's weapon. The bullet holes in the owner's box were given a good run, each blast about two and a half feet across. Then Matt watched his father address a battery of microphones, the backdrop a sea of faces. Milking the moment as only a winning candidate could. Sunday evening after a threat on his life, and the candidate was still rolling hard.

The phone rang as he was washing up. Judy Leigh, the newspaper journalist, sounded breathless. "Sorry to bother you."

"No problem. I've been expecting your call. Is that traffic I hear?"

"I'm in my car."

"Where are you going?"

"Nowhere. I'm parked outside my house. I needed to check . . . Can we talk about what happened?"

"At the game? Sure." Matt sketched out the day's events.

"So you don't think it was a real attack."

"That's just my opinion."

"What do the police think?"

"The police haven't shared their thoughts with me," Matt replied.

"You supply evidence that reignites a dormant murder case. You saved your dad and the Ravens owner, and they're still shutting you out?"

"If you write that, they'll never let me back in again."

"Point taken. Still, their attitude astonishes me."

"There's a lot of bad blood," Matt pointed out. "Some of it your paper's fault."

"Yeah, that comes with the job." She hesitated, then said, "I've been ordered not to have anything more to do with you."

"By whom?"

"The super-boss." She related the confrontation with the paper's CEO, then concluded, "I probably shouldn't be telling you this."

The night was black against Matt's kitchen window. The clock read late. Lights still gleamed from every window of the carriage house. Matt saw figures moving back and forth inside. The house over his head was utterly quiet. A week to go and the candidate ran to a twenty-four-hour stopwatch.

Matt said, "Why would the owner of three-dozen papers fly in and order you to stop talking to a candidate's son?"

"I was hoping you'd tell me that."

"This has to be about money. A lot."

"What can you tell me about your father's latest project?"

"Nothing. I know less than you do."

"Excuse me for saying, but that sounds, well . . ."

"Bizarre. I know." Matt stared at the reflection in the window glass. Memories filled the space where the night should have been. When Matt had joined the Vail police force, his father had been so angry he had wanted to disown his son. Megan Kelly had threatened to leave him. It was the only time Matt could ever recall his parents really fighting. Matt hated his father's business. He always had. It had stolen his childhood. Because of his father's companies, he never had a home. He never had friends. His father did not disown him, but he swore Matt would never see a dime. Matt could not have cared less.

Matt dreaded the next question she was bound to ask. But all she said was, "Can I say something that is going to sound totally absurd?"

"Is this a joke?"

"No, Matt. No joke." Her voice sounded strained.

"Tell me."

Another long pause, then, "I think somebody is stalking me."

———

The taxi driver said, "Here is your house coming in the next block."

"Thank you." Connie said into her phone, "Almost there, Matt. Are you in place yet?"

"Five minutes. Hang back, will you?"

Connie said to the driver, "Could you pull over here and wait a second, please?"

The driver was Pakistani and extremely nervous about carrying a cop. He had balked when the young woman in old woman's garb had climbed into his backseat. The driver had liked it even less after she had flashed her badge. The driver asked, "There is going to be shooting?"

"No shooting. Promise. Just pull into this spot, please." She said into her phone, "We're in a holding pattern, and I think this wig has fleas."

"Okay, I'm pulling down the side street. Wait, I've got a parking spot."

"Do you see anybody?"

"Not yet." A moment's pause, then, "I really appreciate your helping me out here."

"You know how long I've dreamed of being a real cop? I'm the one paying dues, Matt."

She felt the change in his voice as much as heard it. "I really like hearing you say my name."

"Maybe we should focus on the game plan." But she was smiling as she said it. She leaned forward and said to the driver, "Okay, thanks, you can pull out now."

"We drive to the address and there's no shootings?"

"Not a single bullet. Promise." To Matt, "My driver is a little freaked."

"That makes two of us."

The driver said, "This is being the place."

She handed a bill over the seat and said to Matt, "What say we go be cops."

As soon as the taxi pulled up in front of the door, Judy Leigh's husband came down the stairs. Connie said in greeting, "Take my arm and help me out, like you would your favorite great-aunt. That's it. Okay, big hug for the cameras. Can you tell me where the joker is?"

The man was trying hard to sound tough and failing. "Across the street, five cars back."

"Do you see him now?"

"No."

She waved at Judy hovering inside the townhome's front door. "You both are doing great. Okay, reach inside and get my case. Now let me take your arm and go slow on the stairs."

Connie wore gray lumpish hair, baggy sweater, ankle dress, and fifteen inches of padding around her middle. The disguise was Lucas's idea. Headquarters had a slew of bad wigs and clothes one step up from Goodwill. Once the door was shut, Connie stripped down to reveal black biking tights and running shoes. "Mrs. Leigh? Connie Morales, Baltimore Police."

The journalist was as worried as she was pregnant. "Can I see your badge, please?"

"Absolutely." Judy's husband was a small man with a true Irish complexion, right down to the emerald green eyes. Connie thought he looked vaguely elfish, the way he did his two-step in and out of the living room doorway. "Mr. Leigh, maybe you should move farther away from the living room window."

"Oh. Right." He shifted his dance back into the hall shadows.

"We don't want the stalker to observe you being anything but happy over your great-aunt's visit."

"Sure, sure." It was unlikely he heard Connie at all. The only steady thing about him was his eyes. They never left his wife.

Judy Leigh asked, "Where is Matt Kelly?"

"One street over and waiting for my signal." Talking like she'd done this a million times before. Hoping they wouldn't notice the stuttering heart in her own voice. Connie squatted on the floor by her suitcase. "Tell me what you know, Mrs. Leigh."

"I noticed him on the way home. He followed me from the paper down into the Metro. I thought I saw him on the walk up our street, but I wasn't sure. I stayed with other people the whole way home. Then I saw him crossing in front of our house on the other side of the street. I called Matt from our van so I could scout our street. The guy was still there, sitting inside a car."

"Which one?"

"A black SUV. He doesn't stay in it all the time. He was walking the sidewalk the last time I looked."

Connie opened the suitcase and pulled out a Taser, collapsible baton, Kevlar vest, Maglite, Beretta, and ankle holster. Mr. Leigh's eyes grew increasingly wide as she kitted out. "Describe him, please."

"He never approached. Never got very close. Never stayed still. Never looked straight at me." Judy Leigh rested one comforting hand on her baby. "Tall, certainly over six feet. Narrow face. But very strong-looking. Brownish gray hair, military cut. Incredibly fit. He looked about fifty, maybe ten years more; I have no idea."

Her husband said, "I should have confronted him."

"Harry, please."

"Your wife's right, Mr. Leigh. This man sounds like a pro."

Judy Leigh asked, "Did Matt tell you about my problem at work?"

"Yes. Is there a back way out?"

"Through the kitchen." Judy led her down the hall.

"No, keep the light off."

"Yes. All right." She fumbled with the door lock. "The yard is ringed with a safety fence. The gate is rusted shut."

Connie glanced into the night. The fence looked only shoulder high, with a doghouse next door. "Can you keep your neighbor's dog quiet?"

"They're away and the dog is at a kennel."

"Okay. You both stay inside. Move around the front room where he can see you. If you hear me yell 'Police!' dial 911 and say, 'Officer needs assistance.'" Connie flipped open her phone with Matt's number set into her speed dial.

Matt answered immediately. Connie said, "I'm going out the back."

"I see your silhouette."

"Our guy still in position?"

"Half a block away from the Leighs' front door. He was standing for a while. Now he's seated inside a black Tahoe."

"Hold on." She cradled the phone, said to the journalist, "You know what to do."

"Dial 911 if you call out 'Police.' She continued to hold her baby. "Is that Mr. Kelly?"

"Yes. Everything's going to be okay, Mrs. Leigh." Connie shut the door, stepped into the garden, and started for the fence. "Maybe he drove over, parked the car, then went back downtown to follow her. Which means he was after more than just watching your journalist friend, right?"

"I'm too new at this game to guess."

"I'm moving now." She shut her phone and started over the fence. Still smiling.

She spotted Matt as soon as she stepped through the neighbor's shrubs and hit the sidewalk. He was crouched three cars behind the Tahoe. The SUV was not hard to spot. It sat as far as possible between two streetlights, a dark pavement mole. The side windows were tinted.

Connie waited until Matt slipped up on the SUV's other side. Then she came out of her crouch and trotted across the street, moving fast and hard. She took her badge in one hand and the Maglite in the other.

She hit the beam and raised her badge to tap on the driver's window. "Police. Step—"

The door came at her with the force of a battering ram. No click, no internal light, no warning. The door crashed into her chest and shoulder, sending her sprawling. The Maglite clattered on the pavement and rolled.

The man was a very fast shadow. Connie grabbed for the ankle that bounded across her and missed. "Police! Stop!"

Matt dived around the vehicle. He caught the same leg she'd missed, not well, but enough to cause the guy to stumble.

Connie rolled over and pulled the collapsible baton from her pocket. And stopped cold.

The two men were dark spinning blurs. She had never seen anyone move that fast. Their speed and ferocity made a farce of films. The fact that they were utterly silent, save for soft grunts, made it even more chilling.

The guy leaped and launched a double flying kick at Matt's head. Matt blocked with both arms, trying to grip the man's ankle and bring him down. But the man's two kicks were just a feint. The man landed and kicked a third time, this one connecting with Matt's wounded leg.

Matt grunted but did not go down. He punched through the pain; Connie could see the agony on his features. The blow became two, three, four, five, a kick, Matt launching the next before the last was finished, moving so fast it appeared he was not connected to earth at all, all four of his limbs flailing simultaneously. The guy blocked and parried and backed. Until Matt struck him just above the sternum with the flat of his hand. The guy fell and rolled and came up running.

Connie dropped her baton and pulled out her gun. *"Freeze!"*

But she was shouting at an empty night. There was nothing. Not even the sound of footsteps.

The guy was just gone.

———

Connie chased him a half block but knew it was futile before she took the first step. She ran because she felt so foolish. Just lying there being a total rookie while Matt took a dozen strikes. More.

She walked back as he came limping over, carrying her badge and baton. "You okay?"

"Sure. Your light's busted."

"Matt, I'm sorry, I should—"

"You couldn't have done anything."

"Sure I could have. I should have pulled my gun faster."

"Who would you have shot?"

"You kidding? The guy trading blows with you faster than I could count."

"Exactly. If you'd fired, you'd probably have hit me."

Doors were opening up and down the street. Judy Leigh and her husband were huddled together in their doorway. Sirens were wailing in the distance. But all she could focus on was, "I've never seen . . . How did you *do* that?"

"I've been training all my life." He was studying the unseen trail laid down by the fleeing man. "And so has he."

She realized Matt was leaning slightly to one side. "He hurt you."

"Bruised, not broken." He pointed at the Leighs. "Go talk to them. Tell them everything's all right."

On Monday, as usual, the nightmares hauled him from sleep an hour or so before his body was ready. Matt dressed and put on coffee and stretched. He drank his first cup watching early dawn gradually conquer the sky. He picked up the phone and made two calls, apologizing twice for the hour, glad to find both men already awake and willing to see him.

The morning was colder than the previous day, but just as beautiful. The sky held a winter's dusty hue. Autumn trees shone in the crisp air as though imitating the sun that had not yet risen. Matt tried hard to ignore the whispers that ran alongside his car, gnawing at the day with tiny rabid teeth.

The church rectory was located a couple of blocks off Mount Vernon Square. Matt had taken his mother there any number of times, but never been inside. Ian Reeves answered in shirtsleeves and gray suit pants. He showed no surprise whatsoever at Matt's appearance.

"I should have asked to come by later."

"Nonsense. I always make a full pot of coffee in the hopes that someone will help solve a bachelor's worst dilemma." He waited until they were back in the kitchen to add, "How to fill the empty spaces between friends."

Matt took a seat. He knew quite a lot about the pastor. He knew Ian had loved a woman, but she had married another man. He knew Ian's sister had been widowed a couple of years back. They had turned the top two floors of Ian's stone town house into an apartment for her. Matt knew these things because his mother had often spoken of the big ugly man, and done so with an open fondness she reserved for very few. Megan Kelly had deeply regretted Matt's silent disinterest in her church. My men, she used to say. My daily reminders of everything I can't change in this old world.

Matt accepted the mug, declined the offer of milk and sugar, and said, "I need to ask you about my mother."

Ian Reeves was narrow in the shoulders and massive about the waist. His hands were too big for his body and his feet were elephantine. Yet he moved about the kitchen with subtle grace. "No you don't."

He watched Ian set out toast and juice and plates for two. "I don't know where else to turn."

"I hear that one a lot." Ian seated himself. "Matt, listen to me. There is nothing I need to tell you about your mother."

"She was the intended victim all along. This means there had to be some—"

"Let me save you the agony of asking because there is nothing to be found. I knew your mother as well as anyone outside the family. She loved your father. She was faithful to him in every way. She loved you. She was a wonderful woman. There. I've just saved us both a world of unnecessary discomfort."

Matt lowered his gaze to the steaming mug and wished he could feel better about all he had just heard.

"Now, why don't you tell me why you're here."

"I just tried to."

"You're sure there's no other reason?"

The man's voice held a calm almost strong enough to draw a few fragments from his internal vault. "Yes."

"Are you resting well?"

Matt sipped from his mug.

"Stupid question. You're investigating your own mother's murder. Matt, I admire your motives, but I question your actions."

"I have to do this." Matt rose from his seat. "Thanks for the coffee."

Ian did not try to stop him. Nor did he rise. "Far be it from me to stand between a man and his chosen duty. Just remember this, will you? An investigation is only as good as the questions you ask."

Matt headed straight from the rectory to Vic's dojo in the Tenth Ward. When Matt had started attending the dojo at age twelve, Vic had treated Matt as just another uptown kid. Vic ran them in teams. Like with like. The vanilla cupcakes paid Vic's rent. Vic didn't want some mill-town punk from Hamden or Tenth Ward knocking loose a couple thousand dollars' worth of braces. Early on Matt had realized that, if he'd asked Vic to put him with the Hamden kids, Vic would have shown him the door. So Matt had studied the books he could find at whatever library was closest, practiced hard, and waited.

Then his dad had sent them back to their Bolton Hill home for almost two months. Megan Kelly hadn't liked being away from her husband that long, but Paul Kelly's latest deal had him constantly on the road. Finally things settled down, and Paul Kelly called for them to join him. Matt approached Vic the day he learned they were moving to Grand Rapids and asked what he could do to work out at home.

"Do the katas," Vic replied, not glancing away from the mill-town kids going at it hard. Katas were stylistic fighting dances, intended to develop grace and strength. Vic had started the cupcakes with four katas, all less than a dozen moves.

"I'm already doing them."

"So do them again." When Vic realized that Matt had not moved, he said, "You're not in here often enough for me to work with you, kid."

"My dad moves us around a lot."

Vic turned back to the senior class, his silence saying better than words that this was Matt's problem.

"I'm doing the four katas and some other stuff for two hours every night," Matt persisted. "I want more."

Vic ignored him until the senior class worked through the routine a second time. He turned back then and looked at Matt, really looked, for the first time. "Two hours?"

"At least."

"Show me."

Matt ran through the katas together, joining them into one so that they actually formed enough of a workout to kick up his heartbeat. But his breathing was still calm when he was done. Vic noticed this. He noticed everything. "What's your name, kid?"

"Matt."

"Matt what?"

"Matt Kelly."

"Okay, Matt. Widen your stance before the kicks. And stop hesitating. You need to have more confidence in your stance. Loosen up. Stop rushing. You control the time here, not the kata. When you're ready, you *strike*." Vic uncoiled then. One moment he was leaning against the wall. The next, his leg was a rotating blur. Then back to the wall. "See?"

Matt's lungs were pumping now from what he had just seen. "Yes."

"If you're going to do it, if you have to strike, you do it full on. You hold nothing back. You hesitate, you die. Got me?"

"Yes."

"So what's the word, Matt?"

"Full on."

"That's right."

When Vic started to turn away, Matt halted him with, "Can I show you something else?"

"Go for it."

Matt moved into his fighting stance and started another kata. When he finished, Vic asked, "Where'd you learn that?"

"Watching you teach the black belts."

"You know any others?"

"Yes."

"How many?"

"Seven."

"You taught yourself seven katas watching me train the others?"

"And studying some books."

Vic laughed at that, a soft punch of breath. "Sure. I can teach you something else."

Vic started him on the exercise pole, a bare trunk with stubby branches polished by the hands and feet and sweat of Vic's advanced students. The exercise pole taught speed and a tolerance of pain. It toughened sinew and callused skin. Matt learned to hate and love the pole.

Matt left for Grand Rapids with six new katas, three books, and a rigorous new exercise regimen. Calisthenics and running and isometrics. Vic wanted to see how far Matt could be pushed before he ran back to Mama. Vic never said it. But Matt saw it in his pockmarked features and flat gaze. Vic figured it was only a matter of time.

When Matt returned five months later, he ditched the white karate uniform that all the uptown guys wore. They also took pride in the belt ceremonies. Vic kept the front counter full of belts and uniforms and books and DVDs and made a ton off the stuff. The uniforms also made for easy separation of the two crews.

Matt adopted the mill-town garb of cutoffs and tank tops. The mill-town kids who could afford proper gear saved it for contests where uniforms were required. When Matt walked in wearing stuff he had washed with stones until they were suitably ragged, Vic welcomed him back by sticking him into the mill-town crew, who proceeded to deck him with brutal relish.

Matt hid his bruises the best he could. He accepted the pain and the beatings as just another lesson. But he kept getting handed his head. The family moved again. When he came back three months later, the beatings just got worse.

Finally Vic pulled him aside and asked, "When are you finally going to lock and load?"

The last bout had left Matt unable to put weight on his left leg. "I'm trying."

"I'm not talking about trying." He took in the dojo with a quick motion of his hand. "What's this place you're in?"

"Full-contact Sho-Rey dojo."

"Emphasis on *full*, which is what I'm not getting from you. Do you come in here to lose?"

"No."

"Because I don't have time for losers, Matt."

"I'm not a loser."

"So why is it you let those kids use you for a doormat? You've got the strength. You got speed. You're smart enough to watch and react. You know more katas than any of them." Vic leaned in close enough for Matt to smell the cinnamon on his breath. "You're afraid, aren't you?"

"No, I'm not—"

"Yeah, you are. You're terrified."

"They don't scare me."

"I'm not talking about them. Forget them. I'm talking about *you*. Yeah. I can see it in your eyes. You're scared to death of what you got tanked up inside you. Afraid if you let go for once, it'll just eat you up. Isn't that right."

"I'm not afraid."

"Get outta here. And don't come back 'til you're ready to show me." Vic saw Matt's stricken look, and it only turned him mean. "You know what? Don't bother coming back at all. I don't ever want to see your shiny little cupcake face around here again."

Matt stayed where he was because he had nowhere else to go. Certainly not home. There was nothing for him there but more of what he kept tightly clenched up inside. What he had always assumed was hidden from the world. Until now.

"Do I gotta hurt you to make you leave?"

Matt fought down the tremors enough to ask, "Show you what?"

Vic had a panther's moves when he wanted. Fast and silent and scary. He whipped the air about Matt's face, racing through a series of death strikes so fast Matt had no idea what he had just seen. "No. *You* tell *me*. What do you think I'm talking about?"

———

When Matt arrived at the dojo, Vic was leaning in the doorway, drinking coffee and squinting into the warming day. He held out his mug in greeting. "You want any?"

"I'm good, thanks. Appreciate you meeting me."

"Man's got to be somewhere. You want to work out?"

"More than I can say. But I'm not sure my leg is ready."

"We'll do a few katas, hold it to style and balance." Vic tossed out the dregs of his mug. "Maybe you can show me what you've learned, watching the older guys. Like the old days."

The parking lot was empty save for three dusty pickups parked by the Mexican grocery. A group of construction workers breakfasted on burritos Matt could smell across the lot. "That's not why I needed to see you."

"Figured it wasn't." Vic pushed off the doorway. "Let's work up a sweat, then you can hit me with serious."

They went at it for over an hour. The attacker's kick caused his thigh to throb, but not at what felt like a dangerous level. Finally Vic noticed him easing off and called time. Matt followed his old teacher through a series of stretches so ingrained he did not need to watch himself, much less think.

Afterward Vic took up his position against the wall. "Got a call last week from an old buddy."

"From your police days?"

"Before. He was with me in Nam. He's something else now, some government job, got himself a nice suit, cleaned up his talk, can't tell me what he does."

"CIA?"

Vic fanned the air. "I never had time for that federal alphabet soup. Tells me about a pal of his. A Brit who wants to stop by, ask some questions about a friend of mine."

"Allen Pecard."

"Man walks in while I've still got my buddy on the phone. Didn't ask so much as tell. Just bounces ideas off me. Matt Kelly is this, he's that. All the while he's talking, he watches my response. Watches hard."

Matt toweled off, holding to an offhand manner. Or trying. "What did you think of him?"

"That he knows you pretty well."

"Other than that."

Vic pulled a towel off the rail and slowly wiped his face. "You see some guys, they go into serious action and only partway come back. They got the civilian moves now; they hold down steady work; they talk the talk. But inside . . ."

"Something's missing." Thinking not about Pecard, but himself and the last time he had been here. A woman waiting to tell him exactly the same thing. AWOL, but without the warrior's excuse.

"Is Pecard a friend?"

Matt remained silent. Locked inside two problems laid atop each other.

"That's what you need to know. If he's not, you got to watch out, you hear what I'm saying? Stone-cold was made to describe these guys. They do what they do, and they walk away. There's nothing inside to even think the word *regret*."

———

His phone chimed as he was pulling from the parking lot. "This is Kelly."

"Lucas D'Amico. I was wondering when you planned to arrive at the station."

The man's formal tone was an evident warning. About what, Matt had no idea. "I've just worked out. I was going to stop by the house, shower and change, and come in."

The detective cupped the phone, then asked, "Can you give me a time?"

"Is something wrong?"

"I really can't say."

Matt sped out of the lot. "Forty-five minutes. Less if traffic is with me."

"We'll be waiting." He cut the connection before Matt could ask who made the statement plural.

The phone rang again so swiftly he answered with, "Forget something?"

"Excuse me?"

Matt recognized the newspaper reporter's voice. "Sorry. Thought you were someone else."

Judy Leigh sounded almost as edgy as the detective did. "I wanted to thank you for last night."

"The cops taking care of you?"

"They followed me to work, promised to be there when I get home. Look, Matt, I did some checking into your dad's business setup. Did you know he's put all his companies into a blind trust?"

"I told you. We don't talk."

"Last year. And very privately. Not secret, just way in the background. Interesting he would go to all this trouble and not mention it in his press."

Matt pulled up beside the house, carried his phone with him as he grabbed his bag and juggled for his apartment key. "Is it?"

"Absolutely. This sort of action doesn't come cheap. It's almost like he's anticipating trouble and keeping this as ammo."

"Can you find out who are the trustees?"

"Now you're thinking like a reporter. I'm on it."

He let himself into the apartment, dropped his gym bag and his keys. The air to his home congealed, making every word a struggle. "I need to ask you what you've found out about my mother."

"Are you sure you want to go there?"

"This is a murder investigation, remember?"

She sighed. "I've checked. Believe me. So far I've come up with nothing."

"There had to be a reason she was targeted."

Judy Leigh took her time coming back, and when she did, it was to say, "So far I haven't found anything. And that's the honest truth, Matt. I'm still hunting, but very quietly. We're still ordered off the chase. My editor fired off a memo to the publisher and our chairman first thing. Described the attack at the game, your role, and said we had to report it. Not asked. Told. The publisher took all of thirty seconds to respond. He invited her to review her options or offer her resignation. One or the other." She was growing hotter by the moment. "So now I'm on easy assignments, puff pieces, enough to fill the time sheet and leave me space to dig. Which I will. Until we get enough to go front page."

"You and the baby and the job stay safe, Judy."

"Now you sound like my husband." She hung up.

———

Matt shared the elevator with four clerical staff caught up in the transition from home to cop. Matt got off on seven and made it halfway across the bull pen when a voice called, "Agent Kelly?"

"Sir?"

A very dark man in a pale blue dress shirt, checked tie, and a narrow, frowning face walked up. "Lieutenant Crowder. The chief wants to see you."

"Can you tell me where I'd find Detective D'Amico?"

"Kelly, the chief wants to see you *now*."

Crowder led him through the busy outer office and knocked on the major's door. He opened when there was a pause in the conversation going on inside. "Kelly's here, Chief."

"Show him in. No, you stay too."

D'Amico was seated in the same position as the first time Matt had entered the chief's office. His chair was against the side wall, from where he could observe the entire room. Major Bernstein wore a two-piece outfit of fawn suede, with a bracelet of Indian silver and a turquoise pendant. Her hair was neat and full and her looks very striking. "Take a seat, Kelly. Mind running through what happened last night?"

The office was tight with the four of them inside and the door shut. The others did not seem to notice, however. "I received a call from *Times* reporter Judy Leigh."

"How do you know her?"

"I read her work in the hospital. She was the only reporter who didn't harp constantly about right-wing extremists. When I got out, I looked her up."

"So she called last night."

"She asked me about the attack after the football game. I told her." He glanced at D'Amico. The detective had pushed his chair over as far as it would go, giving him a better view of everyone in the room. "Was that wrong?"

"Our department passes all journalist inquiries through Public Affairs. But you're not a police officer, Mr. Kelly. So you can't be ordered to follow proper police protocol. Go on."

"Ms. Leigh had noticed someone following her. She's seven months pregnant and I guess she got spooked. I called Officer Morales. She checked with Detective D'Amico. We confronted the stalker, or tried to. He got away."

"I spoke with Morales. She said you showed some remarkable skills yesterday."

Matt was listening hard, yet heard none of the hostility he had experienced in his previous meetings with Bernstein. Instead, she sounded oddly formal. All three officers watched him with the same detached, professional gaze. "Is there a problem?"

Bernstein asked, "Mr. Kelly, have you spoken with your office this morning?"

It took Matt a moment to realize she was talking about State. "No."

"Well, I have. With a certain . . ." She adjusted her reading glasses. "Jack Van Sant. You know him?"

"He is State Department Intel."

"Mr. Van Sant has been busy. The case involving your mother has been reassigned. It is now federal in jurisdiction. You have been designated officer in charge."

They all gave him the official mask. Matt said, "I don't want it."

"You don't . . ." The chief was halted by a ringing phone. She answered, "Bernstein. Yes. He just arrived. Hold on."

She handed Matt the phone. "Now I'm expected to play receptionist?"

Matt took the receiver. "This is Kelly."

"Van Sant here. I assume the chief has informed you of the change in status."

"With respect, sir, this is Detective Lucas D'Amico's case. I'm the greenie in from nowhere. I don't know enough to go point on anything. I'm just a ride-along, learning as I go."

"You solve this, the publicity could reach as far as Washington."

"I repeat what I said, sir. This is BPD's case. They deserve the glory. Not me."

All the eyes in the room bore down hard as Matt waited for the incoming barrage. Instead, Jack held to an easy tone. "This Bernstein, is she as tough as she sounds?"

"Roger that."

"Bet you caught her flat-footed with that last remark."

Matt glanced quickly across the desk. "Affirmative."

"This is an officially sanctioned investigation now, Kelly. Which means you can handle it however you like. Leave this D'Amico in control or not; that's your call. Whichever way you run the hunt, you can bring in whatever federal help you want. We clear?"

"Yes sir. Thank you."

"I told you. Lose the 'sir.' I should be back to you sometime today with the data you requested earlier."

Matt asked, "Can I request your help with one more item?"

"Go."

"In the original attack, a thumbprint was found in every room. Just one. The same each time. They've run it through the national system and come up with nothing. It's been suggested that it might belong to someone listed as KIA."

Bernstein's eyebrows lifted. For the first time, D'Amico showed surprise as well. Van Sant asked, "You want me to request a search of inactive military files?"

"It's a long shot at best."

"No, no. This can be arranged. Send through the print and I'll see what we can turn up."

"Thank you."

"Standing up for the locals, that's rare in this game, Kelly. I have to tell you, I like it. I like it a lot."

"I meant it."

"My guess is, the ambassador will be pleased as well." Van Sant hung up.

Matt set down the phone. And waited.

Bernstein needed a moment to unfasten her gaze and ask D'Amico, "What have you turned up?"

D'Amico lifted the top sheet from the file in his lap. "The SUV used by last night's stalker was stolen a week ago in Philly. Our people went over it very carefully. Nothing. Not a hair, not a print. Zip."

Bernstein asked Matt, "Neither of you got a good look at the guy you danced with?"

"Tall, stocking cap, dark clothes, gloves, strong. Seriously good with his hands." Matt hesitated, then added, "I think he knew about my leg."

D'Amico said, "He could have seen you favor that side and gotten off a lucky shot."

Bernstein asked, "What about yesterday's attack at the stadium?"

D'Amico resumed his study of the case file. "The perp used a Cheyenne Tactical 408."

Bernstein asked, "Why do I know that name?"

"Our TAC team has been pressing for us to shift over. Things cost a bomb. Called a Chey-Tech among our serious gun nuts. Professional sniper's rifle. Had a matching computerized scope that our guys claim would make it almost foolproof at a thousand yards."

He passed Matt a plastic baggie holding a round. "This is what he was shooting at you."

The bullet was eight inches long, thicker than his thumb, and weighed five ounces empty. Matt handed it to Bernstein. She hummed a note, handed it to Crowder. Just four pros out fighting the bad guys.

D'Amico read, "Cartridge is from Blaser of Germany, projectiles by Lost River High Energy Technologies. Four-hundred-twenty-grain supersonic projectile. Solid nickel-copper alloy, sized through pressure dies to variations less than one-hundred-millionth of a centimeter."

Crowder said, "The old-style fifty calibers would take your shoulder off. Took a special sort of animal to lug all that weight through the jungle, forty pounds for the BAR, double that for the belts. Slam it into position, start plowing furrows."

D'Amico added, "This new version has a gas port on the end of the barrel that represses recoil. Problem with these models is noise. The research students who called in the incident were three city blocks away, call it a quarter mile. They said it sounded like a cannon going off in the next room. Broke windows in all the surrounding buildings."

Matt recalled, "He basically shattered a solid concrete wall."

"So I hear. Our gun guys say the gas port kicks up some serious blowback. Debris and dust and whatever is around the tripod base. And the muzzle still tracks up. You say he kept shooting at a steady line, though."

"Right across the rear wall," Matt confirmed. "At head height."

"Suggesting he knew how to handle his armament. And came prepared." D'Amico was giving him that careful look now. "Strange how he didn't hit anybody."

"Unless he didn't intend to."

D'Amico squinted in pleased agreement. "I never did like this as a hit gone bad."

"He wanted to shake somebody up. Either that or he's playing with us."

"Not for long," Bernstein declared. "So what's next."

"I want to talk with the armory chief. But I'm getting stonewalled. I was hoping Kelly might have an in."

Another glance his way, then, "And Morales?"

"She's out trying to find us a lever we can use to unhinge one of the guys behind the robbery."

"Those Aryans?" Crowder huffed a laugh. "Lotsa luck."

"She might have something. We'll know by tomorrow."

Bernstein motioned a dismissal. But as Matt rose from his chair, she asked, "You have any idea why the mayor's office would try to pull you off this case?"

He thought of his conversation that morning with the journalist, decided to check it out first. "Nothing concrete."

She said to D'Amico, "Add that to your list."

D'Amico headed for the door. "Top of the pile."

D'Amico followed Matt out of the chief's office. He pointed Matt down the bull pen's central aisle and pulled a second chair into his cubicle. "How are you doing?"

"Sore. But I worked out this morning, so it's to be expected."

He nodded once. Then asked again, "How are you doing, kid?"

"Okay. Why?"

"Investigating your mother's killer. Taking incoming fire and doing a heavy tango all in one day. It's a valid question."

Matt thought of his earlier conversation with Ian. "I'm fine."

"You need to talk, I'm here. You copy?"

"Thanks, Lucas."

D'Amico nodded again. "Back to what I was telling the chief. I tried to set up an appointment with the head honcho over at the National Guard Armory. The general over there is one Robards. His aide kept me on hold for fifteen minutes. Came back and gave me a number in New York." He shuffled through the paper on his desk. "Told me I had to run my request through a Major Patches Smith, National Guard Public Relations Office. You believe that name?"

Matt looked down at the bullet in his hands. "If I go through official channels, there's a risk we'd be stonewalled."

D'Amico unbent a paper clip. "Okay. I'm asking. But I don't have to like it."

Matt took out his phone, dialed Pecard's number from memory. D'Amico asked, "You calling that retired spook?"

"Pecard. Yes."

D'Amico sighed and worked the paper clip harder.

Pecard answered with his usual terseness. "I was expecting to hear from you yesterday, Agent Kelly."

"We got caught up in something else."

"If one of the team goes into hostile territory, it is proper conduct to report his safe return."

Matt watched D'Amico snap the paper clip into tense little bits. "We've got a problem. We need access to the senior officer at the National Guard Armory without jumping through a month of bureaucratic hoops."

"Is General Robards still OIC?"

"Yes."

"I want something in return. Is the detective with you?"

"Right here."

"Ask him when he plans to confront Sol Greene."

D'Amico liked the question less than he had Matt's phone call. "That's none of his business."

Matt replied, "It is if we want his help."

"Greene's office. Three o'clock this afternoon." He threw the metal fragments at the trash can and missed. "You tell that fed if he meddles in my case I'll lock him up as an accomplice to murder."

Before Matt could relay the message, Pecard said, "Meet me at the armory in an hour."

———

The National Guard Armory was a monument to ugly. Built in the heyday of Teddy Roosevelt imperialism, the exterior was a belligerent boast. The eye slid off it, like passing a brute who embarrassed anyone caught staring. The stone fortress so crammed a city block at the base of Reservoir Hill, even the sidewalks were constricted. Dozens of rifle-slits were carved into granite walls. The chimneys were shaped like watchtowers. All the doors were steel, blistered with a century of rust and painted army green. It rose into the sunlit sky like a stone tumor.

Pecard was standing outside the armory's main entrance when they pulled up. Ray-Bans masked his eyes. He kept his face pointed at the traffic as they approached.

D'Amico offered no greeting. Matt said, "Thanks for your help."

"Let's go."

The building's interior was no better. The front foyer was as big as a basketball court and shadowed by the bars crossing the tall smoked-glass windows. Halls were squared off, twenty feet to a side, painted a yellowish gray as dismal as the cement flooring. Lighting was too high and too weak.

A noncom stood at parade rest behind a desk bearing forms and a phone. "Help you?"

Pecard replied, "We're here to see General Robards."

"Do you have an appointment?"

"Yes. Arranged through Agent Bannister with the FBI."

"Names?"

"Just use Agent Bannister."

"And them?"

"With me."

"I need your names, sir."

"Make the call, soldier. You don't want to keep your commanding officer waiting."

The MP did not like it one bit. But he picked up the phone and spoke softly. He set the phone down and went back to standing and staring at nothing. Giving them the military freeze.

Footsteps echoed down a hall. A captain in tailored khakis demanded, "Which one of you is the FBI affiliate?"

"That would be me."

"This way."

The MP objected, "Sir, the lieutenant says I need names and IDs for all visitors."

"Not these, Soldier."

"Sir, the lieutenant—"

"Corporal, these visitors do not exist. They are not here." Spelling it out in bullet-sized chunks. "You do not see them. So you can't ask them for anything."

"But I'm ordered—"

"Call your duty officer."

The MP dialed a number, spoke a few words, then handed the captain the phone. The captain turned his back to the room, talked softly, then handed back the receiver.

They waited for the MP to listen and then return the receiver to its cradle. He did not look pleased. The captain said, "Let's go."

The general's office was at the end of the hall. It wasn't as large as a football field, but it wasn't much smaller either. The outer office had four desks and still had room to lose a grand piano. The general's office made up for its size with a total absence of taste. The floor was polished linoleum, the battered desk as big as a boat, the chairs wooden and uncomfortable. A sofa set from a fifties sitcom occupied the far wall. Flags and dusty trophy cases flanked the windows. The general remained seated behind his desk and watched them approach. "You're Pecard?"

"I am indeed, General."

"Bannister and I go way back. He speaks highly of nobody. But he could not say enough about you. That's the only reason you're here. You read me?"

"Loud and clear, sir."

"Show me some IDs."

The captain collected their documents and passed them over. The general lined them up on the front of his blotter. He was a soldier's soldier, grizzled and tough and starched and bemedaled. He touched each ID in turn, then studied the corresponding face. His eyes were a very light brown, dyed to match his uniform. "Bannister assured me that this meeting never happened."

"In and out like ghosts, General," Pecard confirmed.

"All right. Tell me what you need."

Pecard said to D'Amico, "Fire away, Detective."

D'Amico started, "We're investigating a murder, General. Just trying to follow up on some loose ends."

"Of the candidate's wife. The bombing."

"Megan Kelly. Yes sir."

Khaki eyes looked down at Matt's ID, and then up at Matt. But the general said nothing.

D'Amico went on, "Preliminary analysis suggests the explosive device was a decommissioned claymore."

The general snorted. "The bombing was two weeks ago and your department is still on preliminary?"

D'Amico said nothing.

"Okay. So you suspect a claymore."

Pecard spoke up. "We don't suspect, General. We know."

D'Amico leaned forward to look around Matt. "I'll handle this."

The general looked from one to the other. "Well, well."

"Sir, following the theft here, you told the FBI all the claymores were accounted for."

The general's smirk vanished. "Are you asking or telling?"

"Whichever will help me get to the bottom of this."

"Your word, Detective. Will any record exist of this meeting?"

"Not from my end."

The general cut a glance at Pecard, who replied, "Agent Bannister did not ask; I will not offer."

Before Matt could reply, D'Amico said, "He's with me."

"All right. Then the answer is, yes. That's what I said. Sixteen FBI agents spent a month and a day in here. Disrupting our work. Giving us nothing but scorn. Treating me and my men and our operation here like we were no better than the filth who robbed us. So they finally pulled their sting and arrested those punks. Then they asked me. Can I confirm all the claymores are accounted for? I told them what would get them out of my hair."

D'Amico nodded slowly. "May I please ask you, General, what is the truth?"

"The truth?" The general leaned back and laced his fingers across his uniform jacket, just below the lowest of his six rows of medals. "The truth, Detective, is I don't have idea one. You want to know why?"

"Please."

"All right. I'll tell you. My roster calls for seven hundred and fifty active-duty enlisted men and forty-eight officers." He glanced at his aide, who had taken station by the side window. "Captain, what's our roster show this morning?"

"One hundred eighty-nine, sir. Officers and enlisted."

"Hundred and eighty-nine," the general repeated. "And where are the rest of my men?"

"That would be England, General. An air base by the name of Upper Heyford. Sent there in January. On a sixty-day assignment that's lasted over nine months."

"But I'm still getting directives to open my facility to local events. What is it today, Captain?"

"Seniors basketball tournament, General."

"And tomorrow?"

"Dog show. Straight through 'til Sunday."

General Robards asked the detective, "You getting the picture?"

"Yes sir. I sure do." D'Amico matched the general for false ease. "How do you figure the perps pulled it off?"

"They waited for the biggest event of our calendar year. The flower show. They waltzed in unnoticed. They overwhelmed my men on duty at the entrance to our vaults. They burned their way into the two vaults closest to the entrance. They loaded up a dozen empty flower boxes. They waltzed out. End of story."

"You've thought a lot about this."

"Every day and every night since it happened. Don't like closing out my career with a scandal on my watch. No sir. That I do not."

"And you didn't share this with the FBI?"

"They chose not to ask." The smile was a greater lie than his easy manner. "Why should they? We're all just lazy scum, right? Bottom-feeders on the military food chain."

D'Amico smiled back. "The flower show is chaotic."

"Turns this place into a loony bin with silk. Five hundred contestants start wheeling in here long before dawn. Screaming and shrieking and hand-wringing and driving my men totally berserk. You could drive an armored troop carrier through here and nobody'd notice. I begged Washington to let me drop this one event, to move it someplace less strategic. But the flower folks've been coming here since before the Second World War. It's *history*. It's *tradition*. And there's one thing you can say about the flower folks. They've got civic clout."

"Glad I missed that one."

"Yes sir, that you are. Now ask me the other half of your question."

"Your records."

The general's smile broadened. "Bet you're good at your job, Detective."

D'Amico just waited.

General Robards asked his aide, "What'd we receive documentation for this week, Captain?"

"That would be for a shipment of rocket-propelled grenade launchers, sir. Still in their grease. Compliments of that very same air base in England."

"What'd we receive?"

"All the boxes we've opened so far hold carbines. But there might be some grenades in there somewhere. A few. Maybe."

"I assume you have complained, Captain."

"That we have, sir. And I will again. But not to our men. The English countryside seems to have swallowed them whole."

D'Amico rose to his feet. "This helps us a lot, General. Thank you."

"Not at all." Robards came around his desk, handed back the IDs, and shook hands with them all. Pecard last. "Give Agent Bannister my regards."

"I will that, sir."

"Tell him if he wants to waste a bullet on his predecessor, give me a call. I've got some nobody'll ever miss." He nodded a military farewell. "Gentlemen."

When they came back outside, the weather had erased all color from the day. Brilliant one moment, winter dreary the next. Schizoid like the rest of Baltimore.

D'Amico kicked a couple of loose rocks as he crossed the parking lot. Pecard observed to Matt, "The detective looks ready to welsh on our deal." Talking loud enough for D'Amico to hear.

Matt responded at the same volume. "Detective D'Amico is a man of his word."

D'Amico slid into the car, slammed his door, gunned the engine.

Pecard said, "Would you care to drive down with him or me?"

"Why don't we all go together?"

Pecard laughed out loud. The sound was hoarse and derelict. He turned and headed for his own ride.

When Matt slid into the passenger seat, D'Amico said, "I was wrong to go with this."

"We would never have gotten what we just learned. Not in a billion years."

D'Amico burned rubber leaving the lot. He did not speak again until they were well south of BWI. "What can you tell me about Sol Greene?"

"He's my father's best friend. Has been since Nam. They came back and Sol went into politics, my dad into business. But they got together all the time. A year or so back, I heard my parents talking about how Sol wasn't doing so hot. He'd lost three major races in a row. Some folks were saying he'd lost his edge."

"This was when your parents decided to go for the national slot?"

"Around then. Sol had helped Pop with his runs for the state legislature. He'd been after my father for years to try for a seat in Washington. Called him a natural. My mother always liked the idea."

"You and Greene close?"

"It's not that simple." Matt shifted in his seat. "My pop and I never got along all that well. Sol has played the go-between pretty much all my life."

D'Amico glanced over. "You don't have to do this, Matt."

"Yes I do."

Matt readied himself for the argument. But the detective merely sighed and took the exit for the Beltway.

———

Sol Greene's Washington office was on Eighteenth Street a half block off K. He occupied the first two floors of an attractive Napoleon III manor that had once housed France's representative to the court of Pennsylvania Avenue. The brick was French provincial gray, the mansard roof was slate, the ceilings high, the voices muted, the decorations discreetly expensive.

Inside the main doors a receptionist sat at a sculpted desk and talked into her wireless headset. She watched their approach with cold eyes until she recognized Matt, then she cut her connection and came to her feet. "Mr. Kelly, good afternoon; your father is upstairs with Mr. Greene. Shall I show you the way, sir?"

His phone rang. "Excuse me a moment." Matt turned away. "This is Kelly."

"Van Sant here. This a good time?"

"Absolutely not."

"Just the same, what I have can't wait. Something you need to understand. Everybody in this business wants his or her own watch center. A watch center is where the traffic comes in. If the station assimilates as well as gathers, then it's called a fusion center. Having a fusion center means you're the first in the know. It's a status thing. You don't have to go hat in hand to anybody for anything. A major player has his hands on the raw stuff and has it first. This means high-level prestige. Lose prestige, you lose access. Lose access, you don't have the power to dictate budget or anything else. An in-house watch center is a signal to the world that you're operating at the top of the intel pile."

"The ambassador has his own?"

"Takes up most of this floor. What the ambassador likes most about this, besides the power badge, is the speed. The ambassador measures his day in microseconds. Which is why I'm able to call and report there's no record of a murder or bomb attack in the past eighteen months anywhere in the United States using a decommissioned claymore."

"This is news?"

"No, that was the windup." Van Sant was enjoying himself. "But there was one in England. Upper Heyford, to be exact."

Matt hurried to the receptionist desk and made a writing signal. The receptionist came up with pen and steno pad. "The air base?"

"Just outside the main gates. Only reason our system flagged it. Treated the base as U.S. territory. The victim was civilian, but on an army consulting contract. Guy by the name of Barry Simms."

"Spell that last name, please."

Van Sant did. "Air force chopper pilot, retired. Three tours in Nam. Served for the past eight years as a flight instructor on choppers."

"This is extremely interesting."

"Tell me. Same MO as your case. Man opened his door, *boom*, gone. Took out one wall of his house, the rest completely intact. The cops there made an arrest, but there was no conviction."

"So the accused is still at large?"

"And living in the same village. Retired Adjutant Geoffrey Snedley-Cummins. Needless to say he's a Brit." Van Sant spelled that name as well. "I've arranged for you to hitch a ride on a military transport leaving Andrews this evening for Upper Heyford. This flight, you're just a ride-along. You know the term?"

"Yes."

"You sit in the back of the bus. You make yourself very small. You don't hear a thing. You don't speak unless spoken to. Knowing these guys, they won't even see you."

"I owe you big-time."

"Tell me. I'll have the file on this Snedley-Cummins guy messen-gered to planeside. Your flight leaves in three hours. Oh, and a word to the wise. Eat before you board. Air force flights have carried the same meals since Normandy. Smart guys wouldn't eat them then either. I want a full report soon as you're back on American soil."

Matt shut his phone to find the receptionist watching and waiting. He was close enough to smell the spices in her perfume. Matt pulled D'Amico to one side and related what he'd just learned. D'Amico nod-ded several times, then asked, "You sure you want to do this?"

"Yes."

D'Amico turned and said to Pecard, "My show. You got that?"

"I merely have one question I wish to ask."

"Not part of the bargain."

"I assure you, Detective, you will want my help on this."

"Not a chance in the world."

"I have something—"

"My show," D'Amico repeated, the edge sharper.

Pecard sighed quietly and looked away.

Matt looked at the receptionist, who remained standing by her desk. Wearing the same look of bulletproof cheerfulness. A real Washington pro. Matt said, "I know the way."

"Certainly, Mr. Kelly. I'll just tell them you're coming."

The stairway was broad and marbled and formal. A signed Chagall print almost as tall as Matt hung from the right-hand wall. Midway up Pecard said, "I heard you were over with the marines right before the fall. I happen to have taken part in—"

D'Amico did not even glance over. "Don't go looking for a way to buddy up, Pecard. You won't find one."

———

Everything about Sol Greene's outer office was muted. Pastel carpet, shades, lighting, desks, chairs. Soft conversation from a trio standing in the corner. An almost-musical hello from the secretary. She showed them straight in.

Matt's father had pulled one of the visitor chairs over behind Sol's desk. He and Sol were working through a pile of documents when they entered. Paul Kelly scowled at the disturbance. Sol gave them nothing.

The secretary asked, "Would you gentlemen care for anything?"

"They won't be staying that long," Paul Kelly snapped.

The secretary smiled. "I'll just leave you alone then."

Paul Kelly took aim at his son. "You couldn't do the right thing just this once, could you?"

There were only two chairs in front of the desk. Matt walked to the conference table and pulled over a third.

"No matter what it is, no matter what I ask, my son has to go and do the opposite."

Matt seated himself between Pecard and D'Amico. Met his father's gaze. Held to his silence. Just like a hundred thousand times before.

"That's my boy. Never fails to disappoint."

Sol spoke then. Quietly. One word. "Paul."

"No, Sol. Not this time. We are *one week* from the election. There is no reason why my son couldn't back off for that long." His glare smoldered. "I just don't get you. What is it, jealousy? You don't like your old man moving up in the world? Rocks your tiny little boat to think somebody's got more ambition than you have? More drive?"

D'Amico said, "Sir, my name is Detective Lucas D'Amico."

"I'll get to you in a minute." Paul Kelly aimed a finger at his son. "*Now* you call? *Now* you insist on pulling us from a ton of work that can't wait? There has to be some ulterior motive. Something that's eluded me my entire life as your father."

Matt did not speak. The distance opened between them, the same protective detachment he had known all his life. He did not feel rage. At least, nothing anywhere near the surface.

Paul Kelly slammed his fist on the papers. "For once in your life, you will *answer me!*"

D'Amico came back with his steady calm. "It's good to have you both together. Saves us all some time."

"I have called the mayor's office, Detective. I have spoken with his deputy. He assures me that you are here without approval. I intend to bring harassment charges against you."

D'Amico crossed his legs. "Mr. Greene, could you tell me where you were on Sunday afternoon?"

"Don't answer that, Sol."

Sol replied, "Right here. Working."

"Can anyone confirm that?"

"I can," Paul Kelly snapped.

"You were at the game, Mr. Kelly."

"I called him. Twice."

"On his cell phone or his office line?" D'Amico held up his hand. "Please understand, Mr. Kelly. This is an official police investigation. Your phone records can be subpoenaed. If you are found to have lied, you can be arrested for obstruction."

Matt's father developed a tic beneath his left eye. He did not speak.

"Mr. Greene, was anyone else—"

"No. I was alone. But my own phone log will show a number of outgoing calls."

"This is *insane*."

"Paul." Sol was in placating mode. But tired of it. "Let's just get through this and move on, all right?"

Matt said softly, "Barry Simms."

The two men on the other side of the desk froze.

"Chopper pilot." This from D'Amico. "From your expressions, gentlemen, I take it you knew him?"

Paul Kelly cleared his throat. Tried to recapture his annoyance. "What about it?"

"He was murdered," D'Amico replied.

The two men actually flinched. Sol asked, "When?"

"Six months ago. He was attacked in the exact same manner as your wife, sir."

This time it was Pecard who leaned forward to look around Matt. Allen Pecard stared hard at D'Amico. As surprised as the two men on the other side of the desk.

D'Amico pretended not to notice. "A decommissioned claymore mine was wired to his front door. The rest of his home was left utterly intact."

Paul Kelly rubbed his eye, trying to stop the twitch.

Sol Greene asked quietly, "What do you want?"

"Two things. The names of the other men in your platoon who came home. And any reason why somebody might be after you."

"Are you nuts?" Kelly rubbed harder at his eye. "That was thirty years ago."

"I realize that, Mr. Kelly."

"I haven't seen any of them again. We weren't best buddies. We were soldiers. I was their commanding officer. Sol was my number two."

"A couple of them wrote me," Sol offered.

Kelly's hand dropped to the desk. "You never told me that."

"What's to tell?" Sol kneaded a spot just beneath his rib cage. "I never answered."

"Who wrote you, Mr. Greene?"

"Barry Simms wrote me a while back, maybe a year. And one of the enlisted men, Lonnie Eaton."

"Lonnie was a good man," Paul Kelly said quietly.

"He was getting married," Sol said. "Again. Wanted us to come."

D'Amico gave them some space, then asked, "Anybody else make contact with either of you?"

When Sol shrugged his response, Paul Kelly offered softly, "I got a letter once. Sort of."

Sol showed genuine alarm. "What?"

D'Amico asked, "Who wrote you, Mr. Kelly?"

"Nobody by name. It wasn't signed."

"When was this, sir?"

"A while back, I'm not sure. A year, maybe longer. I got a letter from the asylum."

Pecard's chair creaked as he leaned forward.

Sol had gone pale at the news. "Paul, you've got to tell me these things."

"What's to tell? A nutcase wrote and didn't even sign his name."

"This is part of my job."

"Your job is to get us through next Tuesday."

D'Amico asked, "So you received a letter from an inmate at Fort Howard?"

"No. The other one up north. I forget the name."

Pecard said, his voice dangerously soft, "Perryville?"

Sol looked over. "Remind me again who you are."

D'Amico pressed, "You received a letter from an inmate at the Perryville, Virginia, mental hospital. What did it say?"

"Not really a letter. Didn't say anything I could understand. Drawings of bombs and fire. Words scrawled in tight little circles. I didn't even try to read it. I threw it away."

Sol muttered, "Good."

The two men were gone from the room. They did not look at each other. Nor at the people across the desk. Their gazes were dark and far-reaching.

D'Amico said, "Who else came back from that last mission?"

"Eight of us," Paul Kelly said. "We took four chopper loads out. I brought eight men home. For that they gave me a medal."

"Seven now," Sol said.

"That's right. Seven." Paul Kelly shook his head. "Poor old Barry."

D'Amico asked, "The others?"

Sol gave a toneless roll call. "Ace Keeler, Tim Vance, Peter Neally, Chad Campbell, Brett Shuford."

"Old Brett." Paul Kelly shook his head. "Where was he from, Missouri?"

"Arkansas," Sol corrected softly. "The original Ozark whale."

D'Amico asked, "What happened out there?"

Paul Kelly spoke to thirty years ago. "Only reason we're here at all was Barry flew back for us. He's the one who deserved to have the president pin that medal on his chest. Nobody else would land."

"Too hot," Sol said. "They had us in enfilade. Blasting us from the hill we'd been sent to take. And the forests to either side. Sat where we couldn't get to them and tore us apart."

"Told us it was lightly defended. Military intelligence." Paul Kelly glanced briefly at his son. "What a waste. What a total waste."

Pecard took a breath. Said in a voice little more than a whisper, "You didn't mention Porter Reeves."

D'Amico's protest was halted by the expression of the two men across from him. They stared at Pecard in blank astonishment. Sol finally said, "Porter's dead."

"He might be," Pecard said. "But I have very good reason to believe he did not perish during that battle."

Sol had gone gray. "I saw him go down. He got taken out by a land mine."

"A man answering to Porter Reeves's description was a POW," Pecard said. "Guest of Hanoi Hilton."

Sol looked ashen. "You think or you know?"

Pecard asked the two men, "Can you describe this Reeves for me?"

"You heard Sol. Porter's dead." Paul Kelly bolted to his feet. "This has gone far enough. You come in here bringing nothing but ghosts and news we don't want to hear. You've got what you came for. Now get out."

They did not speak again until they were back on the building's front steps. "Hold up there," D'Amico said. "What was all that about?"

"A man from Kelly's platoon by the name of Porter Reeves was listed among the KIA that day. But after the pullout and the final prisoner exchange, one report had a Porter Reeves listed among the Hanoi Hilton survivors. Not the official report. Your official report was supplied by the Vietcong. But the returnees were asked about the other prisoners. Your military intelligence sought to piece together a report of their own. I have no valid record of anything more."

"What was your interest in this man?"

Pecard hesitated, then shook his head. "It was all a very long time ago."

D'Amico closed the distance. "Whose agenda are you working on here?"

"I'm on your side, Detective."

D'Amico squinted up at the sky, as though trying to pierce the gray veil looming over Eighteenth Street. He might have sighed the word *feds*. He asked Matt, "You okay?"

"Yes." After all, he had years of experience hiding his wounds.

"I have to get back to Baltimore."

"I can get a taxi to Andrews."

Pecard offered, "I can take Agent Kelly."

"Walk with me, Matt." D'Amico moved through the bustling foot traffic like the people weren't there. "Can you ask your contacts to check for anything on the records of those guys who survived? Arrests, convictions, current known addresses."

"Sure. You want me to include this guy Porter Reeves?"

"For what it's worth." D'Amico glanced back at where Pecard stood by his midnight-blue Grand Cherokee. Pecard gave no indication he was either aware or interested in their inspection. D'Amico said, "You think maybe you could ask about him as well?"

The interior of Pecard's Grand Cherokee was immaculate and smelled vaguely of cleanser. He drove smoothly through the coagulating traffic until rush hour turned the Beltway into a six-lane clot. Matt tried Connie's phones—home, office, and cell. He left two messages saying he was sorry to break their date but he was called away and would phone when he could. Pecard waited until Matt shut his phone to ask, "When are you scheduled to depart?"

"Two hours. Less."

"Then we shall need to try Plan B." Pecard slid to the emergency lane, floored it, took the next exit, and headed overland. Traffic remained dense but was at least moving. They traveled into Virginia hill country, populated by million-dollar homes and hives of foreign cars. Matt's thoughts weaved like the road.

They crested a ridgeline. A bulldozer idled by a half-demolished farmhouse. Construction machinery was biting new furrows from the earth. A cheery billboard announced the new housing development was already sold out. In the distance a stand of walnut and maple blazed with the season's flare. Matt's gut crawled with nameless dread. For the future. For the past. For all he could no longer control or ignore.

Matt took hold of the only fear he was willing to name. "Do you think my father had some hand in this?"

"I personally can't see either of them as culprits." Pecard's Ray-Bans gave Matt nothing. The silent observer—ever watchful, ever hidden.

"Why did you elect to participate in that confrontation? Though participation hardly describes your reactions."

"I needed to be certain." Matt turned his attention back to the winding road. "It's good to be certain, isn't it?"

They did not speak again until arriving at the Andrews Air Force Base main gate. Pecard pulled in front of the Visitors Center and cut the motor. "Everybody has gifts. Some you're born with. Some you learn from experiences you wish you never had. Yet they are yours just the same. But only if you *claim* them."

"You're telling me to lie, is that it?"

"Everyone lies, Agent Kelly. You certainly should be aware of this fact by now. In this world, truth is the odd man out. What you should be striving for is *control*. Not internal. This is where the world fails to understand the power of British subtlety. Internal control is merely the first step to dominating whatever situation you enter."

The same barely suppressed force Matt had sensed the first time they met emanated from this man. "Who *are* you?"

"That, I fear, is an utterly incorrect question for you to be asking at this point in time." Pecard started the car, gunned the motor, and slapped the gearshift into drive. "You have just failed a critical test, Agent Kelly. Kindly step away from my vehicle."

———

The Andrews waiting hall was a converted hangar in concrete and linoleum and hard plastic chairs. Almost everyone wore uniforms. Matt joined the long line snaking toward a military-style buffet. He selected an empty table next to a cluster of noncoms playing a noisy game of poker. Afterward he went back outside. The wind had freshened. The air smelled of jet fuel and coming rain. He tried Connie's numbers again, got the same messages as before. He then called the Baltimore FBI office and asked for Bryan Bannister.

When the station chief came on, Matt said, "I was wondering if you could give me some background information on Allen Pecard."

"The man is a living legend," Bannister replied. "What else do you need to know?"

"Pecard is becoming increasingly involved in our case."

"Which can only be a good thing for a recruit like yourself. What is that noise?"

"A plane's taking off."

"Where are you?"

"Andrews Air Base."

"What?"

"Hang on a second." The jet roared by, then, "Who is Allen Pecard? Where does he come from? What are his qualifications? These should not be difficult questions."

Bannister was silent a moment. "Pecard is originally from London. He served in the SAS, their equivalent of Special Forces. Toward the end of our time in Nam he transferred over to Military Intelligence. Got himself wounded. Retired a major. He came out and went to work as a consultant. End of story."

"How did he come to work for us?"

"Pecard is one of the best there is at armaments and explosives. We asked. He came."

Matt carefully chose his words. "It's been suggested that he didn't ever fully recover from his time in combat."

"Who told you that? Because I'm telling you they don't come any finer than Allen Pecard."

"Who has he worked with?"

"Everybody. Military police, ATF, us, DEA, the CIA, local cops. He's the guy to call when you can't figure out what's gone off, or who did the deed." Despite Matt's calm, Bannister grew increasingly hot under the questions. "You listen up. I don't care what tag Washington decides to hang around your neck. Chief investigator, senior case officer, king of Nepal. You're still nothing but a green recruit. You want to get ahead in this game, you sidle up to Pecard and you take in everything he offers."

Bannister slammed down the phone.

The brass was late. Matt was kept waiting in the concrete hall until after eight. The plane was a large Gulfstream—not old, not new. The exterior bore no markings save for the ID number on its tail. Nothing said it was military. When the boarding call finally sounded, Matt was the first on the plane and took the rearmost seat. Then the brass arrived—two two-star generals, one three-star, three bird colonels, one lowly major. Before the door shut, the military had their papers spread out and their heads together. The plane taxied and took off. No attendant wished them a nice trip. No pilot spoke over the intercom. The wheels thunked under Matt, and the plane soared through clouds and away from a swiftly setting sun. As soon as they leveled off, a pilot emerged from the cockpit and made his way back to offer Matt a sealed manila envelope. "I was told to give you this."

"Thanks."

"There's a galley up front. We're carrying a tray of sandwiches." The pilot shrugged. "Sort of."

"Is the food that bad?"

"Never met anybody who's eaten on board and lived to complain, sir."

"Any chance of making a phone call?"

"Phone's in your armrest." The pilot started away. "ETA's oh-six-hundred, local time. Five-hour time difference from Andrews."

His seat was a cross between plush first-class and lumpy sofa. Matt wriggled about until the lumps fit his body, opened the folder, and read the contents carefully. Then he went to the galley, poured himself a Coke, went back, and reached for the phone.

When Connie answered, he asked, "Did you get my messages?"

"You think leaving me a half dozen voice mails is going to get you out of the doghouse? You stood me up!"

"Is that a smile I'm hearing in your voice?"

"Absolutely not. Where are you?"

"Thirty thousand feet, somewhere over the North Atlantic, riding in an air force jet."

"Man, if I only had a dollar for every time I've heard that excuse."

"I'm really sorry about missing our date."

"Me too. When are you back?"

"Soon as I can. I better hang up now."

"Call me when you're settled."

"I don't know when that will be, Connie."

"Call me anyway."

Matt replaced the handset and reopened the file. This time he made notes in the margin as he read. He set the papers aside and mulled over the data. But he was tired and the air was stuffy there at the back of the bus. He shut his eyes.

His mind played through recent events like a jumbled collection of film clips. Connie, the Ravens game, working out with Vic, the meeting in the chief's office, the confrontation with his father, Allen Pecard driving him to the airport. The nightmare.

The next thing he knew, the pilot was shaking his shoulder. Hard. "You're wanted on the phone."

For an instant Matt could not remember where he was. "What?"

The pilot lifted his armrest and handed him the handset. "We've already started our descent. You need to finish this fast, sir."

When the pilot started back toward the front, Matt realized all the brass were glaring at him. The three generals looked outraged.

Matt ducked his head, shamed by the prospect of his nighttime terrors having been on public display. He said to the phone, "This is Kelly."

"Van Sant here. You awake?"

Matt glanced at his watch. He was still on East Coast time. It read almost eleven. He had slept five hours and woken up feeling even more tired than before. "Barely."

"We got a match on the print. You ready for this?"

It took Matt a second to realize what he meant. "Yes."

"Barry Simms."

"The guy killed by the bomb over here?"

"One and the same."

Matt stared out the window. The plane broke free of clouds, revealing a wet green world below. "I don't get it."

"That makes about a dozen of us. We're all thinking message, but we don't know—"

The pilot's voice broke through on the line. "We're cleared to land in five. This connection needs to shut down."

Matt said, "Call Detective Lucas D'Amico with Baltimore Homicide. Tell him what you told me."

"Roger that. Good hunting."

———

Tuesday morning Lucas slept in and then made pancakes for Katy. Pancakes were Katy's favorite meal and normally reserved for easy Saturdays. But Lucas wasn't due at the office until noon, and he was trying to make up the interrupted Saturday routine. He called the school and said Katy would be late, then waited for the smells to wake her. A silent celebration, something she loved and he loved doing for her. There was a quiet joy to such mornings, a tiny glimpse into the past, one that meant far more to Lucas than the food. Before June had become ill, he had made all the meals for their little family on Saturdays. His wife usually sat in the kitchen with them, reading a book or the newspaper. Saying little. Quietly enjoying her own downtime.

Katy came downstairs when the smell of bacon and pancakes filtered through her closed door. "Good morning, sweetheart. Sleep well?"

"Is it Saturday?"

"No, honey. Go look at Katy's calendar and tell me what day it is."

She rubbed the sleep in her features and crossed to the calendar on the pantry door. It took her quite a while to decide. "Tuesday."

"Very good, honey. But sometimes we have pancakes during the week. You don't like pancakes just on Saturday, do you?"

"That's silly talk, Daddy."

But there was no playfulness to her tone. Lucas had learned to listen closely to what his daughter did not say. And something was wrong. "Sit down, honey, your plate is ready."

He had melted the butter in a little iron skillet just as Katy liked. She watched him solemnly as he forked open a hole in the middle of the top pancake and then poured in the yellow liquid. "Enough?"

"Thank you, Daddy."

He poured himself another cup and seated himself across from her. "Do you want to pray?"

"You do it."

"Let me have your hand. Lord, we thank you for these many blessings. We thank you for family and friends. Bless this food to our bodies and this day to doing your will. Amen."

He watched her eat. Something was wrong. "What is it, honey?"

She cast another glance at the window. "The sun is shining."

"Yes, it looks like a beautiful day." He let her take another bite, not offering to help her cut up the bacon, even when she slid all the other slices onto the table mat. Katy knew how to ask for help when she needed it. "Is something bothering you, Katy-girl?"

"We were going to work in the garden."

"Who?"

"My friends. I told them I would be there at nine."

"Sweetheart, I'm sorry, I didn't . . . It's just, I wanted to do a family thing."

She did her slow-motion cut with another bite. "We're family."

"That's right, sweetheart. We sure are."

"I miss Mommy."

He set down his mug. This was serious. Katy rarely spoke about June anymore. When she did, it was because something at the dark core of her being pained her. So much of Katy's interior world was a mystery, even to Katy. Talking about June was her way of touching the hidden depths.

Lucas reached for her hand. "I miss her too. Very much."

"She's not coming back."

"No, honey. But we'll join her when our time comes."

"In heaven."

"Yes."

"We'll be a family again then, won't we?"

"Yes, sweetheart. We'll be in God's family."

She cut another piece of pancake, then pushed the plate to one side. "I don't want any more, Daddy."

He rose from the table. "Go wash your face and hands and brush your hair. I'll drop you by the school."

"No, Daddy. I told you, by the home."

"Of course. Where your friends are working in the garden." He watched her put the plates in the sink. Sometimes she remembered to do this on her own, but not often. He kept his tone light. "Who are these friends of yours, Katy?"

"They live in the home."

He set his mug in the sink with her plates, squirted some soap over the dishes, and grabbed the brush. Anything to keep his eyes and hands busy. "Do you want to go live with them in the home, Katy-girl?"

"No."

She did not move from beside him. "Why not?"

"You can't come."

The lump in his throat turned the words very hoarse. "But I could visit you as often as we liked."

She stood there beside him, as still as only his Katy could be. Finally she said, "Family is a lonely thing, Daddy."

Lucas stacked the dishes and the frying pan in the drying rack. He dried his hands off on the dish towel and moved to the downstairs closet. He unlocked the door using the key he always kept with him. He slipped on his holster and armed his weapon. He relocked the door. He stood at the foot of the stairs, wondering if he dared go ask Katy what she had meant. Then the phone rang.

"D'Amico."

It was Connie. "I think I scored, Lucas."

"Tell me."

"I might have a lever we can use for Bert Lang."

"He was the leader, right?"

"Yeah, and his common-law wife was the Division One dispatcher."

Katy thumped down the stairs, turned, and gave him the look. The one that was both sad and resigned. Like he'd been caught doing something wrong. Or he'd disappointed her in some intensely bad way. "Look, I need to run do something with my daughter. Where are you?"

"On my way back home to shower and change. I've been at it since five."

"I'll run by the federal courthouse, get us a writ on Lang, then swing by your house. Give me an hour." He hung up the phone and realized Katy was standing in the hall, watching him with a worried frown. "What's the matter, baby?"

"You have to work."

He walked over to her and started to take her in his arms. But Katy scrunched up her shoulders and shied away. A little girl's way of saying she didn't want to be held.

Lucas dropped his hands, feeling as helpless as he had since standing by June's hospital bed. "I don't understand, honey. It's written down in your calendar. Today is a day when Daddy works."

"I know."

"Then what . . ."

Katy opened the door and stepped outside. She walked down the stairs and stopped in front of the car. Lucas opened her door, then went around and let himself in. He started the car and put it in gear, but stayed where he was. "Katy, I can't help you if you won't tell me what's wrong."

"I miss Mommy."

"I know you do, honey. So do I. Very much."

"Mommy told me I had to take care of you."

Lucas cut off the motor. He reached over and took her hand. "Katy, I want to ask you a question and I need you please to promise to tell me the truth. Okay? Will you do that?" She nodded in her slow fashion, staring out the windshield at nothing. "Katy-girl, would you like to go live in the home?"

"I promised Mommy."

"Sweetheart, Mommy would understand. I know that in the bottom of my heart."

"We're a family."

He felt the confusion and distress beneath those deep, soft, slow-spoken words. So much it threatened to crush his chest. "Yes. Yes, we are."

She rocked slightly in her seat. "I'm alone a lot, Daddy."

The U.S. air base at Upper Heyford was laid out like a wet red-and-green chessboard. The buildings were low and brick. Between them, neat emerald lawns glinted in the rain. A pair of military sedans arrived while the plane was still taxiing. The brass deplaned without a backward glance. Matt waited while they saluted and shook hands and departed. He then started down the aisle to where the pilot waited. Matt asked, "When do you head back?"

"That depends on you, sir."

"Excuse me?"

The Gulfstream was just high enough for the pilot to stand straight but so low Matt had to crouch. It brought him close enough to see the man's spark of humor. "They didn't tell you anything, did they."

"Show up and go, that's about all."

"That last call you got included a change of orders for us. We're to hold here until you're ready to depart."

"Which is why the brass gave me the slow burn," Matt realized.

"Air force pilots are trained not to notice things like that, sir. How long will you be here?"

"I have no idea. I hope not long. Is there a number I can call as soon as I know something?"

"Have your man notify the ready room. They'll know where to track us down."

"My man?"

This time the smile broke through. "Bottom of the stairs. Good hunting, sir."

———

"Mr. Kelly? Brian Aycock, United States Embassy." He opened an umbrella and held it out to cover Matt, not himself. "Welcome to England. Sorry about the weather, sir."

He was young and dressed in a three-button suit that turned him into a fashionable stovepipe. He was also extremely nervous. Matt felt like a liar just shaking his hand.

"I haven't had much time on this, sir. I was only flagged yesterday." He led Matt to a dark Ford Mondeo parked on the tarmac. He opened Matt's door and extended the umbrella to shield Matt as he took his seat. "I've managed to set up a meeting with the head of security here on base, as per instructions from Washington. Other than that, I'm at your disposal. Sir."

Matt put up with it until Aycock scurried around the car and slid behind the wheel. "Hang on here just a second."

"Yes sir. But the senior air force security officer, he—"

"He can wait five minutes."

"Sir, yes sir." Aycock wore the expression of a deer staring down the business end of a rifle barrel. Five minutes into the assignment and he was already going to catch it.

"I don't know what they told you, but I am a total rookie. I've moved around all my life, but I've never been anywhere." Matt realized that made no sense only when Aycock's forehead creased. His own head felt stuffed with steel wool. He had heard of jet lag but never experienced it before this moment. He tried again. "I've never been outside the U.S. I'm not supposed to be here now. I got handed a vague nothing of an assignment and suddenly it's gone ballistic. So you can forget the sirs. I'm Matt. We clear so far?"

"Yes sir . . . Sure."

"Good. The only way I can hope to move forward is if you tell me what you know."

"Not much."

Matt rolled his finger. Go.

"Okay. Two things. You don't want to keep this guy waiting."

"That's one."

Aycock started the car. "Don't expect much from this meeting."

———

They rolled away from the airfield at a sedate twenty miles per hour. Hangars gave way to barracks and offices and gyms and buildings Matt could not identify. The base was far too tidy to be called decrepit. But every building appeared of World War II vintage. They were all mind-numbingly similar, red brick with sash windows and white trim and white doors and little yellow signs with cryptic military code planted by every front walk. The signs all said the same thing to Matt: If you have to ask, you don't belong.

The road's often-repaired tarmac was as striped and humped as lizard skin. "I thought you said we were in a hurry."

"We sure are."

"And this is the fastest you can go?"

"That is absolutely correct."

Matt settled back. "Tell me what I'm seeing."

"Upper Heyford Air Base played a critical role in D-day. Following the end of World War II, it was designated part of NATO operations. The airstrips were extended to handle B-52s and B-1Bs. Security was stepped up."

"The base went nuclear?"

"There has never been official acknowledgment of any U.S. nuclear arsenal ever being on British soil," Aycock replied very carefully. "For the past two years, Upper Heyford has basically been waiting its turn at closure."

"Has it gone well?"

Aycock glanced over, measuring whether he could take Matt at his word. Then, "The official word is, there is no official word."

"So not at all well."

"There are problems at both ends. The Brits can't decide what they want to do with the place. The local government is fighting with both Whitehall and the British army."

"And from our side?"

Aycock glanced over once more. "I have no idea."

"Is that a fact."

"Yes," Aycock replied. "It really is."

"Meaning whatever is happening, they don't want me to know about it."

Aycock drove on in silence.

Military police headquarters had an incongruous white front porch, the only one on the base that Matt had seen. Aycock pulled into the one slot marked Visitors. He asked, "Do you mind if I stay out here?"

Three young people stood at attention in the misting rain, two men and one woman. Their hair was matted flat to their faces. They all wore sodden National Guard fatigues, darkened to almost black by the drenching. They looked very young. All three trembled violently. Matt asked, "What are you not telling me?"

"The station chief wasn't all that eager to help out."

Matt noticed a corporal in fatigues standing on the porch. He leaned against a wooden pillar, his arms crossed, watching the three enlisted personnel. "He refused to meet with me?"

"The ambassador had to speak with the base commander to make this happen."

"The ambassador knows about me?"

Aycock nodded. "Whatever you landed in, it really must be something."

Matt kept watching the three trembling soldiers. "I was told some National Guard units out of Baltimore have been sent over to help shut the base down."

"That is correct." Aycock did a very good job at diplomatic bland.

"Problems?"

"Officially, the base is severely understaffed due to most of its original personnel now serving in Kuwait City."

"And unofficially?"

Aycock pointed at the three shivering forms. "Ask them."

Matt held up the file he was given on the plane. "Have you seen this?"

"No sir."

He handed it over. "Read it. Then I want you to call the judge in Oxford who handled the case. His name is at the top of page four. Ask if we can come by and see him." Matt opened his door. "Make it sound urgent."

———

The young woman whimpered softly as Matt passed by. The two young men gave a hoarse shiver with each breath. The chill was cramping them so that their bodies were slightly bent and their faces taut. Like they were in severe pain.

The corporal was taller than Matt and outweighed him by twenty pounds. He watched Matt's approach with eyes as pale as his close-cropped blond hair. He drawled, "You the guy from Washington?"

Matt climbed the stairs. "That's right."

"You're late." The corporal's eyes flicked over Matt and dismissed him. "Not a good idea to keep Major Stafford waiting."

A dozen off-duty enlisted personnel hoofed by on the road, protected from the rain by military ponchos. Not one looked at the trio in the front lawn as they passed. Cars crawled by on the street. No face glanced their way.

As Matt started for the door, the corporal added, "Overnight spell planted out front would teach you the proper meaning of time."

Matt entered the station.

A grizzled sergeant was seated behind a desk. His eyes were darker, but just as cold as the corporal's. "Help you?"

"Matt Kelly to see the officer in charge."

"You're late, Mr. Kelly."

Matt glanced at two young women seated on a bench beneath the side window. They were scrunched together as far from the sergeant as they could manage. They looked terrified.

The sergeant rose from his desk and made a military drama of crossing to the inner office and knocking.

Matt saw the two young women wince as the voice inside barked, "Come!"

"Major, the fellow from Washington finally decided to show up."

The two women wore the same National Guard fatigues as the trio outside. They looked ready to sell their every remaining day to be elsewhere.

The voice inside drawled, "What does he want to see me about, Sergeant?"

He swiveled around. "You there! What's the purpose of your keeping the major waiting?"

"I wish to ask about the murder of an American civilian."

"Show him in, Sergeant."

Major Stafford was a humorless badger with silver-flecked eyelids and a bony ridge along the crest of his bald head. "Close the door, Sergeant."

"Certainly, sir." The door banged shut. "Can't have the scum in our front office hear the top secret business that kept us waiting all morning."

"That will do, Sergeant."

Matt walked over and sat down.

"We can only assume that Washington has ferreted out some vital new information about a case that is six months dead."

The sergeant took up station beside the major's desk. "Washington is very good at that, sir. Ferreting."

"No," Matt said. "Nothing new on this investigation at all."

"Well now, I find that very strange. Since I've been *ordered* to see you. My commanding officer, who has been on base a grand total of six weeks, *ordered* me and my entire staff to extend you every courtesy." He was not ageless so much as well preserved. A pickled version of the base itself, long stewed in military brine. "As though we had nothing better to do than wait for you to waltz in. Isn't that so, Sergeant."

"Courteous, sir. That's us in a nutshell."

"Strange how Washington would wait six months to contact us at all. Then traipse in here and declare everything so urgent. What would you call that sort of behavior, Sergeant?"

"Best not say, sir."

"So, Mr. Kelly. As you can see, we are extremely eager to help you any way we can."

"The police investigation identified one culprit, a retired Captain Snedley-Cummins. The court then found him not guilty."

"Are you asking or telling, Mr. Kelly?"

"My question is this: Were there then or are there now any other suspects?"

"Of course not. He did it. Cummins murdered the chopper pilot."

"The court decided otherwise."

The two military police smirked. Stafford said, "Obviously we poor air force types don't have access to Washington insider information."

"Could you tell me if Snedley-Cummins has been around these past few weeks?"

The two men stared at each other and burst out laughing. "You travel four thousand miles to ask me that?"

Matt rose to his feet. He had never felt so tired in his life. "Thank you for your time."

"Here, now. I've got a question of my own." Stafford planted two elbows on his desk. "What's happened that this case is suddenly so all-fired important?"

"There's been another bombing. With a decommissioned claymore."

"And?"

"Barry Simms's thumbprint was found at the scene."

It was worth the aggravation, seeing the two men gape like that. Stafford managed, "*Our* Barry Simms?"

"Yes."

"That's impossible!"

Matt headed for the door. "I know."

The federal courthouse was jammed. It took D'Amico five and a half hours to jump through the legal hoops and obtain the necessary writ. Even so, when he finally pulled up in front of Connie's home, she bounded through the front door and gave him a schoolgirl's wave. Carrying a shoulder bag that must have weighed forty pounds, what with the Taser and gun and speedloader and Mace and tape recorder and everything else a rookie could possibly imagine needing for her first trip to the pen. But Connie slung the bag like it was empty and actually skipped down the stairs. Lucas tried to recall the last time he had been so eager about going to work.

She slid into the car. "How're you doing?"

"Feeling seriously ancient." He put the car into gear. "Sorry I'm late."

"Is that a joke, you apologizing to me?"

"It's what partners do when they show up at three in the afternoon." He slipped through the stop sign at the end of her street and headed north. "I got the typical hassle downtown. A perfect example of why I detest all feds."

"Matt's fed."

"He's an exception only because he hasn't been in long enough. Wait a year. You'll see." He noticed she was smiling. "What?"

"Nothing. I'm just hoping you're wrong, is all."

Connie was easy with silence. Which D'Amico liked in a cop. Chatterers wore him down. Only today his thoughts made so much clamor, he might as well have been on the firing range. Connie was only a couple of years older than his Katy. Young and eager and smart and alive. Her whole future ahead of her. So achingly full of life. "Tell me about yourself, Morales. You're from Philly, right?"

"My dad covers the police and courts for the Philadelphia *Enquirer*." She shot him another smile. "Dad really admires cops and made sure I learned that much growing up. Mom died while I was still in diapers."

"I'm sorry to hear that."

She shrugged easily. "My father is the best. I count myself super lucky."

"What'd he think of his daughter becoming an officer of the law?"

"Wild as I was growing up, Dad's happy I'm on this side of the bars. He has his worry moments. I get these calls, usually around two in the morning, making sure I'm being careful. Otherwise, he's so proud he could explode. The guy actually wept at my swearing in."

The state penitentiary had been erected back in the thirties using work-relief labor and federal money. Back then, the area had been a wasteland. Druid Lake, a half mile east, had been country. Now the pen's neighbors were the I-83 extension and Johns Hopkins. A few years back the city had made a big noise at state level, trying to get the legislature to move the prison. But the state had bigger problems and no money. It responded by paying for a new roof, the legislature's way of saying that the pen was there to stay.

The pen was a demented stone castle. The new tin roof shone clean and white, an enormous dunce cap for all its inhabitants and their manic ways. The U.S. government leased one wing for federal inmates.

Cops entered Men's Detention through a sally port on Eager Street. The big metal gate rolled up and down, clanking like a human garbage disposal. When D'Amico drove in, he caught two guards grinning over Connie's wide-eyed expression. Every first-timer reacted the same way. D'Amico leaned over and said what his first partner had told him several centuries back, "Don't worry. The sally port only eats lawyers."

The place shouted hopeless in a wordless prison clamor. Concrete walls, guard towers, coiled razor wire. A lot of this was hidden from the street behind clever construction and high brick walls. All the menace was aimed inside and down.

"Leave all your gear except for the pistol in the car. Did you bring a clip holster?"

"Yes."

"Put that on your belt. Keep your gun at the ready. You're my only backup while the prisoner is in our custody."

They left the car and were buzzed through the official entryway. Connie followed his example, signed in, left her badge and gun, stepped through the metal detectors, and entered a claustrophobic wire-mesh tunnel. They passed through the steel door at the other end. D'Amico handed his federal writ through the slot and told the guard behind the bulletproof glass he was here to collect federal prisoner Bert Lang. They sat on a metal bench in a cheerless antechamber. Today D'Amico found it harder than usual to tune out the prison's constant din. He leaned against the sweating wall and did what a cop does too much of. Wait.

Bert Lang was escorted out by three guards. One held each arm. A third walked a pace back, stick at the ready, telling D'Amico more clearly than words ever could what kind of prisoner he was taking.

Lang was typical hard-core Aryan. He used his body as a sketchbook and rage as his pen. Prison tats decorated hugely defined muscles on his chest and shoulders. Spiderwebs and swastikas and fury ran over his wrists and knuckles and neck. A professional artist had done a flaming third eye on his forehead. Cell-yard build. Swagger. Sneer. Eyes so empty the color didn't matter.

Lang gave Connie the long prison stare while D'Amico took the manacles from the guard and personally chained his prisoner. Ankles first, then the chain up to the padded belt around his middle, and then this to the restraining pads on his upper arms. Finally a pair of cuffs. He went over everything a second time. Only then did he sign the clipboard and formally announce, "I have the prisoner."

"He's all yours."

D'Amico took one arm and led him back through the tunnel. Connie adopted the proper guard-stance, two steps back. Once they were rearmed, her hand never left the grip of her pistol. Lang's chains clattered across the concrete as D'Amico led him back to the car.

As D'Amico unlocked the doors, Lang stared over his shoulder at

Connie. "What's the matter, honey? Afraid to get any closer to a real man?"

D'Amico pushed down on the greasy bald head. "Inside."

Lang kept his gaze on Connie as D'Amico locked the ankle chain inside the bolt welded to the floor of his car's backseat. They climbed inside. D'Amico started the car and rolled forward. The gate ground up and they drove out.

Lang watched the outside world in silence. Prisoners always took a few minutes to reorient to a world beyond bars. Then he spoke to D'Amico for the first time. "Do I know you?"

"My name is Detective Lucas D'Amico. When you get back inside, ask around. They'll tell you the same thing. I only have one forward gear. Straight and honest."

"This means something to me?"

"I don't make promises unless I aim to keep them. If I tell you something, it's for real."

"Whatever." Lang turned back to the side window. He waited through five minutes of silence, then, "We headed someplace special?"

"Police headquarters by way of Lexington Market. What do you say to a corned-beef sandwich? You like corned beef?"

"I was always partial to pastrami."

D'Amico pulled up by the north entrance. "Go get Mr. Lang a pastrami on rye. You want mustard with that?"

"Sure, mustard's good." His eyes tracked Connie as she rose from the car. "Does your honey come with the sandwich?"

Connie stooped down and replied, "The detective has just offered you your first decent meal in six months, Adolf. You like, I could drop it in the gutter, make it taste like home."

"Don't call me that."

"News flash, Adolf. You don't make the rules here."

"You children play nice," D'Amico said. "Go get Mr. Lang his sandwich."

It was hard to say who had the deader eyes. Connie gave their prisoner a full minute, then turned and walked inside.

They drove to headquarters with the aroma of hot pastrami permeating the car. They parked in the underground secure section and took the elevator to seven. A pair of detectives stopped to watch Lang's clanking progress. Lang spoke only when they passed the crime board. "What, you think one of these got my name on it?"

"This way, Mr. Lang." D'Amico kept a firm grip on his arm as Connie unlocked the first interview room. The room was painfully bare. Steel table bolted to the floor. Same for the prisoner's seat. Drop ceiling. Harsh fluorescents. "Have a seat here. Would you like a Coke?"

"I won't say no." He watched Connie leave, then turned his attention to D'Amico as the detective shackled Lang's left wrist to the table and his left ankle to the floor. "Matter of fact, I won't say another word."

D'Amico unlocked Lang's right wrist, opened the drink, set it on the table, and unwrapped the sandwich. "Enjoy your meal, Mr. Lang."

D'Amico left the interview chamber and entered the room next door. Bernstein stood beside Connie. The room's only light came through the one-way glass. Connie said, "What an animal."

Bernstein turned so she did not have to watch the prisoner eat. "How will you play this?"

"Alone," D'Amico replied. "Connie came up with the goods. If anything will turn him, it'll be this."

He waited until Lang finished licking the sandwich wrapper. "Showtime."

———

D'Amico took his time settling the plastic chair across the table from the prisoner. He took out his tape player, flipped the notepad to an empty page, and uncapped his pen.

"What, you think I'm gonna roll over for hot pastrami?"

D'Amico continued with his preparations. He took Connie's sheets from his jacket pocket. Three of them. "I told you I delivered on what I say."

"Yeah. So?"

"I just want you to remember that." D'Amico turned over the first page.

Lang's sneer dissolved. His common-law wife stared up at him from the page. In prison garb. "Hailey used your last name at the trial, Mr.

Lang. Hailey Saunders Lang. Charged with falsifying a police application. Aiding and abetting. Passing confidential police information to criminals. Namely, you. She was convicted of using her position as dispatcher to slow down our response and warn you when the call finally went out about the National Guard robbery. Which is how you managed to escape with those weapons. I'm only telling you this since you might have missed the news. Being inside yourself."

It cost Lang a lot to ask, "What'd she get?"

"The DA refused to plea-down this one. Five to ten. Upstate."

Lang said nothing.

"You know what that means."

Lang did not respond.

"Two parents convicted of felonies. The court has taken custody of your little boy. He's in foster care."

Lang bore holes in the table with his gaze.

D'Amico turned over the second page. A dark-haired child of five stared solemnly up at them.

Lang did not move.

D'Amico turned over the third page. The child had drawn a boat on the ocean. Overhead in rainbow letters was written, "I love you, Daddy." Compliments of Connie.

D'Amico said, "I need information about the claymores, Mr. Lang."

"I want to see my kid."

"A murder took place using a decommissioned claymore. Possibly two. We suspect the bombs originated from your heist. Can you confirm this? Wait, Mr. Lang. I'm not done. I also want a detailed run-through of the heist's planning and execution. And where the extra claymores went. And how many others might be out there."

"I don't say nothing 'til I see my son." Lang's growl was so feral the table vibrated. "And not in the prison. Somewhere else."

D'Amico rose from his chair and went next door. The two women had been joined by Crowder and three others. The observation room was hot and cramped. "What do you say?"

Bernstein asked, "Who put this together?"

"I told you. Officer Morales."

All eyes went to the young woman. Bernstein said, "Fine work."

Connie flushed crimson. "Thank you, Chief."

"All right. Fix it with Social. Make it happen." She started for the door, turned back, said to D'Amico, "Did you get the message from Kelly?"

"I didn't know he'd called."

"Actually it was that guy from his Washington office."

Crowder supplied, "Jack Van Sant. Dude sounds like he snores at attention."

"Matt asked him to phone us. The feds ID'd the fingerprint from their house. It belongs to one Barry Simms."

"The victim of the British bomb?"

"One and the same, if their info is correct." She gave D'Amico a nod. "Looks like you're building yourself a team, Detective."

When she was gone, Crowder asked, "Did I just see the chief smile?"

Lucas turned and winked at Connie.

"Can't be." Crowder headed for the door. "Must be an age thing, my eyes going funny on me like that."

Brian Aycock started the car when Matt emerged from the guard-house. The three young guardsmen still stood at attention in the rain. The corporal still leaned against the pillar, protected by the porch awning, watching the guardsmen with a tight smile. He did not even glance Matt's way. Matt slammed his car door and sat staring at the three drenched soldiers. Brian Aycock reversed from the slot and aimed for the main gates. He did not speak until they rounded the corner and the guardsmen were out of sight. "I don't suppose I need to ask how it went."

Matt unclenched his hands. The two young women had still been cowering inside the guardhouse's front room when he left. "No. You don't."

"The judge will give you five minutes." Brian Aycock crawled along the narrow streets bisecting manicured lawns and stodgy brick build-ings. He turned the wipers on high as he gunned through the front gates. "I'd hate to be in Major Stafford's bad graces."

The city of Oxford might have been pretty. Matt had no idea and did not care. The weather matched his internal state. He was mired in a gray nothingness where random thoughts and emotions flashed, then disappeared. Their view was of snarled traffic and clouds so heavily laden they drifted like unraveled ribbons, falling with the rain.

"Is jet lag always this bad?" Matt asked.

"It hits some people worse than others." The light went green. Brian Aycock threaded a roundabout and merged with sullen city traffic. "You're booked into the visiting officers' quarters on base. But I could find you something nicer if you want."

"The way I feel, any bed will do just fine."

The Oxford Crown Courts possessed broad stone stairs, Palladian windows, columns, and a sense of burdensome duty. The Cotswold stone edifice glistened gray and stern. Matt gave his name, passed through security, and was pointed toward a hard wooden bench. A court official stopped by to say that the judge had been informed and would call a court recess as soon as possible. Matt thanked the official and tried to rub the image of those shivering young soldiers from his eyes. A man and a woman passed by, walking swiftly. The man wore a suit. The woman wore a dark robe and a gray powdered wig with a blue ribbon. They talked in serious voices about something. Matt could not make out a single word.

"Mr. Kelly, do I have that correct?" A tall, big-jawed man in robes and wig halted before Matt and offered his hand. "Edward Compston. So sorry to have kept you waiting."

Matt struggled to his feet. "Thank you for seeing me."

"Not at all. Just popped in from the States, have you?" The judge was Matt's height but had him by thirty years and pounds. He had a cheery voice and very cautious eyes. "Perhaps we'd be more comfortable chatting in my chambers. Do come this way."

At the end of the hall they passed by another uniformed guard seated at a little desk. As the guard buzzed them through the doors, Compston asked, "Will you have anything, Mr. Kelly? A coffee, perhaps?"

His stomach rebelled against the prospect, but he needed to wake up. "Coffee would be great, thanks. Black."

"Charles, would you be so kind?"

The guard was already on his feet. "Certainly, sir. And yourself?"

"Nothing, thank you. This way, Mr. Kelly."

Midway down the adjoining corridor Compston unlocked a door. "I do apologize for remaining in my robes, but I must dash back to finish hearing this case."

The judge's chambers were austere in an expensive and oddly personal manner. Scandinavian furniture matched the light parquet flooring. Narrow bookshelves shaped as a dozen bas-relief pillars marched around the room. A stubby conference table sprouted from the end of Compston's desk, surrounded by beige leather chairs. "Do make yourself comfortable, Mr. Kelly."

The judge kept the conversation inconsequential until the guard brought Matt's coffee. Then, "Perhaps you'd be so kind as to tell me what this is all about."

The judge was two people. One was pleasant and mild-voiced and maintained a steady smile. The other was steely-eyed and asked incisive questions. Matt drank his coffee and related what he knew and wished he could degum his brain. When he finished, the judge glanced at his watch and said, "I can't run much over my ten-minute recess, I'm afraid. There's quite a full docket all this week."

"Major Stafford was not helpful."

"No. I rather imagine he wouldn't be."

"Do you think the right man was tried for this crime?"

"What I *think*, Mr. Kelly, is that British justice ran its proper course. Regardless of what the major might have inferred, there was no question of miscarriage. The prosecutors simply did not have a case."

"That was not what I asked."

"That's as may be. But as an official representative of Her Majesty's courts, that is all I am prepared to say."

Matt was too tired to care. "I appreciate your being willing to see me."

"Not at all, Mr. Kelly." The judge remained seated behind his desk. "Tell me, are you fond of English pubs?"

"I've never been to one."

"You can't possibly visit my country without sampling at least one country pub, Mr. Kelly. It simply isn't done." He reached for a pen and scribbled a note. "Where are you staying?"

"Visiting officers' quarters at Upper Heyford."

"Splendid." He handed Matt the paper. "The Fox and Crown in Sumerton. A mere stone's throw from the base. You could walk it if the weather wasn't so miserable. Shall we say seven o'clock?"

———

Matt resumed his zoned-out state for the return journey to Upper Heyford. Brian Aycock remained silent until they halted before one of the base's faceless brick buildings. "Visiting officers' quarters. Officers' mess is the next building to your right. You're in room forty-nine, ground floor, key should be in the door."

"I'm scheduled to meet the judge tonight. I can do that on my own."

"He knew I was escorting you. If I wasn't invited, I shouldn't come." He offered Matt his hand. "It's been nice meeting you."

"Thanks for everything."

"Here, you'll need this." Brian handed him an umbrella, then Matt's file. "Thanks for the chance to read that. It made for a change from file-clerk duties."

"What are you, CIA?"

"Cultural affairs." They shared a smile. "You can catch a cab to Sumerton outside the main gates. Good luck."

The room was bare in the extreme. Table, chair, bunk, sink, threadbare towel, light over the mirror, bulb in the ceiling, two sheets, one blanket. Matt zonked out for five hours and woke up famished. He showered and shaved using a disposable razor left with a skimpy bar of soap. He dressed in the same clothes, as he had nothing else. Outside his room, people laughed loudly at words he could not be bothered to understand. The noise only heightened his sense of unwelcome.

He walked to the mess hall in the misting rain. He ate alone. No one spoke to him. No one looked his way. The food was very bland. When he finished, it was half past six. He left the mess hall and followed the road to the main gate. He entered the first taxi in line and gave the driver the name of the pub.

Rain fell in soft pattering beats upon the car. What little Matt saw of his surroundings showed a village cut from the same mold as the base—modest brick houses, neat terraced gardens, and quiet lanes. A military town.

A mile from the main gates they left Upper Heyford and entered a narrow country lane. The taxi halted before an ancient two-story inn. A hand-painted sign creaked softly above an arched door of stout English oak.

Inside, large stone fireplaces burned at both ends of a single great room. The bar ran down the wall opposite the entrance. The inn was quiet for being so full. Matt spotted the judge waving from a leather-clad booth and walked over.

"Mr. Kelly, excellent. So glad you could join us. May I introduce

Miles Spending, chief constable of this charming little borough. What will you take?"

"I'd better stick with coffee, thanks. Black."

"I'll get it." The constable was a very neat man, compact and still. He moved to the bar and returned with an economy of motion. Few people noticed his passage. Matt assumed he liked it that way. "Here you are, Mr. Kelly."

Without his wig and robes of office, Edward Compston's dual nature was even more striking. His looks and manner were almost boyish. Straw-blond hair fell over his forehead. He spoke with gentle hesitation. Yet there was a blade-hard edge to his gaze, a judge's incisive ability to slice down deep and draw out the kernel of truth. "Do I need to inform you, Mr. Kelly, that this little meeting of ours is off the record?"

Matt sipped from his mug. The coffee was freshly brewed and very strong. "No."

"Fine. Then perhaps you'd be so kind as to repeat for the constable what you told me earlier."

One of the men serving behind the bar crossed the flagstone floor and tossed a double handful of cedar chips onto the nearest fire. A lady seated in the next booth drank mulled wine. Matt could smell the cinnamon and clove. The constable heard him out in silence. Then, "You've identified the thumbprint as belonging to our victim here?"

Matt nodded. "Could Barry Simms have survived the blast?"

The constable retreated into his glass. "Not a hope of that, mate."

"What about the man arrested for the crime here? Any idea where he was around the time of the Baltimore incident?"

Compston offered, "I doubt very much our man was involved."

"One way to make sure." The constable rose from their booth. "When exactly was the attack out your way?"

"Eighteen days ago."

"Hang on a tick."

As the constable made his way to the bar, Compston leaned forward and said, "While our friend is otherwise occupied, let me share a couple of items. There is no love lost between the base police and our local lad here. The incident in question occurred on what might be classed as disputed territory. Upper Heyford is actually two bases connected by the public road you took to come out here. Barry Simms rented a house on this road. His landlord was the air base. Do you catch my drift?"

The constable was heads-down with one of the barmaids, a frowsy woman with bright copper hair. She picked up a phone from beneath the counter and dialed, leaning over so the constable could hear what she said. Matt replied, "The base police want to treat the village as part of their turf."

"Precisely. Snedley-Cummins, the man accused of the bombing, was effectively handed to the constable on a platter by Major Stafford."

The judge was no longer smiling. Matt could easily imagine the stern face across from him pronouncing the words "ten years to life." "Your constable friend refused to go along."

"That is quite correct." Compston's eyes tightened in approval. "To say the least, Major Stafford was less than pleased. He went to the press and publicly accused the constable of dragging his feet."

"Snedley-Cummins was tried in the public eye," Matt surmised.

"They don't call it the local rag for nothing," Compston agreed. "Finally the crown prosecutor brought forward the case against Snedley-Cummins. Did so despite the constable's objections, I hasten to add. The trial was duly heard by me. The accused was found not guilty by a jury of his peers. The press called it a miscarriage and blamed our constable for faulty handling of what should have been an open-and-shut case. Again, using information supplied by our Major Stafford."

"Did this Snedley-Cummins do it?"

"Geoffrey Snedley-Cummins was assigned as liaison between the RAF and your departing lads. His official rank was adjutant, but unofficially his duties were quite far-reaching. On a smooth-running base, the adjutant handles a number of issues that should never be brought before the base commandant. Unfortunately, Upper Heyford has recently been anything but smooth-running. To put it bluntly, Snedley-Cummins was a snob and a pest."

"He and Major Stafford did not get along."

"That is putting it mildly. Quite early on, the two of them had several legendary run-ins that . . ." Compston was halted by the constable returning to their booth, accompanied by the barmaid. "Is this quite necessary?"

"She insisted," the constable replied.

The barmaid said to the constable, "Go get me a drink, love. A double gin and bitters will do nicely."

The judge protested, "Bertie, really. We were trying to—"

"Oh, do hush up and give a girl some room. That's a dear." She was cheery up close, with bright eyes and a face that looked born to smile. She said to Matt, "Are all American spies as lovely as you?"

Compston inspected the oak beams above his head.

Matt replied, "We're required to take handsome lessons as part of our training, ma'am."

"Oh, get on with you." She motioned to the judge seated next to her. "Look at this one, I ask you. You'd never guess he chased me for nigh on a year, begging me every step for a kiss."

Compston turned bright red. "I never."

She toyed with the strings of multicolored glass baubles around her neck. "Had the cutest look about him, like a little lost pup. Just begging to be picked up and cuddled."

"Bertie, please."

She patted the judge's cheek. "Never you mind, dear. You can play stern with the rest of the world. But I know better, don't I. Oh, my, yes. I know."

Compston harrumphed and straightened his hair. "We were discussing the case."

"Geoffrey Snedley-Cummins's guilty of being a snot. But he ain't got it in him to go planting any bombs." She accepted her glass from the returning constable. "Not the one here nor your'n either. I phoned my friend over at the golf club. Geoffrey hasn't missed a night in weeks. Pops in for a glass around nine, sits by himself, reads the paper, leaves. Poor lad hasn't had a word spoken to him since the trial."

The constable asked Compston, "You told him?"

"The bare bones."

He said to Matt, "According to any number of sources, Geoffrey Snedley-Cummins was as much a petty tyrant as your Major Stafford, only with more airs. The two positively loathed one another. One of Snedley-Cummins's last acts before retiring was effectively to block Major Stafford's promotion by accusing him of larceny."

"That Stafford's a dreadful man," the barmaid added. "If one of them poor soldiers shows up five minutes late for work, you know what he makes them do?"

Matt said quietly, "Stand at attention all night on his front lawn."

She studied his face. "Don't believe I'd want to get on your wrong side, Yank. Oh, my, no."

Matt asked, "Do any of you have an idea as to who was behind the bombing?"

The barmaid settled her ample girth upon the table. Her breath smelled of her spiked gin. "What's your name, love?"

"Matt."

"Well, Matt. You look like a sensible sort. More than I can say for this lot."

The judge sighed.

"There was this Yank, see. Not Barry Simms. This other one. Showed up out of the blue. Worked down the road at the Lamb. Not near as nice as us here. Different sort of place altogether."

"The Lamb is a pub right at the other end of Upper Heyford," the constable supplied. "Known as a trouble spot. The odd dustup in the lot after hours, rumors of items pilfered from the base and sold out the back. The sort of problems you find around any base. Major Stafford and his men do their drinking there. They claim it's so as to keep the place in order."

"You don't believe that?"

The constable and the judge exchanged glances. Neither man spoke.

"This other Yank, he was seen drinking with the major from time to time. Everybody knew the Yank was in the trade right up to his scrawny neck."

"The trade?"

"As in goods off the backs of lorries, love. I wouldn't put it past the major to be taking a payoff for looking the other way."

Matt asked, "Can you describe this other American?"

"Tall, pale, scarred, and very lean. I used to go in there from time to time on account of a friend worked there. Not anymore. Her man's been sent off to Baghdad and she's moved—"

"You were telling our guest about the American."

"So I was." She drained her glass. "Tall as you, I reckon. But a good deal older. Big in the shoulders, he was. Strong for a man his age. Big hands. Very intense in a scary sort of way. Not an ounce of fat on him."

"Do you have a name?"

"Sorry, love. Never spoke a word to him directly." She glanced up at where the constable stood beside the booth. "Saw him drinking with the major, though. Sitting there at the back table with their heads together. Saw it any number of times."

The constable said, "The Lamb claims no man matching his description ever worked there, drank there, stayed there."

"Which is all a load of old rubbish and you know it." To Matt, "Told them and told them, I did. But the copper here did nothing about it."

"No evidence," the constable said.

She sniffed. "Oh, and I suppose the bomb went off all by itself."

The constable sighed. Matt had the impression people did that a lot around Bertie. The constable said, "We did what we could after the blast. Circulated this information and a drawing done on Bertie's description. Came up with nothing."

She asked Matt, "Where are you staying the night?"

"On base."

She looked worried. "That major wouldn't be the least bit pleased to hear there's a chance his claims might be debunked. Not to mention the fact his former drinking buddy, the man who ain't supposed to have existed, is getting fingered for the job."

"Matt looks like a fellow who can take care of himself," the judge said.

"He does that. Well, I best be getting back to work." She slid from the booth and stared down at Matt. "Never met a real live secret agent before."

The judge said, "And you didn't meet one tonight now, did you."

"No, 'course not." She smiled. "Been nice, just the same."

Back on base, Matt went by the ready room. The chamber occupied the entire bottom floor of a brick building midway between the officers' mess and the airfield. The place was empty except for a lone figure in the guards' trademark camo fatigues. The young woman stood behind the desk, staring at nothing. Matt did not recognize her until he was up close to the desk. The last time he had seen her she had been soaking wet and deathly pale and groaning softly.

The young woman bore plum-colored indentations beneath her eyes. Her hair was washed and her clothes were dry. But she still looked shrunken by the previous night. She spoke with a hollow voice that matched her gaze. "Can I help you, sir?"

"I arrived here on a military jet from the U.S. I was told to come here to make arrangements for the journey back."

Something flickered deep in her eyes. A hint of red touched her cheeks. "Sir, Upper Heyford operates on a no-fly rule from midnight to six a.m. But I can call the pilots for you."

"That would be great, thanks."

She checked her log, then phoned a number and spoke briefly. She returned the phone to the cradle and said, "Wheels up at six-fifteen, sir."

"Thank you very much." Matt turned away, bitterly ashamed for the both of them.

Matt returned to his room and its peculiar brand of military monasticism. He dozed but did not fall into a decent sleep. An hour or so later, the nightmares began whispering to him. Not gripping him with their customary talons. Taunting him. Slivers of images, half-heard crystal chimes disturbed by a storm beyond the horizon. He tossed and turned for a while, fighting the reality that distance meant nothing to his internal fiends. Then he dressed and reentered the dark.

The rain was a colorless shroud over the night. Heavier than mist, too light for real rain. It clung to Matt as he walked. His umbrella was almost useless. All the world's sounds were deadened. A solitary car crawled along the lane next to him. Matt noted the insignia on the door and the lone military policeman inside.

He placed his call from the red phone box situated outside the officers' mess. Every surface inside the box was coated with damp. The air felt frigid. He gave the operator his credit-card number and waited through a series of clicks.

Connie answered with a sleepy hello.

"It's me."

"Matt." She breathed his name in a way that warmed him four thousand miles away. "Hi there."

"I'm sorry to call so early, or late—"

"No, no, it's fine. I took a siesta to catch up on some sleep. Been a big day."

"What's going on?"

She stretched and moaned luxuriously. "You called to ask me about work?"

He leaned against the door. "No. You're right."

"So. How's England?"

The box was so tightly enclosed by the mist and the empty night he might as well have been the only person on his side of the Atlantic. One connection linking him to the outside world. One.

"Matt?"

"When I was a kid, I used to dream about seeing Europe. I had a map I put up on the wall of my room. Every time we moved it was the first thing up, the last off. I'd read a book and stick colored thumbtacks where I was going. Take time, really get to know the places. But here I am, running around like crazy and seeing nothing." He banged his head softly on the glass behind him. "Failed again."

"You're not a failure." She was fully awake now. "You're really special."

"A lot of girls have called me a lot of things. But never special."

"Give me a break."

"Shallow, impenetrable, invisible, toneless, faceless, emotionless, ice-man . . ."

"Stop."

"I don't know why I'm telling you this."

"Since when do you need a reason?"

"I've told you that I never talk about myself, Connie. Never."

"Maybe you should try, Matt. What would you like to tell me?"

He leaned over slightly, trapped inside a viselike cramp. Not his body. A cramp so deep it clenched his spirit. He tried but could not say the word—*everything*.

"Matt?"

He straightened in stages. Stared at the glass in front of his face. Watched the home video of past mistakes he was doomed to repeat forever.

"Maybe it would help if I went first. What do you think?" There was a rustling sound, and Matt realized she was sitting up in bed. "I was always drawn by the wrong kind of man. Always after that edge, you know? After that hint of the dark side. I used to tell myself it came just from wanting to make a bad man better. Now . . ."

He knew she wanted him to ask something. Even just repeat her last word and attach a question mark. He opened his mouth. No sound came.

Finally she went on, "Now I build my deck. You've got to come over and see what I'm doing out back. It's pretty nice, Matt. All teak. Charcoal grill, outdoor sink and fridge, even a place for a hammock."

Another pause, another silent invitation. She turned somber after that. "Probably doesn't sound like much of a confessional, me building a back porch. But the work means a lot to me, Matt. It's been my therapy during the bad times. I think better when I've got a hammer in my hands. But sometimes . . ."

His fist clenched the phone so hard it bruised his ear, mashed it into his skull. Outside his red metal world the rain streaked the glass and formed soft halos around the only streetlight he could see. He heard the rasping sound of his own breath. Filling the gap between her words.

"Sometimes I worry about losing touch with the human race. Work doesn't count. I'm talking about normal people and safe things and happy . . ." She stopped to pant in her own quiet way. Then, "You know the worst thing about when Hands accosted me? He was easy about it and he smiled and he talked in this real nice voice. But it was still an attack. And you know what I worried about afterward? That maybe I deserved it. Maybe the life I had, the guys I went after, maybe it has stained me deep where nobody but I can see. Me and guys like Hands."

They were quiet together now. Connie unable to go on. Matt wishing he had the means to give back. Make it better. Make it right.

Finally she managed to say, "Will you at least think about talking with me, Matt?"

He tore the words out. One shard at a time. "I won't think about anything else."

———

He did not notice them until he opened the phone box door.

The car was parked a half block away. The doors opened together. The mist coalesced into three camo-suited men. The car's headlights formed a glistening silhouette of their long wooden clubs.

Matt let the booth door swing shut. "Evening, officers."

"Listen to the guy now." The tall corporal from the guardhouse porch took center position and did the talking. "Gone all respectful on us."

The two other men did not speak. The man to Matt's left was a whistler, a single note that jiggled as he walked, like he was laughing at the same time. The man to Matt's right was a fireplug, solid and silent. He tapped his club on his leg as he approached. His eyes showed nothing. That one was trouble.

"Wasn't so respectful this morning, was he."

They spread out slightly as they approached. They had done this before. Many times.

The tall guard said, "You're coming with us."

Matt backed up against the side of the phone booth. He did so to block a rear attack. He spread out his arms as though clenching the metal. The hand holding the rolled umbrella was now around the corner and out of sight. The squat silent man smiled with real pleasure. The man assumed Matt was scared. The man was right.

Matt said, "No."

The tall guard smiled as well. "I was hoping you'd say that. I really was."

The whistler started slapping his palm with the stick. The night was empty.

"Here's the thing," the guard said. "The major's heard you've visited with a certain judge and a constable. We don't take lightly to having outsiders come in and stick their noses into business that's none of their concern. The major's charged me with making sure you don't carry the wrong message back to wherever you'll soon wish you never left."

Matt recalled the three soldiers standing in the rain and how no car stopped and no pedestrian looked their way. He knew if he screamed no one would hear. Even if they heard, they would not take notice. "Don't do this."

"You took the words straight out of my mouth. We can't have you making trouble for us back in Washington." The tall guard pointed with his club. "So you're now under arrest. We'll hold you long enough for you to confess to whatever charges we decide to lay on. When we're sure you won't be causing us any trouble, why, you're free to go."

The skinny man whispered something. Or perhaps he just made a sound. Trying to spook the prey.

Matt said, "I don't want any trouble."

"Too late for that. Seeing as how you've done nothing but beg for it since you got here."

"It was all a complete misunderstanding." He timed his strike to the last word. He took a single step away from the phone booth. Headed straight at the tall guy. Going for the boss. Moving so fast it caused the tall guard and the skinny one to Matt's left to hesitate. But not the fireplug. He was a fighter. He closed.

Which was what Matt had hoped for.

The fireplug swung with an economy of motion at Matt's chest. His staff was two-thirds the length of his arm, the windup just the span from slightly behind his body to where Matt was closing. But he knew his weapon and his own strength. Matt blocked the blow with his umbrella, holding it at the tip and handle. The umbrella buckled.

Matt bent the umbrella around the club, locking it momentarily. His second step was a windup. He swung his entire body around and clouted the fireplug on the side of his head with the heel of his right foot. The squat man spun in a parody of a dance. The club was attached to his wrist by a leather thong, which now kept it from flying away. The umbrella, however, spun away into the night. The black spinning form caused the tall guard to flinch and step back.

Which left the skinny man exposed.

This third man was brave only in a crowd. His eyes widened at Matt's approach and whatever he saw in Matt's expression. The guard made a half swing, half stab with his club. Matt moved his upper body back while his feet still closed. He deflected the club with his left forearm. His right he drove straight into the man's solar plexus. He brought his left arm down in a vicious chop to the point where the guard's ear met his jaw. The man fell hard.

The fireplug was down on all fours but not out. He shook his head like a wounded bull, waiting for his vision to clear. Matt needed to use this moment, but could not. The tall guard was going for his radio. Matt closed in two strides, launching himself on the third step. The tall guard raised the hand holding the radio. The side of Matt's foot caught it hard, sending it spinning out of the guard's grip. It landed on the pavement and shattered.

Matt heard the huffing breath behind him. Knew the bull was up and taking aim. There was no time to look, and without looking he could not deflect. He collapsed to the ground and rolled.

The bull caught him with a baton swipe to his ribs. Thankfully the squat man's strength had not fully returned. Even so, Matt felt like his lung had been punctured. He did not try to rise. A thousand sessions in Vic's dojo had taught him that much. He rolled onto his back and danced hard with his heels, taking the squat man twice in the stomach.

The tall guard cleaved down with his club, wielding it axlike with both hands gripping the handle. If it had made contact, it would have finished him. Matt rolled away, slick now with grass and wet. He bounded to his feet and ran, or started to. But his foot lost traction and he almost went down.

The tall guard's aim was too high. He lost force re-aiming downward, so the club merely swiped off Matt's left shoulder. Even so it sent him tumbling once more and numbed him to his wrist. Matt fell into the bullish guard who still held his free hand to his middle, huffing for breath. Matt sensed as much as saw the tall guard coming in for the kill. He gripped the squat guard's club and brought it around, hand and arm and all.

The tall guard's blow missed Matt and struck his mate's arm. The bullish man squealed in pain and rage.

When the squat guard bent over his arm, Matt chopped down once with the blade of his hand to the back of the stubby man's neck. The guard fell without a sound.

Matt stepped back and to one side. The tall guard was hesitant now. His motions were cautious. He was not used to having his prey fight back. Nor had he expected any real struggle. Now he was alone. And fear was in his eyes.

Matt tensed and waited, weaving steadily back. He clenched and unclenched his left fist, willing his strength to return.

The guard saw the motion and recognized Matt's weakness. He charged.

But the guard rushed it, and the wet grass was against him. His foot swept right out from under him. He twisted about, flailing for balance.

Matt feinted, as though going for another spin kick. When the tall guard flinched, Matt sprang forward. He put everything he had into a straight-armed jab for the tall man's forehead. It was a dangerous act, for the forehead was the single hardest portion of a man's anatomy. It required the same focused power as striking a stone block. But a solid punch rattled the brainpan. Matt felt the blow all the way to his spine.

So did the tall guard.

His eyes glazed over. He collapsed to his knees, then fell facedown into the grass.

———

This time, when Matt stumbled into the ready room, the young woman looked at him. Really looked.

Which was hardly a surprise. Matt limped slowly. He cradled his left arm. His ribs ached with each breath. He was not breathing hard so much as moaning softly. He was soaked and filthy with dirt and wet grass.

He stopped before the desk. "Can you hide me?"

Understanding lifted her from the desk. "Stafford's men did this?"

"They tried." Matt pointed at the door and winced at the motion. "There are three of them out there in the grass."

Her eyes went round. "You took out three of Stafford's guys?"

"Temporarily. When they come around, there'll be trouble."

She scampered around the desk. "You just come with me."

Matt hesitated when he saw she was aiming him for the ladies' restroom. Impatiently she pulled him forward. Inside she tried the door to the janitor's closet and found it locked. "Use the sink and clean yourself up. I'll be back quick as I can."

Matt washed his face. Took a handful of paper towels and did what he could for his trousers and jacket. Glanced in the mirror. Looked away. Used his fingers as a comb. Washed his face a second time.

She came back bearing a steaming mug, two blankets, and a ring of keys. She opened the janitor's closet, pulled out a wheelie-bucket and a pair of mops. Tossed in the blankets. Handed him the mug. "This should warm you up. Now hide in there."

"Thanks . . . I'm sorry, I don't know your name."

She shut the door, leaving him in the dark.

Matt settled down on the blankets, leaned his back on the painted concrete wall, sipped his mug.

He had no idea how long he sat like that. Quite a while. Long enough to doze off. He would have thought it impossible. But he did.

Footsteps awoke him. Then he heard the outer door swing open. He scrambled to his feet or tried to. But one leg got trapped by the blankets and he slammed against the closet door. Which mashed both his shoulder and his ribs. Matt groaned and almost went down.

The keys jingled in the lock and the door swung open. The young woman said, "Take it easy, will you?"

"Sorry. I tripped."

"It's okay. There's nobody else around yet. Here." She handed him a pair of hangers wrapped in plastic. "I raided the cleaners in the officers' mess. You've just become an air force loadmaster. It's the largest uniform I could find. They won't be looking for a fed in fatigues."

Matt accepted the clothes. "I can't tell you—"

"Don't you even start. Here's another coffee." She handed over the mug. Her eyes appeared clear for the very first time. "The three stayed where you left them until about an hour ago. People were standing about, nobody doing a thing to help. Shame it didn't last longer. But a patrol spotted the crowd and went for a look. None of the three got up on their own. It was a delight to watch." She backed out. "Better get yourself ready. Wheels up in fifteen minutes."

She shut the door. Matt kicked the blankets to one side and stood drinking his coffee. She had dumped in double measures of sugar and fake-cream dust. He downed it like medicine. Then he dressed, testing each movement carefully.

Soon enough the woman was back, this time accompanied by another. "You ready?"

Matt could hear quiet murmurs from the ready room. Sleepy voices getting ready for the day ahead. "Yes."

"Right. Here's how it's going to play." Her voice was tighter now, softer. "Annie here is running routes this morning. She's going to walk you out, just another ranks getting special treatment from the staff. You don't look anybody direct in the eye. Just move fast, straight for planeside."

Matt recognized the other woman as one of the two soldiers caught inside the guardhouse front room. "Whatever you say."

"We get so many visitors through here, one more flight officer who can't find his way to the airfield without help shouldn't cause any notice at all." Talking like she was trying to convince herself and her friend. She asked, "Ready?"

Annie held a metal clipboard to her middle. She gave a tremble of a nod.

"Right." The young woman stepped to the restroom door, scouted quickly, and then said, "Quick march."

Annie stepped forward. Matt followed close on her heels. He smelled coffee and saw several people clustered around a back table. But he saw no one clearly. Just kept his eyes on Annie and his attention focused on staying upright and not limping.

Annie pushed through the outer door and headed for the tarmac. Matt moved up alongside. "Could we go a little slower?"

She eased up a notch. "You hurt?"

"A little."

"Almost there."

The plane was stationed behind a troop transport, white and gleaming in the wet gray dawn. As Matt rounded the larger plane, the jet's right engine fired into whining life.

Annie halted by the jet's stairwell and snapped off a salute. When Matt tried to respond, she grinned and said, "You need to work on that."

"Thanks again."

She touched his hand. "You've just made best friends with every guard on this base."

Matt traveled back across the Atlantic in a semidoze. Two of the generals and a colonel joined him for the flight. They gave Matt's appearance in fatigues a sideways stare, then dismissed him as an apparition of no importance. Matt kept to his seat at the back of the plane, neither awake nor fully asleep. He'd shut his eyes only to jerk upright time and again, drawn by sudden strikes from fatigue-clad enemies appearing in the fog.

Upon arrival at Andrews Air Force Base, Matt made two calls. The first was to Connie Morales. Matt found himself talking with an immensely frustrated cop. Matt tried to pay attention as she described their struggle with Social Services, something about arranging for a prisoner to see his son. How they had finally gone before a federal judge who had reluctantly agreed to personally supervise the meet. Matt knew it was all very important, though his brain remained locked in low gear.

He made the second call through the base operator. "Baltimore Armory."

"General Robards, please."

"Who do I say is calling?"

"Allen Pecard's . . . Allen Pecard."

A pause, then, "Mr. Pecard?"

"No, General. Actually, it's Matt Kelly."

"One of the fellows who wasn't here."

"Yes sir. I've just returned from Upper Heyford."

A pause, then, "You don't say."

"Is there some reason why the base police would intentionally give your National Guard divisions a hard time?"

"Is that what's happening?"

"Sure looked that way to me, sir."

Robards muffled the phone an instant, then, "We're talking hypothetical and off the record."

"This call never happened, sir."

"If a local contingent wanted to rob the government blind, say, by making items disappear before they could be mothballed and shipped home, what do you suppose they would seek to do?"

"Create havoc among the base personnel." Matt willed his brain to work harder but came up with a stuttering effort at best. "Lose or intentionally obscure records. Build a reputation for making mistakes with documents and inventory."

"You ever worked for the military?"

"This is my first run-in with your operations, General."

"Well, you're right on target. Was your trip tied to the murder investigation?"

"Apparently so, sir. Precisely how, I can't pin down."

"How about that. A fed who admits he doesn't know everything." A pause, then, "Can you give me any specifics on what they're doing wih my folks?"

Matt detailed what he had seen and experienced. He received static in response. When the general came back, it was in a volcanic growl. "Son, you need anything, you let me know."

"I appreciate that, General."

"Nobody does that to my soldiers. Robards out."

Matt's elevated status meant a military driver was on call to take him home. He bought a paper at the PX just to check the date. His watch read meaningless numbers, but at least he could be certain they were attached to Wednesday afternoon. They got caught in heavy rush-hour snarl and needed almost three hours to make Baltimore. The driver did not speak a word the entire way.

Matt entered his apartment and stripped off the uniform in his kitchen, listening to his phone messages. There was one from Connie, three from the newspaper journalist, and a dozen from Sol. Matt cut off the machine and limped to his bathroom. His body felt like one huge ache. He stayed under the shower until the water ran cold, then returned to the kitchen. He had not eaten anything since dinner in the officers' mess, on a day that felt centuries ago. He microwaved a meal and ate standing at the back counter. The phone rang while he was eating. Sol again. Had Matt completely forgotten they were at five days and counting? Matt dropped his plate into the sink and walked back to the bedroom. The last thing he heard was Sol's voice ordering him to be somewhere in a half hour's time.

The phone woke him. That and the sunlight. Which was strange, since Matt's bedroom faced west. Matt lay blinking into the light, trying to fit together a day that did not start with a nightmarish jolt. Then he heard Connie's voice come over the answering machine.

He rolled over and grabbed for the bedside receiver. "I'm here."

"I thought you were going to call me."

"I just woke up. What time . . ." He managed to focus on his clock, which read two. "I don't believe this."

"You didn't get my messages?" She sounded borderline frantic. "You don't know what's going down?"

"Connie, I don't know what day it is."

"It's showtime, buster, is all you need to know. You better get your act in gear, or you're going to miss the curtain going up."

———

The Bromo-Seltzer Tower sat alone in the middle of its own little city block. North and west and east grew the new developments of Charles Street, Inner Harbor, and Camden Yards. South was a dreary wasteland of empty skyscrapers and wasted space. His father's billboards sprouted from most of the buildings Matt could see in that direction. A new undertaking from Camden Partners. Seven hundred condos. Hotels. Restaurants. Shopping village. A project large enough to deserve the name Downtown. In earlier days Matt had wanted to burn all such ads. He had refused to enter any company or hotel or business Paul Kelly had under development. Now they just left him cold.

Connie met him on the sidewalk out front of the Bromo entrance with coffee and doughnuts and an update. Matt listened to her description of the meet between prisoner and son, then the prisoner's description of the man who had set up the armory heist. An accountant named Jerry Freid, a secretive little nerd who, according to the prisoner, dealt with very few clients. Completely unknown to the Baltimore PD's gun guys, which was where D'Amico was now. Matt worked at paying attention, wishing all the while they were somewhere else, talking about different things. If only he could.

D'Amico showed up then, bringing along a taciturn older guy in mismatched suit pants and jacket and a splotched wool tie. "You're here. Good. Nice trip?"

"It can wait."

D'Amico nodded. "This is Lieutenant Donovan Meehan. Donovan, you know Connie. This is Matt Kelly."

The man had a cop's gaze, not cold so much as detached. "You the fed?"

"Yes."

Donovan turned away. "Let's hit it."

Inside, the tower was cramped to the point of claustrophobia. The windowless foyer was decked out in art-deco mosaic tile, brass elevator cage, and matching brass chandelier. A cracked marble staircase with brass handrails wound around the elevator in a square spiral. The four of them fit tightly into the elevator, which clanked and rattled as it climbed.

The eleventh-floor landing was the size of a walk-in closet. Three doors opened along the south, west, and east walls. Beside each was the same brass nameplate for Jerry Freid, CPA. North was the elevator and stairway. The east door was cracked open. D'Amico knocked and pushed.

A young woman was seated behind a narrow desk. She pulled the phone a fraction from her ear. "Yes?"

"We're looking for Jerry Freid."

"And you are?"

D'Amico offered his badge. "Police."

She set down the phone. "Is this a joke?"

"No, ma'am."

"I'm sorry, that wasn't . . . It's just, I called you guys not five minutes ago."

The wall to the secretary's right had floor-to-ceiling mahogany cabinets that shrank the space and darkened the room. The office was too small for all of them to stand inside comfortably. Connie and the gun guy stood in the doorway. Matt remained on the landing. D'Amico asked, "You just called the police?"

"About my boss. He's missing."

"How long has he been gone?"

"He never came in after the weekend."

D'Amico turned to Connie. "Radio Division One. Tell them to cancel the call." He asked the young woman, "What is your name?"

"Fairworth."

"Ms. Fairworth, it's a little unusual for someone to call the police on an adult missing just four days."

"You don't understand. Jerry is *never* away. And he gave me strict instructions on what I was supposed to do if he ever vanished like this."

"May I sit down?" Lucas took the office's only other chair. "You say your boss keeps a regular schedule."

"He's an accountant."

"And he's been gone since Monday."

"He's missed a couple of really important meetings. One I could cover. The other guy, he was furious. He came all the way from Jersey."

"Have you checked his home?"

"Like, ten times a day."

"Does he have a vacation house somewhere?"

She laughed in the manner of one considering the absurd. "Not a chance. He *lives* here."

"Mind if I have a look at his office?"

"Sure. But there's not much to see."

She rose and did a sideways slide between her desk and the filing cabinets. "This way."

Jerry Freid's office was larger and the furniture more upscale. But it was still a thirties-era building in serious need of renovation. D'Amico moved around slowly, touching nothing, just looking. When he spoke, his voice had changed. Not a lot. Matt noticed only because he was listening. Quiet and totally controlled. "Is that it?"

"Jerry has the whole floor. But the other room is just old files."

"Would you show me, please?"

She was already moving. The third room was neat as only an accountant could keep it, an eight-by-ten filing cupboard. D'Amico did another slow sweep. "You say Mr. Freid left strict instructions if he disappeared."

She was standing in the doorway, twisting her hands together. "Yes."

"I know you're not certain what you should say or who you should trust." D'Amico leaned against the cabinet closest to the window, farthest from the young woman. Not pushing in any way. Talking as he might to a frightened child. "But you think something is wrong, don't you?"

"He's such a weird guy."

"What makes you say that?"

"Most of his clients are small businesses around here. Super-normal stuff. The dry cleaners, men's clothing store, restaurants, bars, like that. Then he gets these visitors. People I'm not supposed to see. They're so strange."

"Strange how?"

She whispered it. "Evil."

Slowly D'Amico nodded with his entire body. Giving her approval. "Okay. So your boss might be involved in something bad. You don't know. He's gone and you're worried. But you're not alone. We're here. Do you want to tell me what he told you to do?"

She stared at him a long moment. Twisting her hands. D'Amico remained by the window. Slightly stooped. Waiting. Forever if need be.

Abruptly the young woman turned and stepped past Connie and Matt and Donovan. She walked across the foyer and entered her office. D'Amico moved out of the empty office and shut the door. Eventually the young woman returned and held out an envelope. "Here. Take it."

D'Amico accepted the envelope. "Do you know what's inside?"

"I can feel a key. And some papers. Probably his computer passwords. He's the most secretive guy, you wouldn't believe."

"Do you know what the key is for?"

"He has another office. I'm not supposed to know about it. It's under a different name." She saw nobody but D'Amico. "I've seen him go there once. It's on the seventh floor."

"Maybe it'd be best if you stayed here."

The four of them took the stairs down four flights. The seventh floor was scruffier than the eleventh and had cobwebs in the high ceiling corners and trash on the floor. Things the accountant upstairs wouldn't stand for. Ganja music and smoke that smelled of cloves came from the east office. D'Amico knocked on the central door. Again. He called out, "Mr. Freid, this is the police."

The east door opened. An Anglo with blond cornrows and wide eyes looked out. "What's going on?"

"Step back inside and close your door, sir." D'Amico fit the key in the lock. He took his gun out of his holster. Looked at Connie. "Ready?"

She and Donovan had both drawn their weapons. Donovan shooed Matt farther back. Matt knew it was futile to object. Connie said, "Behind you."

"Okay." He turned the lock and opened the door very fast. Shoving it as far as it would go. It banged on the side wall.

The room was smaller than the main office on the eleventh floor. Narrower. A table and two chairs sat in the middle of an otherwise empty room.

Then Matt smelled it. A sweetish funk. Like compost with a putrid edge.

D'Amico shouldered his weapon, said to Connie. "Call the coroner's, have them send a wagon and an ME. Then get back to Division One, ask for uniforms to back us up."

"Okay, Lucas."

"Then I want you to clear all the civilians off this floor, and get back upstairs and take the lady's statement." He slipped a tape machine from his jacket pocket. "Use this."

Matt stepped inside the room. Donovan walked to the grimy window and shoved hard. When it refused to give, he holstered his gun and banged with both hands. The window creaked open. Traffic and siren noise drifted up from the street.

Matt tapped what looked like an ordinary stucco wall. It gave back a bass thunk. He turned around. The two detectives were watching him. D'Amico knocked on the opposite wall. Same hollow sound.

Matt tried to ignore the stink, which was stronger by the wall, even with the window wide open. The wall's only adornment was a double socket down near the baseboard. Matt bent over. Tapped it. He felt it jiggle. He pushed with three fingers. The socket slid around on an invisible hinge, revealing a lock.

"Would you look at that." Donovan bent down beside him.

Matt held out his hand. "Could I have the key?"

D'Amico handed it over. "That's a new one on me."

The key turned easily. A rattle sounded in the wall as a bolt pulled free. Matt rose and pressed on the wall. A hinge clicked, and the wall sprang out.

The smell almost knocked him flat.

———

Matt hung on okay until the medical examiner finished and things began winding down. His shoulder and ribs ached, but he helped haul the armaments out of both wall units and carry them down to the waiting wagon. It felt good to move about. It kept his mind occupied. The police were there in force. The building was evacuated and the area taped off. News vans showed up, but not until after the coroner's wagon had left and the guns were stowed, so there wasn't anything to film and they soon left. Donovan and the ICU firearms specialists were agog over the haul, especially coming from an arms dealer none of them had heard of before. A corporate techie showed up, took one look at the typed sheet from the envelope D'Amico had taken off the secretary, and got to work on the accountant's computers. Everything in full cop mode.

When Matt came outside the last time, the sunset was doing wonders to the sky. A flock of starlings swirled overhead, their shrill cries echoing over the city traffic. He leaned against the tower wall. The smell from upstairs was in his clothes, his hair, and his skin. His tongue felt coated with a putrid tar.

Lucas found him there. He gripped Matt's arm and said, "Let's walk."

"I'm okay."

"I didn't ask how you were. I said let's walk." He lifted the tape and motioned for Matt to pass under. They crossed the street. Away from the clustering cops and the talk. Matt coughed and tried to clear his lungs. But the smell refused to dislodge.

"First time at a homicide is rough. I should've sent you outside. But I'm not accustomed to ordering feds around."

Matt took up station against a rusted metal railing. Stairs led up to a brownstone door, but the door was sealed with plywood and a county renovation notice. His father's company logo was stamped on the paper and the wood.

"It's still hard for me, and I've been at this a long time." Lucas leaned one foot against the bottom step and stared at the sealed door. "It's a first glimpse at your own end. You get hit deep by everything that's not done, or not done the way you want. You see how short time is and what's happening to the time you got left."

Matt took a ragged breath. Convicted and sentenced both.

"The best way I've found of getting through this is by confronting the honest fact. Everybody's going to face death sooner or later. Right now, though, there's still a chance. It's never easy. But if you try hard enough, you can make the days that are left to you into something of value."

D'Amico patted him on the shoulder. "Something I never thought I'd say to a fed. You're a good cop and a better man. It's an honor to work this case with you. Just don't let this harden you. Don't stop caring about the people you are supposed to serve. Our work is about creating a shelter where good people can live safely. So don't you go hard on me. Find a way to keep caring." He patted Matt again, then turned and walked away.

Matt stared at the cracked sidewalk at his feet as a second set of footsteps approached. "Matt?" Connie came up and touched him the same place as Lucas. "Hey."

He wanted to lift his head. But he was afraid of what he'd find there in her eyes. Another conviction waiting to happen.

"Arnos on Charles Street," she said. "Dinner. Seven o'clock. We don't talk about this or anything else from copland. You got me? Not a word."

She hugged him then. Fast and fierce and gone. "Be on time."

Matt drove from the crime scene to his apartment. He spotted his father's car as soon as he pulled onto the side road. When not riding in the campaign bus, Paul Kelly drove a black-on-black Lincoln Navigator. Several campaign staffers clustered by the car's open window. Matt locked his car and aimed for his apartment door.

"Hey, mister!"

Matt heard a car door slam shut behind him and footsteps hurry in his direction. He kept going.

"Turn around when I'm talking to you!"

His father was jacketless and angry. He strode forward in a starched gray pinstriped shirt and dark silk tie. "You've missed three crucial events! Sol has been going crazy with worry."

Sol rose from behind the wheel. He pushed through the staffers and started forward. "Paul."

The candidate grabbed for his son's arm. "You're coming with me, mister! And I mean right now!"

Matt deflected his father's grip, then planted his hand in the middle of Paul Kelly's chest. And shoved.

His father's face swelled with rage. Sol moved faster now. His father looked down at his shirt, "Look what you've . . ." He sniffed at himself. "What is that stench?"

"The smell of my mother's killer." Matt unlocked his door, stepped inside, and slammed it in his father's face.

He locked the door and leaned against it. Matt's head was pounding.

His father started around the side of the house, yelling that his son had ruined his clothes and he had to go change. Shouting at Sol about rescheduling the shoot.

There was a tentative knock. "Matt?"

"Not now, Sol."

"Matt, son, we've got to have a word."

Matt unlocked the door.

Sol stepped inside. "Matt, we've been so worried. Why didn't you get in touch?"

"I got back last night from England."

"What?"

"Mom's death is connected to Barry Simms. The thumbprint we found upstairs was Simms's. He was murdered by an American, one whose description fits a man I saw out behind our house the day of the explosion." Matt shaped the words without thinking. He took out a glass and poured himself a glass of water. Then he set it down on the counter. He didn't want to drink anything until he'd washed the taste from his mouth. "It all goes back somehow to Pop's time in Vietnam, Sol. There's no question."

Sol stepped forward. "Look at me a second, Matt."

"And there's been another killing," Matt said, still talking to the back window. "An arms dealer. The guy who supplied the bombs that got Mom and Simms. He's gone."

"Do you even hear yourself?" Sol took another step toward him. "Matt, listen to me. There's a killing every day. That's Baltimore. Somebody got another dealer. Arms, drugs, so what? Go look at yourself in the mirror. You're coming apart."

Sol started to take another step. Matt raised his arm. Not pushing. There was no need with Sol.

Sol stared in horror at Matt's hand.

Matt looked at his own hands. They were stained as dark as old blood. "It's gun oil, Sol."

"Matt, I'm talking to you as a man who's known you since before you were born. Give it up. Let it go. You're too close to all this. It's not worth it."

"I can't do that, Sol."

Sol sighed an inaudible protest and left the apartment. Matt stood there a moment longer, staring out the window at the campaign staffers staring in. Then he turned and went back to the bathroom.

He wanted to throw away all the clothes he was wearing, but settled for packing them into a plastic garbage bag and tying it shut. He brushed his teeth and gargled and showered twice. But he came out still certain the smell clung to him. He dressed in starched denims and a knit shirt and running shoes. Knowing it was not fashionable enough for dinner, but not able to work at finding anything else just then.

As he was leaving the house, his phone rang. Matt waited for the machine to answer, thinking it might be Connie.

It was Judy Leigh, the journalist. "Matt, me again. I really need—"

He picked up. "I'm here."

"Where have you been?"

"England."

"Really? On the case?"

"I can't talk about that yet. Soon. I hope."

"What about today? There's a cordon up around the Seltzer tower; you know about that?"

Matt swallowed hard. "I can't talk about that either."

There was a pause. Then, "Okay, it's my turn anyway. I'm having a tough time running down the structure of Camden Trust. That's who is holding your father's business. Everything is being operated through a law firm in D.C. They're not talking. They didn't like the fact that the paper contacted them for details. Not a bit."

"If your boss is one of the shareholders and he hears you called, you could be in serious trouble."

"Credit me with some sense, okay? I brought in an intern from Maryland U. I listened in, fed him the lines. Made his month, playing big investigative reporter, rattling the legal cage."

"You want to see if your boss reacts."

"If he comes back to us again, we got him," Judy agreed. "Oh, and I heard something from a contact in Rolf Zelbert's campaign head-quarters. If elected, he intends to wrest control of the police from the city. Claims Baltimore is out of control and the current system isn't working. He wants to beef up the Homeland Security presence, bring in a new commissioner who would work closely with the feds. Make one unified anticrime force. City, state, and federal acting together."

"Can he?"

"Sure. A century and a half ago, Baltimore was so rough we were known nationwide as Mobtown. The national elections of 1850 got so rowdy families and whole companies fled the ensuing murder and mayhem. Afterward the state and federal governments placed the city's police under their direct control, the only time such an action has been taken in America's history. This remained in place until 1976, when William Donald Schaefer became mayor. But the legal structure is still there. I got all this from Zelbert's staffer."

"I don't see how it could tie in."

"No. Me neither. But I thought I'd let you know. Seeing how you've helped this reporter a time or two."

Lucas just had time to run by home, shower and change, help Katy dress, and speed off for dinner with the Bledsoes. Not even his partner's illness could stop the routine of Thursday dinners. Which was ridiculous only on the surface. Sharla, Clarence's wife, had not invited him just so he and Clarence could eat meat loaf and talk cases and football. Which they did. Sharla wanted Lucas and Katy to have a regular taste of family. Which was the first thing she said when he protested that they should wait until Clarence was feeling better. "Since when does family wait for the good times, Lucas?"

"I just don't want to be a bother."

"You just hush up with that mess. Hello, honey. What a pretty bow." Sharla hugged Katy so hard and long Lucas got a swollen throat. Strange how little things were hitting him where it hurt these days. "What's new in your life?"

"I got a gold star in school today."

"Why am I not surprised? You go on back; Tony's in the playroom making a mess with something." Tony was their five-year-old grandson.

"I like Tony."

"I know you do, honey. Go brighten up the boy's life."

The two of them watched her head back to the playroom, listened to her chat with a child who would soon grow up and leave Katy behind. Lucas had been watching it happen with her playmates for twenty years, and it had never seemed to bite like this evening.

Sharla waited until he turned back to say, "I had a talk with Ian Reeves today."

"I didn't know you and the pastor were friends."

"We're on a board together. Downtown kids. He's worried about you, Lucas."

"Here it comes."

"Now don't you get all huffy on me, mister. Not unless you aim on eating in the kitchen tonight." Sharla was a timeless woman, tall and intelligent and softly defiant. Her hair was copper and determinedly straightened, her nose aquiline, her eyes almond and very aware. "Ian had something important to say about Katy."

"I don't want her to go into a home."

"We all know what you want and what you don't want. But what we don't know is what's best for Katy."

"She needs a family, Sharla."

"Lucas, listen to me. I am not here to argue. I'm just going to ask you one question and then I'm not going to say anything more. And I don't want you answering me either. I want you to *think*." She settled a hand on his arm. Waited until she was sure he saw nothing except her. "How much family has Katy been getting for the past eighteen months?"

She gave him another portion of that measuring look, patted his arm once more, and then said, "There. You see how easy that was? Now, go tell my husband he better be up and dressed and shaved unless he aims on eating in the kitchen with you."

A voice at the top of the stairs said, "I heard that."

"My two misbehaving boys," Sharla said and returned to the kitchen.

When Lucas entered the bedroom, Clarence said, "I would've called and warned you. But she told me I'd be on bread and water if I did."

Lucas pulled the chair over close to the bed. "How you doing?"

"Ready to go. I *been* fine for days now. Now tell me what's going on."

So Lucas laid it out. Doing what he'd been doing for years, talking it through with this trusted friend, letting a step-by-step passage through the case help him see it better.

Clarence heard him out in silence. He was back on the bed, dressed in starched Levis and a freshly pressed short-sleeved shirt. Neat and pristine even when ill. When Lucas finished, he said, "That was a fine move, getting the goods on the Aryan like that."

"I thought so too."

"Good to know your new partner's got more going for her than looks."

"Connie's not my partner, Clarence. She's a rookie doing gopher duty."

"'Course, you'd never let the fact that she's a drop-dead stunner cloud your judgment. Not even a tiny bit."

"I'm treating her like just another cop, Clarence." He had to smile. "And she's loving it."

Clarence coughed once. Trying to keep it trapped inside. Even so, the sound made Lucas wince. His partner wiped his mouth and observed, "Other than what the rookie's done for you, sounds like the only real progress is based on work by your two tame feds."

Lucas gave him nothing. "I was just thinking how you light up a room."

"That's the other guy. I'm his evil twin."

"Matt is very good," Lucas conceded. "He's got the makings of a top officer. Not to mention the fact he gives Connie a run for the money in the eager department. I just hope they don't rework him down in Washington, turn him into just another backstabbing federal roadblock."

"I don't hear the same glowing report on the Brit, what's his name?"

"Pecard. No, you don't." Lucas waited out one long beat. Then he asked it again. "How are you doing, Clarence?"

This time his partner let it sit for a while. His eyes were tinged with yellow and his color was almost gray. "They want me to hang out here another week."

"If that's what they say, you—"

"They're talking desk, Lucas." He paused for a cough that sounded like an ailing cement mixer. "Desk or early off. I don't want either."

"Who's talking to you here?"

"Headquarters sent over a doc; she had me redo all the tests. They say maybe both lungs are scarred." The expression on Clarence's face approached terror. "I don't know what to do."

Lucas settled back in his chair. Focused on the wall beside the bed because looking at the pain in his partner's face was too hard just then. "You want me to talk to you like a partner or a friend?"

"Your call."

"When June got sick the last time, we started counting the days. Closer to the end, we started naming the hours. The last couple of days, it was minutes. Trying to hold on to each and every one, afraid we might miss one heartbeat of happiness, one breath of love." D'Amico lowered his head, remembering. "You're the best partner I ever had. But I tell you the truth. If taking desk means you gain another few years to enjoy with Sharla and the kids, grab hold with both hands. I'd give anything . . ."

He stopped because he had to. And sat there looking at the floor between his feet until he felt the hand on his shoulder.

He looked up to find Sharla standing there, biting hard on her upper lip. The woman stared at him for a long, burning moment, then said in a hoarse voice, "Don't you ever again ask me what you're doing here in this house." She drew him up and hugged him hard. "Why the Lord didn't make more men like you I will *never* understand. Now y'all come on down to dinner."

Matt walked the six blocks to Mount Vernon. The Japanese woman at his dry cleaners accepted his garbage bag without a qualm. He left and walked through the gathering night, not headed anywhere in particular, just walking. At quarter of seven he turned onto Charles Street. The place was full of lights and fragrances and happy faces. Music streamed from cafés. People took advantage of the warm night, filling the sidewalk tables and standing outside the bars. The talk was cheerful, the feeling alive. He arrived at the restaurant on time and saw Connie standing on the sidewalk outside the front window. He stepped closer to the building he was passing so as to study her unseen. She wore a pleated red skirt that stopped well short of her knees and a jacket of something that shimmered in the passing headlights. She moved in time to music pouring from the neighboring café, swinging a little red purse with both hands. Matt left cover and started forward.

When she saw his jeans and knit shirt, she grinned. "You didn't have to dress up all formal just for me."

"Connie, I'm sorry, I just . . ."

"Hey." Using the same voice she had that afternoon. Soft, accepting, warm. "Why don't we go inside."

She gave her name to the server, who showed them to a table by the large front window. A bar ran down the back wall, with a wood-burning pizza oven in the corner. The place was loud and packed and full of life.

Matt looked around and said, "This is great."

"Really?"

"It's so good to be out tonight. That doesn't make any sense, I know."

"Makes all the sense in the world."

He studied her face. "How do you do that?"

"What?"

"Go from cop to child to woman. In your face. And your eyes. You change."

The waiter came and handed out menus neither of them saw. When they were alone again, she said, "I'm a walking advertisement for multiple personality disorder. I know it. There's nothing I can do about it. What can I say? I'm a woman. It goes with the territory. Part wolf, part dove."

He started to say something more, but she stopped him with a touch to his hand. "No, Matt. No questions. I was the one who did all the talking when we were on the phone. Tonight it's your turn."

"I told you. I don't talk."

He expected any of the dozen responses he had known before. Hostile, suspicious, angry, demanding. Instead, she just looked at him a long moment, then said, "Best book."

"Excuse me?"

"The book you grab when you're down and you're looking for something to remind you that life really can work out the way you want."

He did not have to think. *"Touching the Void."*

"I give that a pass."

"Two guys climb the western face of the highest mountain in South America. One of them breaks a leg. The other almost dies getting them down."

She tilted her head. "I'm trying hard to understand here. How is this supposed to help you get through a really bad day?"

"They risked it all to face what had always before been considered unconquerable."

She waited. "And?"

"I read a page." He felt the sweat bead. The internal conflict tore at him. He desperately wanted to shut up. And wanted even more to talk. "Just one page. That's all it takes to feel their wild hunger for the unknown. Putting everything on the line. Hanging on the verge. Staring down into the void. And carrying that home."

She leaned closer still. "You know what? I like that."

"Really?"

"Yes, Matt. I like it a lot." She reached for his hand. "I never did feel comfortable around guys who hanker for the normal life, whatever that is. Listening to you say that makes me want to go buy a ticket to somewhere we've never been, hike to a hidden lake, spend a month exploring the ruins of some lost kingdom."

He stared at the hand on top of his. Pearl-tipped fingers, long and graceful. But strong. He could feel the calluses, see the muscles in her wrist. "Machu Picchu."

"Where?"

"Peru. Andes. A place like you were describing."

"Was that one of the colored dots on your map?"

He wished every word he spoke to her did not feel like his last confession. "Absolutely."

The waiter returned then. She asked if Matt wanted her to order for them both. He nodded, not lifting his gaze from her hand. Part of him heard her order duck sausage pizzas and spinach and Roquefort salads. The other part was elsewhere.

When the waiter left, she asked, "What are you thinking about?"

"FLETSE."

"What?"

"The new federal law enforcement training center outside Savannah."

"Wow, Matt." Her smile displayed an easy joy. "You romantic guy, you."

"Sorry."

"No, hey, I really want to hear about it." She tightened her hold on his hand, as though fearful he was going to pull away. "This is my passion too, remember?"

"The guys down there call it Club Fed. They have a saying you hear your first day inside, 'Happiness is FLETSE in my rearview mirror.' They're right."

"Tough, huh."

"Tough," he agreed. Her grin was gone, but the light was still there in her eyes. Drinking him in. Like what he said was just so very important. "Sixty federal agencies use it for training now, everybody but the FBI. The DEA is there but split off. Everybody else is lumped into the same squads. Classes run eight to five, six days a week. Outside of that is physical training. Sunday you hunker down and study, because Monday mornings you're tested. Fail one test, you start over with the next incoming squad. And you don't want to start over."

The waiter came back with their salads. Connie held to tight impatience during the interruption. "Tell me everything."

So he did. Through the salads and the main course. While a band cranked up downstairs. On through coffee. He told her everything but the reason he had been thinking about it in the first place. He described how the classes and the fieldwork were jumbled together at a super-intensive pace. Locksmithing, forced-entry procedures, hostage raids, copter jumps, forensics, handcuffing, arrest strategy, team strikes, undercover ops, criminal analysis, boat ops, surveillance. He described the lingo and the jokes. How the place had once been swamps and now all the water was trapped in lakes, how some mornings the ducks were out of the lakes and waddling around the jogging paths. How punishment details on those days were dreaded events, because teams were sent into the lakes to net the gators and haul them back over to the surrounding swamps.

He told her about Billy Bob, the fictitious culprit used in every attack and arrest situation. He told her about the northern guys being indoctrinated into grits their first morning, how they were graded on what amount they could keep down.

Matt talked and he watched her, and it warmed him more than he thought possible to make her smile. So much he could almost wipe away the image of himself standing by the barracks' lone telephone that last day, calling the last lady in his life, listening to himself beg for another chance he didn't deserve.

When he finished, she bolted in with another instant question. "Secret talent."

"What?"

"The special ability nobody knows about."

"That would be karate."

"No, Matt. It's not secret anymore. Something else."

Her potent mixture of eagerness and perfume and energy made it almost easy to say, "Close your eyes."

She set down her cup, planted her elbows on the table, leaned forward, and shut down.

Matt had the keen sense of her waiting to be kissed. Not in the way she held herself so much as the air that surrounded her. Of trust and openness. It would have been so easy, just another step down the short road leading to the precipice called inevitable.

Matt turned to the window and sorted through the voices in his head. He listened closely to Lucas D'Amico, then mouthed silently and fit himself into character.

Then, "All right, Morales. I want you in Bernstein's office. Give us a rundown on how you wasted your day."

"Wow."

He knew Connie was watching him. So he shut his own eyes to hold onto the internal discourse. "What say we go out and fight some crime."

"Not tonight." She touched his arm. "How do you do that?"

As usual, it took a moment to reclaim his own voice. "Couldn't say."

"It sounded like Lucas had just walked in and plopped himself down beside us."

"My mom used to love me to do it." He smiled at the memory. "She'd laugh like crazy, then go sad."

"I can understand that. Wondering what's inside her little man, feeding that ability of his to step so far outside himself."

Matt took the words like a slap to his soul. Rocking back in his chair. "That was a terrible thing to say."

"No. It wasn't."

"I'm so sorry. I never could control what came out of my mouth." Her lips twisted into a worried parody of humor. "Case in point."

He rose from his chair. "Ready to go?"

She did not protest. But as soon as they left the restaurant, she wrapped an arm around his waist and grabbed his hand with the other. Molding to his body. Saying in more than words all he needed to hear.

Which was why he let her lead them back toward her Nissan XTerra, as red as her dress, the rear packed with building materials and tools. At the door he spoke before she could, saying, "You mind if I walk back?"

She recovered well. A lady who rarely if ever lost her balance. "If you want."

"I think it would be best, Connie."

"Okay, Matt. If that's what you want." She unlocked her door, then gave him a heat-seeking missile of a gaze. "This time."

The nightmare clawed at Matt. Jet lag added supplementary chains to keep him submerged. The feral beast in his head made up for the previous missed night.

Which was why, when the phone woke him, he answered panting and sweating hard. "This is Kelly."

"Lucas here. Catch you working out?"

"Hang on a second." Matt swung his feet to the floor, padded to the bathroom, pulled a towel from the rack, wiped his face, leaned his forehead against the wall, and waited for the chimes to fade. He avoided his reflection in the mirror both coming and going. "I'm back."

"I've never found a way to make bad news go down easy," D'Amico told him. "So I'm just going to hit you with it. Our geeks have finished going through Freid's records. He duplicated his system in an electronic lockbox in case his computers were zapped. A real freak for backup, everything totally up to date. Our gun guys found some major league surprises, stuff that'll keep them busy for months. But that's not what this call is about. His last appointment was for Sunday afternoon. You with me?"

"The Ravens game."

"Right." D'Amico paused, then hit him with, "The appointment was Allen Pecard."

"No way."

"Goes further. They did a search. Pecard has been in three times before. First time was to make a buy. Second time was early January, trading information for weapons."

"The armory heist."

"Pecard handed Freid the how and the when. Freid supplied the gang. They split the arms. Pecard took the claymores. Only the records show Freid held back a few. Which might have been what got him killed."

Matt walked into the kitchen. Poured a glass of water. Drank it. Another. Willing his hands and mind to steady.

"You there?"

"Yes. I have something too." He related the conversations at the pub in England, the tall, broad-shouldered Yank who came and went with the night.

"We need to get a photo to that barmaid," D'Amico said. "See if she can do a positive ID."

"I'll handle that."

"Good. But first we're going in. Connie is over waiting to see a federal judge in chambers. We wanted to do this quiet and official, seeing as how your man is so well connected."

"I need to inform Bannister." When D'Amico did not respond, Matt pressed, "Part of this whole deal was improving relations with the feds. This is important. Bannister is SAC."

"And Pecard's buddy."

"We need to do this, Lucas."

D'Amico went to full cop mode. "You don't tell him a thing. You got that? Not the what or the who or the why. He comes, or he doesn't. That's his choice. You drive him out personal and you make sure he doesn't use his phone once we get in range."

"I can do that."

"We need a place near Pecard's house where we can meet."

"There's a mini-mart and service station about two miles north of his drive. On the left."

D'Amico held him there through a few more breaths. Not pleased. Then, "We rendezvous in two hours."

Bannister complained in terse agent-in-charge style over not being told where they were going. But he came just the same. The early afternoon held a very dense quality. The day was hazy, the sky down tight against the earth, just high enough not to be called fog. Everything they passed looked drained of color. Cars, houses, billboards, fields, all looked stained with the day's monotone. The forests were filled with the bare bones of empty limbs.

When it became clear where they were headed, Bannister vibrated on the seat next to Matt. He held off erupting until Matt pulled into the service station parking lot and drove to the far side, where D'Amico and Connie stood between an unmarked Pontiac and a sheriff's car. At that point he demanded, "Are you *insane?*"

Matt cut the motor and rose from the car. Bannister came out in stages, giving each of them a good long glare. D'Amico stood beside the sheriff, drinking coffee from a mini-mart cup. He said to Matt, "I believe this is your show."

Bannister slammed his door and danced around and got tight in Matt's face. Matt told him everything. The sheriff was a tall, heavyset man who enclosed his vast gut in an oversized leather belt. He moved in behind Bannister and listened closely, evidently hearing it for the first time. Matt focused his attention on the sheriff so that he did not need to watch Bannister's rising rage. When he finished, Bannister came back with a blast intended for all of them. "Allen Pecard is a highly decorated member of the federal network. I am ordering you men to stand down!"

D'Amico motioned at Connie with his head. She approached Matt, not Bannister, and handed him the warrant.

"Give me that." Bannister ripped it from Matt's grasp. The chest of his suit heaved as he read. He made a mess of refolding the sheets. "Mister, you are so far out of line you're not even in the same *country*."

"I've called this in," Matt said. "Washington has given us the green. We're going."

"I'll take that," D'Amico stepped forward and slipped the warrant from Bannister.

"I am lodging a formal complaint!"

"You do that." D'Amico pointed Matt toward the unmarked car. "Let's roll."

Bannister continued to move even when sitting tense and silent in the Pontiac's rear seat. When they pulled down Pecard's drive, he muttered, "This is an *outrage*."

D'Amico rounded the car in front of the garage so that he could study the house. The sheriff pulled his wagon around beside D'Amico, angled for a quick getaway.

"We're talking *serious* error of judgment on *everyone's* part."

D'Amico quietly sighed. Connie gave no sign she heard Bannister at all. The house was utterly silent.

Bannister sprang from his seat. "I'll handle this." His footsteps scrunched up the raked gravel walk.

Matt opened his door. "Stop right there."

Bannister wheeled about. "Are you *ordering* me, mister?"

Matt said, "Not the front door. Not any door."

"Of course," D'Amico said. "Silly me."

Bannister glanced at the house, then Matt, then the house again. Showing uncertainty for the first time.

Matt moved to the garage window, looked inside, said, "His Jeep's gone."

The sheriff asked, "How do you want to play this?"

Matt looked at D'Amico. "Your call."

"Okay. Connie, you and the sheriff head around the garage. Check out the windows; don't approach the doors there either. Scout out the rear of the house. But don't approach. You follow?"

"Look but hold back."

"Right. Check your radio."

She lifted the handset and said, "Test, one." Her voice crackled from Matt's belt.

"Give us the word when you're in position." D'Amico spoke to Matt. "I say we go for the side windows, stay well clear of the porch."

"Works for me."

"Let's move."

Time gradually congealed as they crossed the lawn. Jays flittered from one tree to the next, mocking them and the strident day. D'Amico moved quickly, his breath a half-formed whistle. Bannister pounded his broughams into the grass but kept silent.

Connie radioed as they rounded the house. "All quiet back here."

D'Amico started for the middle window. He was picking his way through the azalea hedge when Bannister stepped toward him. "One last time, Detective. I'm telling you this—"

Bannister stopped because D'Amico pitched forward into his arms.

There was no sound except the quarreling jays and the rustling hedge and a soft grunt from D'Amico. Like he'd suddenly been taken by utter surprise.

Bannister stumbled but stayed upright. He held D'Amico in a parody of a dance, wearing an expression of confused outrage.

Matt saw the red stain on D'Amico's shoulder the same moment a splinter of brick popped beside Bannister. He leaped forward, taking the two men down. The hedges cracked and flattened and hid them from view.

D'Amico groaned.

Matt ripped the radio from his belt. "Officer down! Officer down!"

Shots rang out from the rear of the house.

Bannister rolled from the hedges, still in denial. "This can't—"

Matt scrambled, not upright, but almost. He gripped D'Amico by the jacket and hauled. Two more shots sprayed pink dust from the wall. *Help me move him!*

Bannister struggled up. Together they dragged D'Amico around to the front. Only then did Matt realize he had left his radio on the grass. He shouted, "Connie!"

There was a reply from somewhere out back, too faint for him to hear. "Connie! I don't have my radio! Lucas is hit!"

He was answered by more gunfire.

Bannister was crouched over D'Amico, still in shock. Matt punched him on the shoulder. Bannister looked up. Struggling to focus. Matt yelled, "Call for backup!" He ran and kept on shouting. "Ambo! Chopper!"

He ran around the outside of the garage. "Connie! Coming at you!"

He turned the corner and almost fell on top of her. She was crouched over the sheriff, who was down with a leg wound. "I can't move him."

"Grab his arm!" The garage's rear wall was pitted with shots. Matt pulled with one hand and waved his pistol with the other, but saw nothing to aim at. "Where is he?"

Connie did not respond until they were back around the side. "I haven't seen a thing."

"Woods," Matt decided. "Silencer. Scope."

As he crouched and moved back forward, Connie cried, "Wait for backup!"

"We've got two men down and an assailant who could move around and take us all." Matt went low, looked around the corner, saw nothing but a forest wall. "Give me cover fire."

Connie slapped a fresh clip into her pistol and moved up beside him. "Go!"

Matt jinked right, then headed straight in. Waiting all the while for a bullet to take him down. He hit the first line of trees just as Connie stopped firing. She called, "You okay?"

"Here!"

"I saw a flash! One o'clock from my angle!"

Matt hunkered behind a large pine, glanced back. Then to his left. Saw movement in the trees. Heard the crashing of branches. Someone running away. He fired twice. And ran.

The going was hard. The brush tore at his clothes. The ground was slippery with pine needles and autumn leaves. He lost sight of their attacker after ten paces. He stopped, crouched again. His training came to the fore. Never race forward when you don't know what you're up against. He listened hard. Nothing.

Then in the distance he heard a car engine come alive. Something heavy spun with four-wheel fury and tore away.

Matt ran ahead until the sound was lost. He turned then and started back. Connie ran across the lawn to greet him. He suddenly felt very weak. But not from the chase. From knowing she was all right. But she was a cop, and he was a professional. So all he said was, "Gone."

It was just after dark by the time they finished at the house. Bryan Bannister pulled in a full team but managed everything from a quiet distance. He walked from room to room in Pecard's house, his gaze hollowed.

Bombs had been wired to both front and rear doors. The structure was chillingly familiar, though Matt had not seen it before. A hole had been chivied through the carpet and baseboard. A reinforced plywood box was set inside the hole, angled so its open end faced the door. The box was fitted with a metal plate for a base. Its interior was filled with carpet torn from the floor and insulation from beneath the baseboard. Wires dangled where the FBI's bomb squad had disarmed the firing mechanisms and extracted the claymores.

Matt drove Connie back to town in D'Amico's car, numb with exhaustion. They stopped by Maryland General, where a nurse informed them Lucas was out of surgery but still in recovery.

Matt asked Connie, "How do you want to do this?"

"Dorcas told me there's some kind of problem with Lucas's daughter."

"Take the car. See to her."

"Call me soon as you know something, all right?"

"Of course."

Connie started away, then turned back. Very hesitant now.

"What?"

Connie did not speak. She just looked at him. And did that thing with her eyes. Going from hard and flat to open. Yearning. Her face changed as well. Losing the day's tension. Turning about twelve years old.

Matt wanted to ask her again how she did that. But was suddenly unable to find the breath.

Connie said, sounding a little breathless herself, "I'm going off duty now, okay?"

He nodded.

She planted one hand on his chest. And kissed him.

She leaned back. Slowly she opened her eyes. She touched her tongue to her lips. Like she was tasting him. Then she smiled.

He did not know what to do with his hands, the day, the kiss, the look, the hunger. "Connie—"

She touched a finger to his lips. Replaced the finger with her own mouth. Then turned and walked away.

The ER nurse looked at his face, then at the gun exposed by his open jacket. She hummed a note. "Honey, you bring a whole new meaning to armed and dangerous."

———

Lucas D'Amico came back to life in careful stages. Thirst hit hard. His mouth was so parched his tongue felt swollen. But he could live with the thirst. He moved his fingers and toes. Felt them all. Very good sign. He was an old dog now and knew the tricks. Feeling his extremities bit by bit eliminated a lot of things he no longer needed to worry about.

He opened his eyes.

Matt was conked out on the next bed. Lucas knew instantly that Matt was not another victim because the kid still wore clothes dirtied by the assault that had landed him here.

A woman's voice said, "Lucas. You're awake."

He knew the voice but didn't. He moved his eyes and saw Hannah Bernstein standing at the end of his bed. He peeled open his lips. His first word was, "Katy?"

"Connie fixed her dinner and stayed until Sharla got off work. Katy's spending the night with the Bledsoes." Hannah moved over and fitted the straw into his mouth. "You deliver a warrant with two rookies and you're the one to take a hit. What am I going to do with you?"

Lucas drank and sighed at the cool pleasure and drank some more. He said, "I don't want Katy to know about this. She worries so."

"Sharla said the same thing. As far as Katy is concerned, her daddy is off doing work stuff." She set down the cup. "The doctor says the operation on your shoulder went very well. You'll be in rehab, but he expects a full recovery. I've also heard all the gruesome bits, if you're interested."

"Later."

"Feel any pain?"

"Far, far away."

Matt snorted and turned partly over. Hannah Bernstein didn't even glance his way. "Don't mind him. The kid is gone. We've had doctors, nurses, a couple of fibbies, ringing phones. That's the first time he's even moved."

"He saved my bacon."

"Yeah, I'm hearing good things. Him and Connie both. The FBI agent, Bannister, he's taking this very hard."

He made a feeble motion toward the cup. Hannah moved swiftly. "Let me. You want to hear more?"

"Shoot."

"A joke. Guess the doctor was right after all." She seated herself next to his bed. "There's an East Coast APB for the arrest of one Allen Pecard. The FBI is in this big-time."

Lucas waited. This was not the sort of news to tense the chief up like she was just now. There was something more.

Hannah Bernstein appeared to choose her words with care. "I want you to hear what I'm saying, and I want you to think about it very carefully. Crowder is retiring in three months. I'm putting you up for division lieutenant."

"I'm going to heal, Chief. I'm putting this behind me."

"Lucas." She started to reach over and touch his good shoulder. But she caught herself and settled the hand back into her lap. "You are a good detective. But you are also a good leader. Look at what you've done with a rookie cop and a green fed. You've made them a team.

You've taken a cold case and you've brought us to the point of issuing warrants. Our division needs this kind of leadership. You'll never know how rare this gift is until you get in my position. Every cop in the division respects you. They'll listen. They'll *follow* you."

Her force of personality was so strong he could not say no, which of course was what he was going to have to tell her sooner or later. But just then, he was a little overwhelmed. So he lay there and he looked at her. She was an extremely attractive woman, even when in full commander armor. Her eyes were clear and intelligent, her face strong and determined and unlined. He could think of worse things to do with his idle hours than lie here and study her face.

Hannah was also comfortable with the silence between them. Which was a very strange thing. Good, but strange. When she spoke, it was in a voice he had not heard before. Soft. Warm. And something more. "Lucas, what you say with how you act and who you are speaks louder than a billion leadership seminars. I want those lessons taught to all the people under my command. I want them to know just how fine a cop can be. I want . . ."

She rose to her feet. "I better go before I make a fool of myself."

She turned to the other bed and shook Matt's shoulder. Harder.

"Wha . . . Chief?"

"Come on, Agent Kelly. We need to get you some coffee and talk over a couple of matters that can't wait."

Matt pushed himself upright, rubbed his face, asked, "Lucas?"

"He's fine. You can see him tomorrow. Let's go get you cleaned up."

Lucas nodded to Matt, but his gaze remained fastened on Hannah Bernstein. He followed her departure, so uncertain how he felt he could not find the words even to say farewell.

Matt spent half an hour with Chief Bernstein. Just two pros handling a tough case. He checked by the campaign office as soon as he returned home. The office was filled with earnest faces and exposed nerves. The clock was hammering down. The staffers had all witnessed the altercation between him and his father after the gun dealer had been discovered. That plus his filthy state troubled them. But when Matt asked what the candidate had going that night, the staffers had no reason not to tell him.

He returned to his apartment and set coffee to brew while he showered. The sleep in D'Amico's hospital room had taken the edge off his exhaustion, but he was still both sore and tired. He drove the short distance back to Mount Vernon and parked by the darkened church.

The Engineers Club was a bastion of old Baltimore. Rooms were occasionally rented out for weddings and charity events. But the rest of the time it held power within a private and luxurious grip. The club occupied one of the largest estate homes on Mount Vernon Square. The church, the Peabody, and the modern art museum were all better-known neighbors.

The walls were oiled wood paneling. The carpets were all Persian, the chandeliers Austrian lead crystal, the paintings antiques. Behind the main restaurant, leading off the corridor to the ballroom, were two discrete meeting chambers. Matt stationed a leather chair beside the door to his father's room. He remained seated as the doors opened and the cigar smoke and the rich laughter rolled out.

His father and Sol moved into the final backslapping stages of farewell. All their guests bore the grand smiles and satisfied voices of having spent an evening carving up future spoils.

Paul Kelly kept his smile in place and his gaze on the last departing man as he addressed his son. "It's been a long day. I'm going home now."

"We need to talk, Pop."

"Wrong. We needed to have you around last week. Now it's nothing but too late." He snapped his fingers. "Let's go, Sol."

"Pop—"

"You want to talk with me, call the office like anybody else."

Matt followed them through the main salons. He waited while his father and Sol spoke with a few cronies. Sol did not once look Matt's way. Paul Kelly let the maître d' personally help him with his overcoat. Matt trailed along behind them as they stepped outside.

The two men came to a halt on the club's top stair as a trio of police rose from their patrol car and stood waiting.

"What is going on here?"

Matt took control of the outer door and shut it in the manager's face. He then said to his father, "The case involving Megan Kelly has now officially gone federal."

Paul Kelly pointed a finger at the police. "I asked you about them. Not your shenanigans downtown."

"There are both state and federal warrants out for Allen Pecard. This afternoon he shot a sheriff and the detective who recently met with you."

Paul Kelly continued to stab the night. "Tell me what they're doing here!"

"As of now, you are under twenty-four-hour guard. There is a jurisdictional issue. Soon as the election is over, it will change to Secret Service. But for now—"

Paul Kelly continued to glare at the cops. "You're telling me I don't have any say in the matter?"

"You can refuse. If you do, it will become a federal issue. Either the Secret Service or the FBI will maintain discreet surveillance. But it will require a lot more manpower. At least twenty agents. I'll be moved out of my apartment and they—"

"No." Paul Kelly dropped his arm and started for the car. When one of the policemen moved to the driver's side of Paul Kelly's Navigator, he snapped, "I'll drive."

"No, Pop." Matt remained where he was. "Not anymore."

"I always drive!"

Sol spoke for the first time. The quiet, almost-resigned voice he used so often when addressing Matt's father with Matt around. "Paul. Enough."

Paul Kelly wheeled about. He glared at them, back and forth, and then stalked to the passenger side and wrenched open the door. "If you're going to drive, then drive!"

Sol hurried to catch up. Matt watched them drive away, then walked off into the night.

Saturday morning Matt called the hospital and then went for a long run. His shoulder and chest still ached somewhat from the attack at Upper Heyford. His thigh gave warning twinges but no longer throbbed. He took it easy for the first three miles, until his motions became smooth and the discomfort settled farther into the background. Then he pushed. Not for long, but a push just the same. The first time since the blast, and it felt very good. Upon his return he stretched for almost an hour, working the thigh and shoulder and upper body until everything moved smoothly. By eleven he felt genuinely ready to start a tough day.

Matt phoned his Washington office and left a long message for Van Sant, detailing what had gone down the previous day. He showered and dressed and drove to the D'Amico residence on Eastern. The house was an old Baltimore brick townhome, a corner unit in a single structure that ran the entire block. The street fronted Patterson Park, once a haven for nearby blue-collar communities. Now the city paid street performers to draw people in, but only during the day. At night the place was ruled by gunfire and sounds the locals had come to dread.

D'Amico's front door was opened by a striking middle-aged woman named Sharla with skin like cinnamon. She hugged him hello as though it was the most natural thing in the world. Matt endured the coffee and small talk, trying hard to see Katy through the affection Sharla and Connie showed. Then he drew Connie outside.

"I spoke to Lucas this morning," she said. She started to reach for his hand and hesitated, as though she was wondering where the boundaries were after the previous evening. Matt wanted to sweep her up. Seize her so hard he breathed for them both. Instead, he did what she had started to. Reached over and took her hand. Connie looked down at their hands and then up into his face. Just looked. But it felt better than any other woman's fiercest embrace.

"Lucas doesn't want Katy to know about him taking a hit," she said. "He's been away before. He'll be back soon. That's all."

"Fine."

"She's such a sweet girl. She has school during the week. I've taken today off; I'll have her while Sharla's at work. Sharla is Clarence's wife."

Matt assumed it was a flaw in his own nature, having been unable to see more in Katy than a shapeless woman in black sweats cutting designs from a book and singing about bluebirds. "Who's Clarence?"

"Lucas's partner. Out with a chest thing."

Eastern Avenue was the connecting artery between Fells Point and Little Italy. Saturday traffic thundered by. Matt felt the diesel wind of passing trucks but saw only her. "I want to make a run to Perryville. It's probably futile, but I need to check something out."

"The chief would probably have something to say about one of her officers talking shop while holding hands with a fed," Connie said.

"Then I'm glad the chief isn't here." He squeezed the hand, felt her gaze in his bones. "If you talk to Lucas, tell him I'll stop by on my way back."

"Then you'll come here, right?"

"You betcha."

She skipped to the front door, smiled down at him like he had recited poetry. "I'll be waiting."

———

The journey north was a tumult of emotions and conflicting desires. Every meeting with Connie threatened to lift the lid off his internal cauldron. Yet he ached for more of everything—more time, more closeness, more connection—hungered in a way he had never known before. Connie asked for nothing but him. He had no idea who that was. Which was no surprise. Any number of departing ladies had tossed the question at him. What terrified him most was that for once he wished he knew the answer.

Camp Perryville was a hollow place. After passing the empty guard station, Matt entered grounds military in their precision and neatness. Even the oldest houses along the riverside lane held a faded charm. The newer structures were solid and glaringly white against the gray autumn day. Yet there was a lifeless quality to the place. Even a fife-and-drum corps would have sounded funereal. An old man sat on a bench beneath huge shade trees that dripped colors around his feet. He wore a faded robe and rested a cane between his legs. He was surrounded by a platoon of empty benches. He stared in the direction of the water. Matt drove directly across his line of vision and the old man did not even blink.

The Records Building was one of the camp's oldest, a wooden structure five stories high. Paint flecks covered the front lawn in patches, the only disorderly spot Matt noticed on the entire base. The steps were warped. Wires dangled above the double front doors where a light had once hung. The left-hand door did not have a knob, just a plastered-over hole. The interior was worse. The linoleum floors were ribbed and peeling back. The air smelled of mold. A ribbon of wallpaper snaked almost to the floor. The windows were filthy and the screens ripped. A woman in a nurse's uniform was seated behind the information desk, typing into a computer. She gave him a minute to take in the place. "Pretty awful, huh."

"I'm trying to find something nice to say."

She liked that enough to rise from her chair. "We were scheduled to move out last year. Now they're saying January. I'm pretty sure I can hold out that long. But I have my doubts about the two doctors they've got stuck upstairs."

Matt stared at a ceiling stained in patches the color of old oak. "They let people upstairs?"

"They were both retired, then brought back to help out with troops coming back from Iraq and Afghanistan. What can I do for you?"

Matt showed her his ID. She inspected it without expression. "State Department Intelligence. After all this time, you'd think I'd have seen everything. But that's a new one."

"I have a problem."

She leaned on the counter.

"I'm investigating a murder."

"Here?"

"Baltimore."

"You think it was one of our former patients?"

"Probably not."

She actually smiled. "Yep. Sounds like a problem to me."

"I've got a list of names. All vets. One of them may or may not be involved in our case. What I want to know is whether any of them were ever patients here."

"Veterans from which war?"

"Vietnam."

She straightened in stages. Her smile was gone. She gave him a long, unblinking look. Then, "We don't keep records from that far back. They'd all be in the DOD vaults outside Crystal City."

Matt knew he had said something. But for the life of him he could not figure out what it was. "What about backup computer records?"

"Computer. Backup. Hah." But she was not laughing.

"So there's nothing here that might help me?"

"Only the doctor's own case files. Long as they're on staff, we keep all their case files on-site."

"Can I show you the list?"

She shrugged. "Free country, isn't that what they say?"

He unfolded the handwritten list from the confrontation in Sol Greene's office. She went down the short list of names. She stopped at the bottom. Just looked. Long enough for him to say the name aloud. "Porter Reeves."

She lifted her gaze. Gave him nothing.

"You've heard that name before, haven't you."

"Like I said, all case records are strictly confidential."

"How can I get access?"

"Formal request to DOD, go through channels."

"That could take years."

She didn't respond.

"I would appreciate anything you can give me," Matt said, pressing as firmly as he dared on each word. "Anything at all."

"You need to talk with Dr. Turminian."

"Could you spell that, please?"

"I'll go one better." She turned back to her desk, wrote on her pad, then tore off the sheet. "Alexis is one of the doctors who's been brought out of retirement. He's been around here since Nam."

Matt saw it was a street address in the neighboring town. "You want me to phone his home on a Saturday?"

"Go on over. I'll call and give him a heads-up. Guys like this, they live and breathe work." She looked at him then. Passing another of those indecipherable messages. "You want answers, he's your best chance. But even there I'd say it's slim to none."

———

The warming day had burned away the clouds by the time Matt emerged from Records. He followed the nurse's instructions back to the main highway and took the bridge across to Havre de Grace. The bay sparkled and autumn colors lit the shoreline like a flaming necklace. Havre de Grace was a well-preserved hamlet, a waterfront market town that had served northern Maryland's outlying regions for over two hundred years. Main Street was a dense collection of shops and cafés overlooking the waterfront. Marinas and hordes of tourists crammed the street's other side. Traffic moved at an easy weekend pace. Sails spread over the blue waters, moving as easy as the traffic, the wind as gentle as the sun.

The base psychiatrist resided in a Victorian manor one block off the water. Peaked turrets adorned both ends. Two rows of late-blooming azaleas framed a long front porch. Matt climbed from the car and spotted a man trimming rose vines from a side trellis. "Dr. Turminian?"

He did not rise from his stooped position. "You're the young man Sally phoned me about?"

"Matt Kelly."

The man dropped his shears and stripped off work gloves. "I suppose we can talk. But there's little I can do for you."

Matt followed him onto the porch. The doctor was slightly bowlegged and moved at the fragile pace of one well aware of his advancing years. "Anything you can tell me would be more than I have right now."

The psychiatrist had a slight accent Matt could not place, Greek or Armenian perhaps. Age had shrunk him into a tanned figure with skin too large for his frame. His energy had receded with his hair. He was not hostile so much as watchful. "Sit yourself down, young man, and tell me what it is that's brought you out from the city. But if it has anything to do with patient records, the answer will be no. I must warn you of that at the outset."

Dr. Turminian had a psychiatrist's ability to listen with his entire being. He sat in a rocker pulled up to the porch railing and watched Matt go through his story. Then, "I take what you say very seriously, Mr. Kelly. But I can only repeat what I've already told you. All patient-doctor records are confidential. The same vow I have kept for forty years would force me to refuse even a direct order from Washington."

"Could you at least tell me whether you have ever treated a patient named Porter Reeves?"

Something flickered deep in those dark eyes. There and gone. "I'm sorry. No."

The doctor was ready to dismiss him. Denial was cemented into every fabric of his being. But Matt needed more to put his plan into shape. He searched for a question—any question would do, so long as it caused the doctor to speak.

He touched the list in his pocket. Thought about the mystery of a man who might be both bomb consultant and bomber. He asked the doctor, "Why would a man lead two lives in two opposite directions?"

Alexis Turminian relaxed a fraction. General questions of personality were clearly open territory. "You'll excuse me for saying, it seems rather interesting to hear that a young man is investigating his own mother's death."

"It started out differently. I just wanted to make sure the police did their job."

"And now?" When Matt did not respond, the doctor nodded. As though he took Matt's hesitation for the proper response. "It is remarkable how life moves us in the most unexpected of directions. One moment, we think we have everything under control. The next, and it has all changed. A man suddenly finds himself old and no longer required at the work that has defined his life. A mother is taken from her son. A patient . . ."

A trio of tourists walked past the house. One halted to take a picture. The doctor shifted his face so that it was hidden behind the late-blooming azalea. When the tourists continued on, Turminian said, "What you ask is in effect a question of identity. How can a personality become fragmented? How can someone arrive at the point of lying even to himself over who or what he is? Would you agree?"

Matt answered very slowly. "I'm not sure."

"You must understand, Mr. Kelly, misleading friends and strangers is part and parcel of most people's daily life. They feel they must hide some dark stain. For some it is rage, for others a past misdeed, a mistake, a secret lust, a shame, an anguish. Every person is different, every reason unique. But my profession is based upon the precept that each patient is also very much the same. Most people have something that shames or pains them so much they cannot bear to reveal it. Not all, but most. So they lie. The lie takes many forms. But again, simplifying my work, at its core these lies all have certain common traits. A psychiatrist's task is to help the imposter connect with what he seeks to hide from others and from himself. Do you see?"

The air was cool and dry. The afternoon was an autumn lullaby. Yet Matt felt caught within his own internal furnace. He licked his lips but could not find any word that fit the moment well enough to utter.

"The type of person you ask about has taken this to an entirely different level. They lose touch with their identity entirely. So much is suppressed, the true self might as well have died. There becomes a total separation between the internal and the external. They feel a visceral need to deny the internal self's very existence. They hunger to become someone else. They absorb, they masquerade. They lie so effectively to themselves, Mr. Kelly, that the truth no longer matters. Does that answer your question?"

———

Matt drove to Havre de Grace's outskirts and located a quiet strip mall. He turned behind the buildings, passed the employee parking, and parked between two garbage Dumpsters. He cut the motor and listened. When he was assured of silence, he sat and he practiced. Over and over.

Starting first with words he recalled the doctor using. The implied message coming from his own mouth drilled at his gut like well-aimed blows.

He had always had the mimic's gift. Only now did he wonder if this was part of living so tightly separated from his own internal state. So dissociated from who he really was he could grab hold of another's voice and verbal mannerisms, and claim them. For the moment. Claim them and then move on. Back to his stonelike state.

He dialed the Perryville number and spoke to the base operator. He was passed over to an internal line, which rang and rang. Then the woman he had spoken to that afternoon said, "Records."

"This is Alexis."

"If I hadn't forgotten my keys, you'd have missed me."

"So sorry to bother you. But I was wondering if you would please pull a file for me before you go."

"Not Grimes again."

Matt was caught totally off guard. He pulled the list from his pocket. There was no Grimes among the survivors.

"Hello?"

He cleared his throat. "Yes. Sorry. Grimes."

"The kid got to you, didn't he."

"Yes. Agent Kelly was . . ."

"Totally different from that other guy."

Matt worked his mouth, but no sound came.

"I'm telling you, that other guy totally freaked me out."

Matt managed, "Did he mention a name?"

"You asked me that before and I told you then. No name."

He started to ask when, then decided he could not risk it. "Just leave the Grimes file on my desk. I'll come by later."

"Whatever you say, Doc." She paused, then asked, "Did you tell him?"

He gaped again, then reshaped the question as a statement. "Tell young Mr. Kelly."

"About what happened with Grimes. What we found out."

"No, no. It is strictly confidential."

"And I'm telling you it's bound to come out sooner or later." But she did not sound certain. "Was I wrong to give him your number?"

"Not at all. We had a most interesting discussion."

"Okay. Well. Good night, Doc."

"Good night."

Matt cut the connection and sat staring at the mall's blank rear wall. Wishing the pieces of what he had just heard could somehow be fitted together.

Matt worked his way through a variety of stores well away from the touristy waterfront. It took him until after dark to collect everything he required. He then ate a leisurely meal. Matt took his time over coffee, wishing the restaurant's cheery din could somehow erase the doctor's words from his memory. When it was late enough, Matt took the highway from Havre de Grace back toward Perryville. The bay waters were oily black below the bridge. Perryville's waterfront was much darker than Havre de Grace. Where the base met the shoreline there was no light at all.

Matt turned off the bridge onto the road leading to the base's main gates. A half mile farther along, he turned left onto a gravel road he had spotted that afternoon. The road led down to a forest clearing, where a building or a range or something had been started and then abandoned. Matt backed his car behind a stand of loblolly pines and cut the motor. He stood beside the car and listened. The night was as warm as the afternoon. The air smelled of pinesap and earth and the bay.

He moved to the trunk and changed into the clothes he had purchased—black sweatpants, T-shirt, socks, and running shoes. He fitted the workman's belt around his middle and snugged it up tight. He loaded the belt with the gear he had acquired and set off.

He kept the bay's waters in sight but stayed well back from the shoreline. He had spotted only one patrol car for the entire base. The forest was silent, empty. Matt stopped in the last line of trees and searched.

The base appeared desolate. A half-dozen night-shift cars were in the lot by the main clinic. There was no movement on the street or the grounds. The Records Building was utterly black.

Matt left the forest at a trot. He crossed the lawn, moving from tree to tree as much as possible, staying well back from the bay. No need to offer a moving silhouette against the water.

He was breathing easy when he arrived at the back of Records. He stopped again and listened. Bats flittered overhead, chasing insects and slicing razored fragments from the stars. An owl hooted from the forest. Then nothing.

The rear porch was identical to the front, two windows deep and framed by slender pillars. At one time the structure had probably housed a proper clinic. Now not even the night could hide its forlorn state. Matt carefully tested the corner post, then climbed the railing and vaulted onto the porch roof.

More than likely a building long slated for demolition would not have an alarm system above the ground floor. But Matt did not want to take any chance of being wrong. He crossed the roof to the drainpipe and tugged. There was a rattling noise and the pipe came away in his hands. He moved down the roof, hugging the wall. The roof sagged in places and once moaned under his foot. The second drainpipe rose alongside the porch roof's opposite end. Matt gripped and tugged hard. The pipe held.

He reached up and took the pipe in a two-fisted hold. He pulled his legs up to his chest and clamped his feet to the pipe. He started climbing.

Length by length he moved up. He kept his feet well clear of the wall, for fear of pushing outward and dislodging an old bolt.

His left shoulder and ribs began aching. Paint flaked away with each new hold of his hands and feet. He could hear the patter of rust and old paint striking the porch roof below him.

Between the third and top floors, he paused and leaned out to study the roof eaves. The overhang looked far greater from this perspective than it had from below. If he went for the roof door as planned, he would have to trust his entire weight to the rain gutter, then flip himself over the edge. He glanced to each side, weighing his options. The pipe ran midway between tall sash windows, about five feet away. He decided to risk the roof.

He hugged the pipe, reached up, and took a new hold. Then the pipe crumbled below him.

One moment his feet had been gripping rust-flaked pipe. The next they flailed about the wall for purchase.

The pipe overhead rattled dangerously. Matt went very still. The pipe groaned and shifted a fraction. He reached down with his right hand and took hold of his hammer. He hung twenty-five feet above the porch by one hand, from a drainpipe that threatened to give way at any moment. The fall would probably not kill him. But it would most likely leave him unable to flee.

Matt turned the hammer around, hauled back, and slammed the hooked claw into the wooden wall. The force of his blow drove him out. Moving out dislodged the pipe. He flattened his head to the wall, gripped the hammer with both hands, and waited through the rattling rain of dust and old pipe.

Trying not to shift his body even a fraction, he searched with his toes and found a narrow opening. He jammed his left toe inside. He stretched out with his right hand and found the window ledge. His right foot found another ledge, this time a loose board. He released the hammer and took a two-handed grip on the ledge. The old-fashioned sash windows were deep and framed in oak, old and as hard as stone. He shifted over until he was in the middle of the ledge and hauled himself up.

When one foot was over the ledge, he rose by jamming his hands into opposite sides of the window frame, like he was scaling an open-ended chimney. By the time he stood upright, his entire body trembled from the strain.

His toes were well set into the frame, but most of his feet hung on air. His face lay planted upon the wall above the window, so tight he could feel the paint flecks scarring his cheek. He did not have time or strength to go for his knife and try to unhinge the window catch. Breaking the window would only add to the clamor and increase his risk of capture. He freed one hand and rammed his palm against the window frame. It creaked but held. Matt gripped the frame, took a breath. One more try. He opened his mouth in a silent roar and hauled. There was a groaning crash from inside, and then the window flew up.

Matt tumbled inside. He fell over a desk and rolled across the floor. He lay there sweating and breathing hard. Waiting for his heart to stop trying to clamber from his chest.

He rose to his feet and went back to the window. Out in the distance the lights of Havre de Grace glimmered upon the water. There was not a hint of breeze. The owl hooted again from the forest.

He closed the window, reached for his flashlight, and went searching for the right office.

Matt arrived at Maryland General just after eleven that night. Lucas D'Amico's room was two floors below where Matt had lain after the attack. The memories of the explosion and its aftermath compressed the air. He knocked on Lucas's door. At a sound from within, he opened it and said, "Mind if I run something by you?"

Lucas used the remote to cut off the television. "Pull up a chair, give me something to do besides watching the empty screen. You want a drink or something?"

"I'm good, thanks." Matt seated himself and relayed first the meeting with the Perryville nurse and the psychiatrist.

The only time Lucas spoke was when Matt described what he had read in the doctor's file. "Do I want to know how you got your hands on confidential military data?"

Matt went quiet.

Lucas pushed himself up slightly in bed. "Rookies."

Matt explained that the file was not in the name of Porter Reeves at all, but rather one Richard Grimes. Grimes had come home in the first wave of POW exchanges. He had previously been listed as KIA. No living relation. He had been captured after a firefight at Phuoc Long. Spent almost a year as a POW. Was among the first POWs released by Hanoi because of his injuries. He spent nine months in Perryville's medical wing. His doctor there brought in Alexis Turminian because of evident emotional damage that the first doctor could not hope to cure.

The psychiatrist's early notes were in his own handwriting, and at times almost took the form of a personal journal. In Richard Grimes's entire stay at Perryville, no one came to visit. Gradually this young man who had nothing and no one began to trust the doctor.

It was then that the patient had confided his name was not Richard Grimes at all.

The admission had been accidental. Then denied. Then spoken of again. As though wanting to test the doctor's reaction. The truth came out in tiny fragments. It was another eight months before the patient ever spoke his real name.

Porter Reeves had entered the army because the judge at his first felony conviction had given him a choice. Seventeen years old, facing either conviction as an adult or Vietnam. His mother died while he had been at boot. He had been disowned by his father. His first week in Nam his former girlfriend had broken off their engagement. He had nothing left of his old life.

Richard Grimes had been Porter Reeves's best friend. Perhaps his only true friend. They had both been snipers. Grimes was an orphan, another misfit with no past. But by all accounts a very good man. Nine months before Phuoc Long, Richard Grimes had been struck by a mortar round. Porter had never fully accepted the loss of his best friend.

There was a gap here, something that had happened just prior to the patient's capture that he refused to speak of. A period that had lasted from the death of his friend to that final battle. The doctor's records described in detail how Porter Reeves changed whenever the doctor tried to delve into this nine-month period. A certain fluid power began to emanate from the patient, a darkness so strong that the doctor became alert to how alone he was. How vulnerable. The patient declared that he wanted to put that behind him. The doctor agreed with relief.

The psychiatrist repeatedly wrote of how little he had to offer this man. How could his patient build upon a life that had been so utterly destroyed? Then the patient began showing an interest in developing an existence that had no connection to the past at all. He discovered not just the strength to go forward, but a purpose. He wished to reinvent himself. Of course the doctor helped the patient. How could he not? The psychiatrist helped arrange court documentation for a name change. The old files were sealed; a few were simply made to disappear. The man who was no more simply vanished.

———

Matt had no trouble with the silence that followed. He sat and let Lucas script out the data upon the ceiling. For himself, it was good to feel tired. Yet sleep was not welcome. The psychiatrist's words had branded him. No, it was good to have someone to sit with through the dark and adversarial hours.

D'Amico finally said, "I don't see a connection. Not to our case, anyway."

"What about Pecard coming to ask about this same guy?"

"If it was Pecard at all." D'Amico shrugged. "So Pecard knew some guy was a POW. So what?"

"We still don't have a motive for why Pecard would go after my family."

D'Amico nodded slow agreement. "That's been bothering me. And the chief. Bernstein brought Pecard's file last time she stopped by. Basically what we already know. British army, military intel, long list of decorations. Wounded while doing some classified investigation in Vietnam." D'Amico shrugged his good shoulder. "Doesn't help us much."

"So you don't think I should phone Washington with what I've found."

"Midnight on Saturday?" D'Amico actually smiled. "Oh. I get it. A fed's idea of a joke. Cute."

Matt rose from his chair. "I better let you get some rest."

"You mind if I ask a favor?"

"Sure."

"Could you take Katy to church tomorrow?"

"Today," Matt corrected, pointing at the clock. It was just after midnight. "No problem."

"Sharla can swing by after. Katy's going over there for lunch anyway. But Sharla sings in her own church's choir, so it'd be tough for her to make the morning run. Katy really doesn't like missing her church."

"It's fine, Lucas. I'll stay for a while and take her to your partner's home afterward."

Matt started for the door. But his feet would not follow through. He found himself trapped within the same old struggle. Only tonight Matt heard the words he wished he was able to say. About the nightmare. And what the nightmares were based upon. The moment he had left his body. The instant he had died. Wishing he could figure out this sense of missing purpose, the reason he had come back. Wanting to figure out why he was so *dissatisfied* all the time.

About Connie. About all the past mistakes he wished he could just make go away.

Lucas asked, "You okay?"

"No." Slowly Matt returned to his chair. He stared down at the floor. And forced out the words he had been carrying for a lifetime. "Nothing seems to fit."

Lucas just let the words hang there.

Matt felt clammy from the struggle. "No matter how good the moment, it all stays wrong. And I stay empty."

Lucas made sure Matt was done for the time being. Then, "Fill up that cup, will you?"

Matt plied the pitcher, then refitted the top and straw. All without looking directly at the other man.

Lucas drank most of the cup. Sighed. Settled back on his pillow. "Year after I made detective, I was chasing this punk. My partner was three years from retiring and I left him in my dust. Took a lot of pleasure in that. Running down this kid in gang-wear and cornrows and flash shoes. Only the punk had a round left in the gun I thought was empty. When I trapped him in the alley, he got off his shot. I took one high in the chest. Punctured a lung. Only reason I'm talking about it today is my partner went back for the car and scouted alleys until he found me."

Matt remained unable to lift his gaze. But he listened. And no longer felt such mortal shame over having spoken.

"I was laid up for three and a half weeks, off active duty for another four months. Being on desk almost killed me. But what was worse was the *fear*. I dreamed about that punk and his gun for a long time. The dream was always the same. How he walked up and looked down at me lying there gasping for one more breath, and surprise, he had *another* round. It started having an effect on our marriage. Took me six months to go crawling to my pastor, Ian Reeves. He told me the same thing I'm gonna tell you. The stronger the guy, the harder it is to be weak. But everybody is, Matt. Everybody. Forget death and taxes. The one rule you can take to the bank is this: Everybody is weak at one point or another. And when one weakness is revealed, out come the others. Which makes it a bad time for guys like you and me."

"Terrible," Matt murmured to the floor at his feet.

"There's a chance here, though. A chance to learn a secret about yourself. I had two taught to me then. What terrified me most was losing June. I didn't deserve her. But she loved me and we were happy. So long as I didn't face up to my fear, I was pushing her away. My denial actually made the fear a reality; you see what I'm saying?"

Matt wished he had the strength to lift his head and meet the man's gaze. It was not much to ask for, but impossible just the same.

Eventually Lucas went on, "I learned to take it one day at a time, love her the most and the best I could. Then, when she really did have to go, I could at least feel like I'd done the most I could with the days we had."

Matt tried to remember if he had ever talked like this with anyone before. He wondered why it felt so normal. Which gave the moment a bittersweet edge. He clenched himself up hard, lifted his head, found the strength to ask, "And the second lesson?"

Lucas D'Amico had eyes that burned with a fire that threatened as much as it sparked. "That I couldn't do it alone."

Judy Leigh's Sunday morning call caught Connie as she was running Katy a bath. "What did you have planned for today?"

"I was thinking of going home, washing my hair, trying out my new hammock. Yesterday I played housekeeper for D'Amico's kid. Matt's due any minute to take her to church."

"Is that her I hear singing?"

"Yeah, that's our Katy." Connie lowered her voice. "And if I hear another round of the butterfly song, I'm going for the Mace."

"Bad?"

"No, Katy's a sweetheart. But I miss playing with adults, you know?"

"Not yet. But I will soon." Judy sighed. "My husband's making noises like he wants me to go freelance after the baby's born. I hate how appealing that sounds."

"You looking for Matt?"

"No. You. I just spoke with Lucas. He said you might be available." The reporter hesitated, then said, "I've got something. About the family."

"His father?"

"Partly."

"His mom?"

"You could say so."

"Bad?"

"I have no idea."

She checked her watch. "Matt's due here in twenty minutes. Tell me where we can meet."

———

Sunday morning's nightmare was as subdued as the gray dawn, a faint smudge against the window of his brain. Matt dressed, ate, and left the house. Rain threatened but did not fall. Even the wind seemed to be holding its breath, gathering for a push hard enough to shove an entire world from one season to the next.

Matt drove to the cemetery and walked out to stand by his mother's grave. It was the first time he had been there since the funeral. The simple black headstone was so perfect for Megan Kelly he could have wept. But there was a bitter weakness to weeping over a rock yet not for his mother. So he put it down deep with all the other emotions he did not know how to express.

Matt knew that the reason he hunted the killer was in order to give some concrete expression to his grief. He also knew his mother would not have cared about vengeance.

The headstone had one segment that was polished and inscribed. It flowed naturally from the rest, which had been left rough-hewn and jagged. Natural and flawed and polished and elegant. So much perfection in being left imperfect. It was a lovely stone. He leaned forward and traced his hand over the rough and the smooth. If only he could give his mother what he knew she wanted from her son.

A hesitant wind pushed leaves across the path as he headed back. Dusty pale sheaves of time past, whispering fragments of all that was lost.

———

The Sunday morning newsroom was a vacuum that smelled vaguely of yesterday's stress. Connie said, "It sure is quiet."

Judy Leigh wore a dark smock that billowed like a pirate sail as she led Connie back to her desk. "Yeah, but come the hour before deadline on a big day, you could drive a pack of mastodons down the center aisle and nobody'd notice unless they were short a headline."

She pointed Connie into a seat. "I've been thinking. The paper and the force, we're not supposed to be the best of pals, right?"

"Nobody knows I'm here, Judy."

"And I'm not telling a soul you're working for the dark side."

They shared a grin. Connie said, "Tell me what you need."

"I've got two possible leads. Both may be nothing. But I also have a problem. I assume Ugly told you about my being ordered off any story to do with his family?"

"Ugly?"

"My in-house name for young Kelly. It helps keep things in perspective for an old married woman like myself." She picked up a pencil and began tapping her desk. "What about you, you tied down?"

"No."

"Girl, what's your problem? I'd be after that hunk in a heartbeat. He didn't like it, tough. That's why the city gave you cuffs and a gun."

Connie felt her face flame. "We were talking about your problem. Not mine."

"Sure we were." But Judy was grinning. "Here's the deal. I give you what I know. You go ask questions I've been ordered not to ask."

"So if it proves to be nothing, then your paper isn't involved."

"Right. And if it is, we share."

Connie reached for her bag. "Let's roll."

———

Lucas was late shaving because he'd been on the phone with his partner for almost an hour. Clarence had been ordered to stay away from the hospital, for fear his lung infection was contagious. So they talked by phone each morning. It was the sort of roundabout discussion two guys would be expected to have, kids and doctors and work and football. Anything but what was really on their minds. Even so, it was a bright spot to his day.

Lucas was almost done shaving when Hannah Bernstein knocked on his door. She pushed it open, not waiting for a response. "Oh, I'm so sorry."

"Hannah, no, don't go." Hastily he wiped his face with the bath towel.

"I can come back later."

"What for? I'm done." Lucas couldn't believe how glad he was to see her. "You look great."

She wore a smooth rich blue turtleneck so soft looking it had to be cashmere and slacks one shade darker. She wore another turquoise-and-silver pin, her only jewelry. "Do me a favor and push this table out of the way, will you?"

"Of course." She rolled the table over beside the window. When she started to rinse the bowl and razor in the sink, he said, "That's what nurses are for."

"I don't mind."

He liked watching her move, liked the way she filled the room's empty spaces. So much so it was not until she came over and sat down in the chair by his bed that he noticed. "Something the matter?"

She waved it away. "How are you feeling?"

Now that she was close and his surprise had faded, he could see the tension. It tightened her lips and crinkled the skin around her eyes and pulled the skin of her face back until she looked pale beneath her blusher. But it was not his nature to press. "They say I can go home Tuesday. Wednesday at the latest."

"That's good news, Lucas." She tried to put some feeling into it. But missed.

"Matt was in here last night. Left me with a tapeworm of an idea. You know the kind. They twist and weave and get in everywhere."

He waited for her to ask what it was. But she started toying with her watch dial. Giving him the impression he was observing a lady do her best to turn back the clock.

So he went on, "I've spent a lot of time laying here thinking about Katy."

She looked up then, connecting with him at last. "There's a problem with your daughter? Why didn't you say something? I could have—"

"Not with Katy. She's fine. We talk two, three times a day. She's staying nights with my partner and his wife. Connie has been over there in the day. Using her free time to look after my little girl. Can you believe it?"

A note of sorrow crept in. A fragment of whatever she had brought with her but wasn't ready to release. "Yes, Lucas. I absolutely believe Connie Morales is delighted to help you out."

Lucas told her about the talk with his pastor. And what Sharla had to say. And Katy's words that morning after the failed pancakes. Then about the church-run home. "It was set up a dozen years or so ago. A wealthy parishioner had a severely disabled son. She was getting on in years and she had all these problems, diabetes, weak heart, you name it. She wanted her boy to have a nice place to live after she left. So she turned her home into a managed-care facility. When the place next door came on the market, she bought that one and made it a hospice. She lived out her last days there, with her son next door. The facility has fourteen single rooms. Communal living and dining. Nurse on duty 24/7. Doctor always on call."

"It sounds lovely."

"Katy likes it there a lot. She has friends. She gardens."

Hannah was watching intently. "You'll miss her."

"It's not like she's moving to Mars. The place is two blocks from our church."

"But it's not the same, is it. She won't be living at home."

If there was a strangeness, confessing his deepest worry to his boss, Lucas could not find it. "Since June died, the hours I keep, it hasn't been much of one. A home."

She studied him with those intelligent gray eyes of hers. "There might be something else at work here. She might be growing up in her own way. Did you ever think of that?"

He had to look away. Swallow hard against the lump. "No, Hannah. I hadn't. But you're right."

He looked back. Ready to thank her. But Hannah's features were stained once again by whatever it was she had carried in with her. "Can't you tell me what's the matter?"

It was her turn to swallow audibly, then speak in a voice that sounded choked. "I've been sacked."

"What?"

"It was messengered to my house this morning. Terminated. Effective immediately. The letter was written like I'd been convicted of a felony. My personal effects will be collected and shipped over. There is no need for me to reenter police headquarters, and if I insist on doing so, I must have a police escort at all times. Like that."

"They can't do that."

"I'm a mini-major, remember. Political appointee. I serve at the mayor's pleasure."

"Hannah, you're the best chief I've ever known."

She patted his arm, said nothing.

"Who do they plan to replace you with?"

She continued to pat his arm. Not speaking with anything except her gaze.

———

Matt's progress out of church was slowed to a crawl by all the people who wanted to speak with Katy. He stood back a fraction and watched. They hugged her with such warmth he assumed they knew about Lucas. But no one said anything, not to her, nor to him.

Even so, Katy knew enough to ask the pastor, "Is my daddy all right?"

Ian Reeves stood by the rear doors, glad-handing with a genuineness all his own. "Of course he is. Don't you talk with him on the phone?"

"Every morning and every night."

"Then why would you ask such a question?"

Katy had a bland sort of voice that did not inflect. "Because you tell me the truth."

Ian blinked slowly. "Katherine D'Amico, your father is coming home."

Katy turned and walked down the stairs without another word.

Ian waited until she had moved well away and been enveloped by yet another group to ask Matt, "How is he really?"

"Good. Getting better."

"Give Lucas my best and tell him not to make a liar of me. Will you do that?"

Matt was halfway to the Bledsoes' before he thought to turn on his phone. Katy watched him pull up to a stop sign and slip it from his pocket. "Daddy does the same thing."

"Does he?"

"After church." She nodded. "Every time."

He was surprised to find he had nine messages. On a Sunday. In two hours. But Katy was watching him in that somber way that left him feeling like he was doing something wrong. So he started to put it away, when it rang.

"Daddy's does that too," Katy said, talking now to her window.

"This is Matt."

"Lucas here. Where are you?"

"Pulling up to the Bledsoes'."

"You gotten my messages?"

"No."

"Drop Katy off and head straight for headquarters."

"What's wrong?"

"Call me back when you drop her off," Lucas said. "Hurry."

Matt bounded through the elevator doors and entered an entirely different homicide division. Detectives stood around wearing expressions of the shocked and bereaved. Matt asked, "Anybody seen Connie?"

Lieutenant Crowder and the reporter, Judy Leigh, were talking by the case board. "In the chief's office."

Matt pushed through the outer door. A heavyset officer Matt did not recognize was seated at one of the desks. "Help you?"

Matt broke stride only to smack open the chief's door.

"Hey! You can't—"

A narrow man with slicked-back hair stood behind the chief's desk. He had eyes the color of congealed mud and a slit of a smile. "It's all right, Sergeant. We were just talking about Agent Kelly. Weren't we, Morales."

Connie turned to him. She said calmly, "They've fired the chief."

"Hannah Bernstein is ancient history," Lieutenant Calfo corrected. "We were talking about your own career, Officer Morales."

"There's nothing to discuss, Hands. The minute you set foot in this office, I was already gone."

Matt said, "Don't do it, Connie."

She didn't even bother with heat. "You think I'd work a minute for him?"

A fraction of teeth glinted in Calfo's smile. "The girl's right, Kelly. She'd be up on charges if she stays. We're talking disciplinary hearing, IA, who knows, maybe even the courts." Back to Connie. "Save us the trouble, Morales. Quit."

"Don't give him what he wants," Matt said.

But Connie was turning for the door. "I'm already having trouble finding air, the stench is so bad."

"Connie, listen to me. Since when did you ever do what Hands ordered?"

Calfo said, "She's smarter than you, Kelly. She knows what's good for her."

"Lucas told me to tell you, Connie. Hang on."

She seemed to crawl out of a hole she had dug for herself somewhere deep inside. "Lucas said that?"

"Oh, right." Calfo was sneering now. "Like D'Amico's got any business offering advice."

"He said if you quit, they can say what they want to the press. If you stay, you force them to level charges. Which means proof. Which they don't have."

"Morales—"

Connie chopped a hand toward Calfo. "I couldn't spend five minutes working for him. Not after seeing what it's like to work with real cops."

Calfo flushed. "You're out of order, Morales."

"You don't have to," Matt said. "I've spoken with Washington. You're hereby seconded to the Homeland Security office as senior liaison. Assigned to work with me on an ongoing federal investigation."

She let her hand drop. "For real?"

"What investigation, Kelly?" Calfo gradually shifted from sneer to genuine rage. "We've already made the collar for you."

"You found Pecard?"

The laugh was coppery and too loud for the room. "We're not interested in whatever grudge match you feds are carrying on. No, Kelly. We've gone after the real culprit. The original one."

Connie gripped his arm. "This is futile. Worthless. Let's go."

"I had a word with the deputy commissioner, Kelly. He's lodging a formal complaint with Washington. How you undermined a police investigation to protect one of your assets." Hands stayed behind his desk, chasing them with his voice. "Talk about twisted! Just like a fed, Kelly. Covering your tracks even when it means shielding the murderer of your own mother!"

———

"Matt. Focus. Down here. Look at me."

They stood in the free-fire zone between the bull pen, the chief's offices, and the elevators. He released the steel band around his chest. Took a breath.

Connie obviously saw a difference. She relaxed a trifle and demanded, "What are you doing here?"

"Lucas sent me to make sure you didn't do anything rash."

"He sent you to make me behave?" Connie developed a tic in the right edge of her mouth. She rubbed her nose. "That's a good one."

"What's so funny about that?"

"Man, when you zoned out there at the end, I was about ready to call for backup."

Matt glanced at the closed outer door. "One little bullet, Connie. That's not so much to ask."

Lieutenant Crowder stepped into his line of vision. Judy Leigh trailed a few paces back, close enough to catch it all, far enough away to dive for cover if required. Crowder said, "I believe the rule book's got something about shooting a police chief inside headquarters."

"Hands is not a chief."

"Mayor's office says different. I called, just to make sure."

Connie asked, "Who'd they arrest for the Kelly murder?"

"Some Aryan dude. All I know is, Hands used his chums over in Division One for the collar. Guess he figured we'd laugh in his face."

Connie said to Matt, "I've got friends over there. Let's go ask around."

Matt was still looking at the office door. "Hands is not a chief."

"You said that already." Crowder poked his chest with an iron-hard finger. "Now you get out there and catch us some bad guys."

———

The jail had special interview rooms available for arrestees to meet their lawyers. The rooms were the size of cells, windowless, and empty save for two metal stools bolted to either side of a dented metal table. Calvin

Hogue was in one, seated across from his court-appointed attorney, when they all trooped in. The attorney rose to his feet. Calvin did not. He couldn't, being chained to both the table and the floor.

The attorney demanded, "What is this?"

They entered single file. First Matt, then Connie, then Vic Wright, then Judy Leigh. The chamber's dense air seemed reluctant to make room.

Calvin was just as Matt remembered from their last encounter, at Vic's dojo the morning before his mother perished. The same bald skull, heavy beard, muscles, tattoo, sneer. Only the chains were different.

Calvin was all attitude. "What is this, a parade?"

The lawyer protested, "We're holding a confidential attorney-client meeting."

"Oh, you want them to be here," Vic said. "Believe me."

"And you are?"

Vic pointed at the man chained to the desk. "Ask your man here."

Then Calvin said to Matt, "I know you."

"Hello, Calvin."

"You're that fed." He tracked to Vic and back. "Sure."

Matt said, "You had nothing to do with the murder of Megan Kelly."

"Are you asking or telling?"

Vic replied, "I'm here to tell you this is for real, Calvin."

The lawyer demanded. "How about you showing me some ID."

Everyone but Vic did as he asked. The attorney demanded, "And you are?"

"Don't mind him, man. Vic is cool." Calvin said to Matt, "I ain't diming on nobody."

Matt said, "I'll do everything I can to get you released. My help is not contingent on your helping us with anything, Calvin. Sooner or later, the charges against you will be dropped. It may take a while. But I'm going to see to it. Personally."

The attorney took his time over the IDs. "Baltimore police, Department of State, and the *Times*."

Connie said, "Boggles the mind, doesn't it."

The attorney handed them back. "You're stating for the record that my client is innocent of the charges leveled against him?"

"We are not the arresting officers, and we don't have the required evidence yet. But we know the charges against him are trumped up, and we're going to do our best to get him cleared." Matt looked at Calvin. "I have a question, but you don't have to answer if you don't want to."

"So if I answer, it's something for nothing, that it?"

"Yes."

Calvin liked that. "So ask."

"Ever heard the name Porter Reeves?"

Calvin thought a second. "Nope."

"How about Richard Grimes?"

Something came and went, very fast, very deep. "That's question two."

"But you know him."

"What if I don't say?"

"I told you. We are going to work for your release regardless."

Calvin shrugged with his beard. "The name. Yeah. I heard it."

"Where?"

"Around. He's bad news."

"Dangerous?"

"Man, walking the streets in this town is dangerous. Richard Grimes, we're talking dead and gone."

"He's a gun for hire?"

"I mighta heard that."

"You know where we might find him?"

"I heard he lives around Baltimore someplace. We done?"

"Yes." Matt was the last to leave. He stepped out the door, then backed up far enough to say, "Richard Grimes is not Aryan?"

"'Course not." The smirk was back. "Only reason we're talking at all."

———

Lucas lay in bed counting holes in the popcorn ceiling, so bored he hummed Katy's butterfly tune in time to the heart monitor. He missed Katy. It was the longest they had been apart since his wife's death. Katy's absence and the void in his life from June's departure had somehow gotten tangled together. He knew there was no way around the situation.

He thought back to the last day with June. He had come into the hospice where they'd moved her, the one separated from Katy's house by the garden. He had walked into his wife's room and asked how she was. June had looked up at him and replied, "You know what they say, hon. The times, they are a'changing."

Lucas jerked to full alert. He realized how he had just shaped that thought. *Katy's house.*

Which was how Connie found him when she slipped inside the room. Wide-eyed and convicted. "Lucas, hey, how you doing?"

"It itches." His wound and the truth both.

"You want me to find somebody?"

"No, no, come on in. I'm bored, that's how I'm doing. I'd pay good money for some company."

"I come cheap." She dragged over a chair. "But I need some advice."

"Fire away. Sorry. Cop humor."

"I've found out something about Matt's family. We have a couple more people to interview this morning, but it's just confirmation now. I'm pretty sure we've got the real goods."

Talking only drew the dark worry Connie was carrying closer to the surface. Lucas went into work mode, what Clarence called "the gentle inquirer." Not pressing. More like inviting. "So you've found out something about Matt."

"His parents."

"His father?"

"Some. Mostly it's about his mother."

He caught the edge. "Do you want to tell me what it is?"

"I'd rather wait until I know for sure."

"That's a good idea." He gave her a minute, then suggested, "You're worried about telling him?"

She nodded and kept on nodding. Like it was such a relief to have it out, some kind of motion was required.

"My guess is, he already knows."

"He can't."

"This is one sharp kid, Connie. He was the one who came to us, remember? He's turned up one key factor after another faster than me, and I've been on the force a long time. He might not know exactly what you're going to say. But he's got some idea."

"It's bad, Lucas."

"Yeah, I suspect it probably is. But he's a strong kid. And the way you're looking at me, I can tell you something else. He won't have to confront it alone."

She sat there awhile. Lucas liked this about her, the stillness, the way she was comfortable in her own skin. Which made what happened next all the more surprising.

Her breath caught up short and the strength in her face gave way. The hard defensive wall a good cop needs abruptly turned into a window. For a single instant Lucas could look through the window and see her soul. Then she built the wall back up through sheer determination, a lesson every cop has to learn in order to survive out there on the street. Lucas knew what it cost, being strong like that. And how much she needed to let go just then. But she had to do it.

He said, "It's okay, Connie. Whatever it is, you can tell me."

She looked like an athlete strained to the ultimate level, every angle in her face and neck and shoulders pulled beyond taut. The strain couldn't hold. She folded down.

Connie rested her forehead on the side of his bed. She said something to his bedspread.

"Lift up, I can't hear you."

She waited until she had her breath under control. She kept her face hidden, but he caught it now. "I love him so much."

He didn't need to ask. But he did so because she needed him there with her. "We're talking about Matt."

"Yeah." She pushed herself back into the chair. A tear dislodged from one eye and rolled down her cheek. She looked about ten years old. "I'm such a loser at love. Wrong guys, wrong moves. That's me."

This was a new one for Lucas. He wanted to fold her in his good arm, stroke her face, wipe her eyes, and call her sweetheart. But this was a cop. And his subordinate. Which made things almost funny.

Connie spotted the smile he thought he had hidden away. "You think I'm stupid, right?"

"No, Connie. I think you're incredible. Smart, street-sharp, beautiful, and good-hearted. I think Matt Kelly is so lucky I could slug him."

She half-laughed, half-cried. "He's also locked up inside tight as a vault."

He nodded. Playing the detective. Loving this. A beautiful young woman seated in his little white world, spilling out her heart like he had the answer to anything. Loving it. "So we've got two problems, not one. First, there's how you keep from making old mistakes all over again. Then there's Matt. And the best way I've found to solve problems is to separate them out. So maybe we should take you first. Okay so far?"

She pulled a tissue from the box on his bedside table and wiped her nose. "I tried to talk myself out of coming over here. But I was right to come. I knew it then and I know it now."

"I'm sure somebody's told me something that nice before. But I can't put my finger on exactly when." He shifted. "Push that button and raise me up a notch."

"How's that?"

"Better. Okay. When I was just starting off, we had a system of pairing the new rookie detectives with old guys nearing retirement. My first partner was this guy, Malloy, what a piece of work." Lucas let the smile out this time. He hadn't thought of Malloy in years. "A real fighting Paddy, taller than your guy, strong as an ox even at sixty."

She made a better attempt at a smile this time. "My guy. I wish."

"Malloy was real Irish Catholic. Mass every day, always worked it into shift. Did his rounds with a rosary, wore it across his front like a watch-chain. There were a lot of guys like that back then. Tough as old iron but bighearted. All you hear about these days are the rogues, the guys who went on the take. And there were some of them as well. But not as many as the papers would like you to think. But good guys don't make for headlines."

She was breathing easier now and listening carefully. Which was what he'd intended all along with his trip down memory lane. "Malloy told me something early on, soon as he decided I was actually listening. If it's not part of your core, the street will eat you up. Your goodness, your caring, your love, everything that connects you to the rest of life beyond your job. All gone. Unless you make it part of your core."

Connie gave him time, then asked, "How do I do that?"

"That's exactly what I asked him. I mean, we were two cops, out there facing the worst the world could throw at us. You know what he told me?"

"No."

"He said, you accept the fact that you can't make it happen on your own."

Lucas waited for her to give it back. How he wasn't making sense. How she'd come in with one question and he'd given her something she didn't need.

Instead, she leaned back. Nodded once. Said very softly, "Okay."

Lucas did not realize he had tensed up. He released half a breath and felt the confidence to say, "I'll tell you one thing more, and this one is from me. Out there, most people want you to think nobody can change. You get hooked into one life and one view of people and relationships and the world at large. They're right, but only if you let them be. Only if you buy their take on things. Only if you go it alone."

She spoke the words softly, tasting them with the easy manner of trusting him fully. "And Matt?"

"You can only give what you've found for yourself, Connie. That's the simplest way I know to tell you."

———

Connie sat and argued with love. Nothing else could have brought her here. The love was real, at least from her side. And what Lucas had told her upstairs was right. All she could really deal with was herself.

As if that wasn't enough.

Connie had the hospital chapel totally to herself. The place was not much larger than a standard hospital room. It was fitted out with rows of padded wooden benches, an empty podium, and two false windows dressed up with stained glass lit from behind. The floor was heavily carpeted. The air conditioner sighed a constant hush that drowned out most of the hospital noise. Lilies on a corner table filled the room with their fragrance. Connie stared at the cross on the front wall, filled with images of her own dire need.

A small part of her wished she could retreat from the talk with

Lucas, just wave her hands and forget it ever happened. This same whispering voice kept telling her the whole thing was insane. She was a *cop*. She was paid to be tough. Connie wiped one cheek and wished the AC could ratchet up another notch, go loud enough to shut out this internal clamor. Because the truth was staring her in the face. She had spent a lifetime making her own choices, proudly stepping out totally on her own. And look where it had gotten her. When it came to love, Connie had a dead-solid lock on bad moves and worse men.

The hardest part was not in acknowledging she had made mistakes. What was far worse was accepting she had known they were mistakes going in. But she had made them anyway. Taken pride in all those wrong moves. Like the acts had somehow made her stronger. Tougher. Defined just how independent this one woman was.

She took both hands to clear her cheeks. A box of tissues rested upon the altar table, saying in silent eloquence that here, in this place, it was all right to cry. She gripped the pew-back in front of her, momentarily tempted by anger. It would be so easy to reduce Matt and her feelings to simply another reason for turning away.

Then she just gave in. A soft sigh was all she showed the outside world. A shake of the head. A weary lowering of her eyes. Nothing really. Just another person seated in just another empty room. Looking for the strength to take the next step.

Matt drove to Washington beneath a sky so dark and sullen it looked almost green. Van Sant had called and ordered him to report in person. The traffic was light until he hit the Beltway, where it grew as dense and surly as the weather. Matt carried his own cloudy dilemma with him. He entered the top floor of State Intel to find Van Sant with two allies from Homeland Security. Matt made his report and lodged his formal objection over the firing of Chief Hannah Bernstein. He fielded their questions the best he could. Van Sant walked him back to the elevators and said something about the job he was doing. But the buzz in Matt's brain was too tight for him to hear it clearly.

It was long after dark when he finally drove back to Baltimore. The earthbound glow turned the clouds a sickly orange. Matt was chased home by the same illogical certainty that had followed him south. He was missing something big.

Just after ten, Matt turned off Howard onto the back alley that brought him up behind the house. He locked his car and entered the yard by way of the carport gate. He unlocked his apartment and turned on the light and dropped his keys on the kitchen table. All the normal actions of coming home.

Then he stopped. He stood beside the sink, looking out over the back lawn. All the lights in the carriage house were off except one. Some staffer had failed to cut off a desk lamp. A streetlight glowed above the carport. Otherwise the back of the house was dark. There was no sound. Matt sensed at deep gut level that something was seriously wrong.

He cut off his light. Stepped outside the door. Listened carefully. The house was utterly silent.

He unholstered his weapon and walked toward the front of the house. The police car parked by the front stairs came into view. He scanned up and down the street. There was no sign of movement.

He slipped through the front gate and stepped across the street. He turned around and studied the house. A couple of the downstairs lights were still on, which would be normal if the cops had taken up position inside the house. But Matt lived in this house. He knew how it breathed. There was an undercurrent he could sense even from this distance.

Matt had been around people like Vic, whose natural abilities had been honed in various war zones. He knew what it was like to be around somebody with eyes in the back of their head and the ability to smell a fire before it was lit. He had never wished for such a talent until now.

A silhouette passed across the second-floor window where his parents' bedroom opened into the central hallway. Moving fast. Far too tall and broad-shouldered to be his father.

Matt sprinted across the street and around to the back of the house. He feared the front door would be watched—or wired. He clambered up the wrought-iron balustrades supporting the kitchen porch. He searched inside the hanging flower basket for the emergency key and opened the rear door. He took the safety off his gun and stepped inside. He pulled the door to but did not relatch it. And listened.

The air smelled of cordite. Matt crouched low and checked the central hall. It was empty. He stepped to the side passage and entered the dining room. The sideboard had been overturned and the dining table shoved off the carpet, scarring grooves in the polished wood floor. The living room sofa lay on its back. One of the cops was sprawled on the carpet and moaning slightly. Matt crawled over and checked. No visible wounds.

Matt continued on. The door leading from the living room to the front foyer was drilled with two gunshots. There was glass everywhere, and the interior front doors were hollow frames, the stained-glass panels shattered. The second cop was down by the front door. Matt could see now what had happened. The first cop had answered the doorbell. He was brought down. The second cop fired. Missed. Was taken out. What by, Matt was not sure. Because neither man was bleeding. Matt put his head to the officer's chest and heard the slow, steady thump. He shook the man. There was not even a groan in reply.

Matt threaded his way through the glass and started up the stairs.

When he hit the middle step, all the lights in the house went out.

Matt froze. He breathed through his mouth, waiting until his eyes fully adjusted. Then he holstered his weapon and flipped over the stair railing. He slipped down so that one hand held him by the stairs' edge and the other by the railing post. He hung out over nothing and began inching himself up. He came to the top stair and worked his way around the corner, moving down the outer ledge of the upstairs landing. He heard nothing. Five feet farther on, he strained and drew himself up just high enough so his eyes came above floor level.

For an instant he saw nothing except a hall in disarray. As though his father had come out of his bedroom, seen the attacker, and started tossing everything within reach between himself and the assailant. Matt felt a tight pleasure in the fact that at least his father had put up a fight.

Then a shadow detached itself from the wall.

Matt watched him move. Tall, incredibly strong, lithe, silent. Illumination from the streetlights and the moon turned him to liquid ink. He wore a ski mask and dark clothes and gloves. He carried Paul Kelly over one shoulder. Even so burdened, he was light on his feet. He moved to the top of the stairwell, so quiet all Matt could hear was his own heart's violent thumping.

The attacker took aim with something and fired down the stairwell. There was a sharp *zing*, then a tight little flash. Matt realized that the attacker held a stun gun, one that fired energy-darts connected to the handheld power-base by spring wires. The attacker jerked the darts free from the stairwell wall. There was a zipping sound as the darts rewound, then the soft, upward-rising hum of the gun recharging.

The attacker stood there a moment longer, then started down the stairs.

Even if he could have reached his gun, Matt could not have fired without risk of hitting his father. Matt waited until he was midway down the stairs before scaling the railing. As he flipped over the rail, the landing creaked beneath his weight.

The attacker spun about. Something thumped the side wall, perhaps Paul Kelly's head, because he let out a moan. Matt leaped down the length of the hall, tumbled and rolled at the top of the stairs, gathered himself by gripping the carpet with his hands, and leaped out.

But the assailant was not there.

Matt flew over the attacker's crouch, reaching down, gripping at nothing but the dark stairwell. Like the assailant had the ability to transfer into smoke at will. Matt was saved only by landing hard on the cop. He rolled and scrunched across the glass, searching for cover. Only to come up with the assailant's leg directly beside him.

Matt grabbed and jerked. Or started to. The assailant fired the stun gun from point-blank range.

The darts pinched into Matt's chest. The zinging noise joined with a humming as violent as a billion stinging bees. A voice growled, "This time you'll lay down and *stay* down."

Matt was knocked far, far away.

The next morning, Matt drove two ladies to the pastor's house. Connie was in the passenger seat of his BMW, Judy Leigh in the back. Neither woman spoke. Connie watched him with the same caring concern she had shown up with half an hour earlier. Matt drove with single-minded intent, struggling hard to keep a firm grip on the day.

As they turned onto Charles Street, Connie said, "You don't need to do this."

The buzzing in his ears had passed. His muscles no longer jumped with tight electric aftershocks. He was left with a dull metallic taste and a vague throbbing deep inside his skull. "Do you have any aspirin?"

Connie fished inside her shoulder bag and took two from a plastic container. "I'll tell you everything I find out."

He chewed the aspirins and swallowed them dry. He turned onto Mount Vernon and looked for a parking place. "I have to be there, Connie."

Her only response was to reach over and take his hand. And look at him. Clearly not caring that Judy Leigh could see her emotions unsheathed. "You're not alone in this. Tell me you understand what I'm saying."

Matt did not know how to respond. Given what lay ahead, she should have been in full cop mode. Instead, Connie was showing him a side he had never known before. One so deep he felt that he could dive into her gaze, lose himself in the warm, dark concern.

His phone granted him a reason to pull back. "This is Kelly."

"Van Sant. Any word?"

"Hang on a second, let me finish parking." He handed Connie the phone, then repressed a groan as he strained and turned and wound the wheel. He cut the motor, retrieved the phone, and reported, "Nothing so far."

Matt had awakened on the floor of the house's front foyer when one of the cops he'd found unconscious had shaken him hard. He'd spent hours answering questions, first from the local officers and then a second time when Bryan Bannister had arrived and formally taken charge of the investigation. Finally Matt had escaped downstairs and slept badly to the tune of cops at work overhead. Three hours later he had given up and risen to call Lucas. Morning had spread a sullen gray light upon the sight of five campaign staffers standing in front of the carriage house, fretful and scared. A cop and a fibbie were both questioning them. A crowd of reporters and onlookers clustered behind the police barricades. Television news vans had dug furrows in the park grass across the street from the home's main entrance. Antennae sprouted among the autumn foliage. Then Connie had arrived and delivered the news that had shattered his world even further.

Van Sant asked, "How are you?"

Sore. Tired. Both were understatements. Back at the house Bryan Bannister had explained they'd been struck by a stun gun rewired to heighten the charge. But Matt didn't want to get into that. "What have you found?"

"There is no official record of any kind for either Richard Grimes or Porter Reeves. Bank, driver's license, credit cards, nothing."

"So he lives and works under a third name."

"What we figured as well."

"Thanks, Jack. I need to go."

"Updates, Kelly. That's what Washington runs on. Keep us in the loop here."

Matt hung up and dialed the hospital. D'Amico answered on the first ring. "I need help with something at the local level and I don't know who else to ask."

"So talk."

Matt relayed what they had learned at the prison the previous afternoon. "I asked Van Sant to check for a last known address. He came up with nothing."

"I'm still having trouble making a connection between Pecard and Grimes."

"It's a long shot," Matt agreed. "But I've got this hunch . . ."

"You want me to ask around."

If only he could clear his head enough to think in a straight line. "Maybe you're right. Maybe we should drop it."

"No, no. Can't hurt. Besides, it'll be nice to play detective for a while, even on the phone. Hannah's coming back over in a while; I'll ask her to help."

Matt hated the idea of involving the chief with something so nebulous. But he had no strength for arguing at that point. "Calvin knew a Richard Grimes. Which means Grimes is probably living around here. Somebody on the street might have an address, a hangout, something."

"I'll get on this." D'Amico paused, then asked, "Is Connie with you?"

"Right here."

"Can I have a word?"

He handed over the phone. Heard her answer. Matt used two knuckles to press at the throbbing in his temples. Maybe the physical pain wasn't altogether a bad thing. Maybe it would distance him from what he was bound to discover inside.

Connie handed back the phone. Still watching him with a calm that suffused and unsettled in equal measure. "If we're going, let's go."

Matt opened his door. "Judy . . ."

"I'll stay." She raised her pad. "I've got plenty to keep me busy."

Matt did his best not to limp as they headed down the street. He pressed Ian's buzzer and then asked Connie, "Mind if I ask what Lucas told you?"

"He wanted to know if you were doing this thing. I said yes." She spoke with a softness that matched the gaze. "He said to be strong for you."

"Connie—"

Ian Reeves answered the door in his off-duty gear of rumpled slacks, corduroy house slippers, and yesterday's dress shirt. "Matt. Always a pleasure."

"Ian, this is Connie Morales."

"The young police officer who called earlier." His smile was so warm and genuine it momentarily fit his face into proper form. "And with you. How nice."

"Ian, we have to ask you some questions about Mom."

"Matt, I've repeatedly told you—"

"And Porter Reeves."

The smile was gone. "Porter is dead."

"We have to do this, Ian. Here or at police headquarters. And it has to be now."

The pastor looked from one face to the next. Then stepped away from the door.

They followed him inside.

———

The house's parlor was almost English in its seedy grandeur. Matt pulled over a hard-backed chair because he knew if he gave in to the sagging sofa, he would not rise again that day. Connie remained standing by the door.

Ian glanced over. Nervous now. "Won't you join us, Officer . . ."

Her voice had resumed its flat cop tone. "I'm good here, sir."

Matt knew there was probably a way to ease into this. But not today. "Porter Reeves is alive, Ian."

The blood did not drain from Ian's uneven features all at once, making him pale in splotches. "That's not possible."

"He's been living under the alias of Richard Grimes, and at least one other name."

Connie asked, "Have you been in contact with Porter Reeves, sir?"

"What? Didn't you just hear me?"

"Tell me about Porter and my mother."

Ian dropped into the sofa. Becoming a lumpy human cushion. "You're sure? Porter's alive?"

Matt turned to Connie and nodded.

"Reverend Reeves, we know Porter Reeves was your older brother. You grew up together in Fells Point. Porter worked at the bar run by

Megan Kelly's mother. Please don't bother denying this, sir. It's all confirmed by a variety of witnesses."

"I'm not denying anything."

"Porter Reeves and Megan Kelly were engaged to be married. Reeves took part in a bank robbery that went wrong." Connie was doing a good job playing the hard cop. "Because Porter Reeves was a first offender, the judge gave him the choice of army or jail. Reeves enlisted and was sent to Vietnam."

"And look what it cost him." Ian spoke to the distant past. "Poor Porter."

"After Porter went to Vietnam, Megan Kelly began dating—"

"No," Ian said.

"—a young seminarian named Ian—"

"No!" Ian Reeves bounded to his feet. "That's absurd. I introduced your parents! Paul Kelly was my friend!"

"Reverend Reeves—"

Matt held up his hand. "Ian, when did you introduce them?"

"Is this really so vital, Matt?" The appeal was desperate. "Do you have to ask these things?"

"Yes and yes."

His spine bowed to support the invisible weight. "About a year before . . ."

"Before the robbery."

"Porter wasn't right for Megan. I knew that from the first moment they started seeing one another. Megan was meant for greater things. She could go anywhere. Make something of her life. Just like your father. Paul Kelly grew up ten blocks away, but he occupied another world. He was always driven, your father. Always determined to break free. He was going places. It was only right he take Megan with him."

When neither man spoke, Connie said, "Reverend Reeves, I have the testimony of numerous witnesses who say that after your brother left for Vietnam, you and Megan Kelly began—"

"It wasn't like that." Ian punched himself in the chest. "Look at me!"

Connie glanced at Matt, then continued, "The neighbors all described Megan Kelly as—"

"Wild." Ian began pacing. Talking and moving in time to his words.

"Wild and carefree and beautiful and so incredibly alive no one could look at her and not smile. Not want to be with her. Not . . ."

He stopped by the front window. "Out there is a world that chants a mantra in chaotic unison. That people can't change. That life is as it is. Yes. I loved your mother. We all did. I loved her so much I gave her the only thing I could. A chance to hear a *different* voice. A chance to lead a *different* life. One where she could go *beyond*. Not just physically. *Beyond*. I knew she couldn't do it alone. Nobody can."

Matt let Connie ask the next question. "Sir, do you have a photograph of your brother?"

Ian looked at Matt a long moment. Matt sat and waited with him. Finally Ian moved to a wall cupboard, unlocked the bottom doors, selected an old frame. Looked at it. Brought it back and handed it to Matt. Facedown.

Ian returned to his position at the window. "It's the only one I have. Porter sent it to me before they shipped him out. My parents . . ."

Connie supplied, "They disowned your brother after his arrest."

"The bank thing was just the last straw." He shook his head to the storm-laden day. Said once more, "Poor Porter."

Matt's phone rang. He glanced at the readout, saw it was the hospital. "This is Kelly."

D'Amico said, "I got your information."

"Hang on." Matt patted his pockets, found he had forgotten his pen. He looked over. Connie was already digging in her purse. "Okay, go."

"Your man Grimes is supposedly living in an area of Oella known as the Hollows." As D'Amico spelled out the address, Matt could hear a woman talking in the background. "Hannah is trying to get the assistant DA responsible for Calvin Hogue's arrest to meet you as well. Your rendezvous point is the Ellicott City train station. It'll be on signposts once you get into town. The cop who heard about Grimes will meet you there."

Matt thanked D'Amico and rose to his feet very carefully. "We have to move."

Ian followed them to the door, watched them leave, then called after them, "Matt, you have to listen to me. Megan came to me because she was alone and frightened and needed help. But not mine. Never mine."

Connie waited until Ian had shut the front door to say, "He didn't tell us everything."

Matt handed her the photograph he had still not seen. "Yes, he did."

———

Back in the car, Judy Leigh asked, "How did it go?"

"Later," Connie said and stowed the shoulder bag at her feet.

Matt followed her directions out of town, constantly aware of the framed photograph protruding from the open bag. The pain in his head was gradually easing. Either the aspirin was taking hold, or the day was simply too full to permit the pain much room. Connie kept glancing over, giving him that look. The one that unsettled and soothed at the same time.

The impact of what he had just learned kept building. All the unanswered dilemmas of his childhood, his father's constant dissatisfaction, the condemnations, the friction. All there.

They pulled up to a stoplight. Connie reached across and touched his arm. He looked over, almost wishing she would speak and give him a reason to push her away. Connie's quiet concern left him sensing dangerous currents working beneath his own surface. He wanted to open up and tell her what kept beating at him inside. Say all the things he had spent a lifetime learning never to reveal.

Judy Leigh shifted in the rear seat, as though reminding them both they were not alone.

Connie appeared not to care. She kept that gaze leveled on him. And said quietly, "It's okay, Matt."

It wasn't and it never had been, he wanted to respond. She was amazingly like his mother just now, able to peel back all his protective layers and see the hidden, the unspoken, the secret cauldron. She *crowded* him.

What was more, she challenged. The silence weighed heavy, a softly prodding glimpse into what *might* be. Which was why he wanted to tell her to back off.

If only he could.

The assistant DA was parked where Lucas had said she'd be when Matt, Connie, and Judy Leigh pulled in. She called over, "You Kelly?"

"Yes." Matt waited for Connie to join him. "This is Officer Morales."

"And her?"

"Judy Leigh, *Baltimore Times*."

She smirked but said nothing about the combination. "Hannah Bernstein promised this trip wouldn't be a waste of my time."

"We can't say anything for certain yet. But I hope the chief is right."

"Bernstein also said the arrest warrant had been issued for the wrong man."

"That I can definitely confirm."

"So the information supplied to me by the new chief of Homicide is bogus."

"Totally."

Riva Pratt clearly favored red. As in red leather skirt, jacket, nail polish, lipstick, and heels. Her hair was a sordid mousy brown, in striking contrast to the rest of her. "You're State, did Hannah get that right? Must pay good, whatever you do at State, to afford those wheels."

Matt let that one pass. "I haven't been able to find the address Lucas gave us on my map."

"Yeah, that sounds like Oella." She held out her hand, took the paper, said, "Sure, I know this. It's back in the Hollows."

"That's what Lucas told me."

"The Hollows are why Oella will never be totally tamed, no matter how many fancy D.C. types build weekend houses along the ridgeline." Riva Pratt had compressed a fifty-year veteran's attitude into her thirty-year frame. "When I first started out, I coulda bought a house out here for nine thousand dollars. Coulda, shoulda. Last month I heard somebody sold the place next door for half a mil."

She handed back the paper. "Hannah Bernstein tells me this might also have something to do with your father's abduction."

"It might." Matt explained what they knew about Porter Reeves and Richard Grimes. While he was talking, two patrol cars rolled up. Connie walked over to talk with their occupants.

The DA told him, "If what you're suggesting is true, it doesn't say much for the charges brought by the new Homicide chief."

"Actually," Matt corrected, "it says a lot."

The DA pointed to the patrol cars. "And they are?"

Connie answered, "Lucas said we ought to roll with backup."

"Fed, cops, newspaper, DA." Riva Pratt started for her car. "Sure hope this party isn't for nothing."

———

The road wound along the left-hand side of a tight valley, about midway between the river and the ridgeline. Oella was spread out over miles, forking off into several branch vales. It was more a geographic designation than a town with a center and a sense of life. A shotgun house with weeds and junk for a front lawn stood in schizophrenic fashion beside a million-dollar McMansion. Next came a pasture with a For Sale sign from Sotheby's. Then a trailer with two rusting pickups and a forties-era sedan on cinder blocks. Trees pushed in tight every now and then, further constricting the valley. Matt occasionally caught sight of the Patapsco River running brown and morose along the valley floor.

Riva Pratt turned left onto a one-lane road so pitted and scarred it was more gravel than asphalt. A half mile on it passed between two granite faces and dipped steeply into a forested ravine. The Hollows.

She parked in a small pasture and waited until all four cars crammed in. "If this is a for-real situation, we had better walk from here."

Matt turned to the reporter. Before he could speak, Judy Leigh snapped, "Don't even start. I'm coming."

Their footsteps sounded harsh in the close afternoon gloom. Riva Pratt said, "Six-years back, Oella erupted in gang warfare."

The oldest of the cops said, "Sure, I remember that. Only they didn't call it gangs."

"Clans," she agreed, the scorn in her voice deep. "The violence overwhelmed the local sheriffs. Before, Oella resisted being incorporated into the city. Then, they didn't have any choice. Each of these Hollows is claimed by one clan or another. They set up meth labs here, gun shops, you name it."

The old cop said, "I thought I recognized you."

The DA glanced back. Said in a hard-timer's voice, "How you been?"

"You know how it is. Same dance, different tune."

Matt said to the cop, "Lucas said you had heard something about the guy we're after."

"Lucas being the homicide detective who took one last week, right? Yeah, I heard of this Grimes. Supposed to be all muscle and bad news."

They passed through a copse of birch. Beyond, the ridge closed in, a steep-sided bowl with just enough room for the road to turn a tight circle around a pair of ancient elms. The property supposedly rented by Richard Grimes was an old humpbacked trailer that had morphed into a clapboard house. The raw stone cliff rose a hundred feet, perhaps more. The sky hung heavy and grim just above the ridge. Stunted pines and snarled undergrowth crammed into the sides of the house. Matt doubted the place saw more than an hour's sun on the clearest day.

The DA said, "I checked the records. There's no Richard Grimes on the rolls."

The older cop replied, "Oella might be Baltimore now and the guns might be back in the closet, but these hollows run by their own rules. Out here, it's a cash-only kind of life."

"When the judge signed the warrant I'm carrying, she ordered me to use it only if I was satisfied." Riva Pratt gave the old cop a very hard look. "You're certain Richard Grimes lives here?"

"I checked with two locals who've done me good in the past. They both said this was his."

"They tell you anything else?"

"Not a thing." The cop squinted at the place. "Knowing them, that says a lot."

"Okay." The DA handed Matt the warrant. "You got your green light."

The three younger cops had their weapons drawn before the DA finished talking. One of them weaved back and forth, two-handing his weapon. Already dead-aiming at the unseen target. The older cop said, "You. Fredricks. Holster your firearm."

"Sir?"

"Lighten up. This isn't the gun range, and the subject is not a confirmed suspect. Got it?"

All three cops eased back. The older cop, looking tired, asked Matt, "How do you want to play this?"

"If it's our guy, he's a bomber. We need a narrow way in, bathroom window, skylight, something he wouldn't bother to wire."

The old cop said, "Okay, you guys scout around."

Connie found it. A narrow dip in the wall, like the house had once ended there and then been extended, had become dislodged. The young cop called Fredricks went back to his car and returned with a professional-length crowbar and Maglite. He and one of the other cops took hold of the clapboard panel and heaved. They pulled out four sections, enough for Connie to slip through. The young cops didn't like the idea of a woman taking point. But they didn't say anything.

Three minutes later she opened the front door. "Clean."

They piled inside. The house had a sterile quality. The floors were old plywood, buckled and worn. But they had been swept and washed and scrubbed so hard Matt could see scars from the wire brush. Same for the walls. Only the windows had not been cleaned. They by contrast were so gray they looked painted in shades of slate.

There were five rooms in all. Each held only a couple of items of furniture. In one a bed. In the next a metal rack and two wooden crates for clothes. In another, one table and one chair and one floor lamp. The kitchen held one pot, one plate, spoon, fork, knife, mug, towel. Even the food was spare—mostly canned goods and sacks of dried beans and rice.

Riva Pratt watched the cops tap the walls and floors, use the chair to push aside ceiling panels, and declared, "This is such a total waste."

Connie said, "We need to check the grounds."

"Be my guest." She headed for the door. When Matt followed her outside, she said, "Next time you speak to Hannah, be sure and thank her for me."

Matt said, "Could you leave me your card in case we find something?"

She didn't like it but fished one from her jacket. "If you bother me again, it better be with a signed confession."

———

Matt stood in the dusty front area, staring up at where the sky should have been. The air felt densely compacted with all that had happened, and everything he could not decipher.

"Matt?"

He turned to where Connie and Judy Leigh were coming down the front stairs. "I need to go check something out. It's most likely just another waste of time. But I have to be sure."

Judy looked from one to the other and then said to Connie, "You need to tell him."

"We don't know anything for certain."

"We know. We just don't know what it means."

"Then come with me," Matt said to Judy Leigh. He asked Connie, "Can you finish up here?"

"You know the answer to that." The calm concern was back in Connie's face. "Are you all right?"

The unspoken was far clearer than her words. Enough so that he felt the steel grip of his internal locks grinding shut. "Yes."

She turned away. Matt watched her disappear into the house, trapped once more by his inability to even pretend to be whole. The first drops of rain began falling as she stepped back into the shadows. He said to Judy, "Let's go."

———

Matt took the I-695 loop around Baltimore. It was longer and the rain slowed traffic. But he felt his ability to focus waning. Judy Leigh's voice moved in and out with his attention. He plugged his car between two large trucks and let them forge ahead for him.

Judy Leigh talked the entire way. She sketched out the interlocking details of his father's business in minute detail. On any other day, he probably would have classed it as grating yet important. Today it only competed with his rising headache.

When he took the turnoff for Lutherville, Judy asked, "What do you think?"

He told her the truth because anything else was too much bother. "I don't see what this gives us. Pop has spent his entire life buying stuff and rebuilding and selling and moving on. Now you're telling me that in each deal he's set a minority portion aside for people who can do him favors. Only in Downtown, he's the minority guy and a lot of people you can't identify own the major share. Right?"

"Pretty much."

The rain was coming down so hard he almost missed the highway for Gunpowder Falls. "So?"

"He's given total control to Sol Greene."

"Sol is my father's oldest friend. Maybe his only friend."

"Still, he's gotten into this Downtown deal because of Sol. We know that much. Now Sol is controlling the trust. Your father hasn't put any balancing force into the trust's control. It just seems radical for . . ." She stopped because of his expression. "What?"

"You didn't tell me that. About Sol getting Pop into the Downtown project."

"Sure I did."

Matt did not argue. His body pulsed in time to his head. He could have missed anything.

"Why is that important?"

"I don't know. It's a first, that's all. Pop loved the hunt, loved coming up with his next prey."

"Sol Greene is connected to some major D.C.-based players. Maybe they put the Downtown deal together and just needed a local face to front for them."

"Maybe." But he had the feeling of a hook in his craw. Telling him he was missing something important. "When was this?"

She checked her notes. "Six years ago, close as I could figure. Maybe seven."

About when his father first entered politics. "Sol was never interested in Pop's business. Every time they got together, Sol would be after him to drop it and run for office. He always called it moving into the majors."

"I don't . . ." She hesitated when Matt swung off the main road onto the forested gravel drive. "Where are we?"

"Allen Pecard's residence."

"Really?" She peered through the rain. "Why?"

"I told you. I just need to check something out."

The sheriff's car was parked between the house and the garage. Matt pulled in close. A bored young man rolled down his window and said, "This is restricted property, folks."

"Agent Matt Kelly." Matt handed over his ID. "I'm just going to have one more look around."

The deputy passed it back, streaking Matt's wallet and his sleeve with rain. "You were here when the sheriff took the hit."

"How's he doing?"

"Got out this morning. What about your guy?"

"The doctors are saying Wednesday. Look, we're going to be here at least an hour. Why don't you roll out for coffee?"

"I could use a break, sure enough."

"Front door open?"

"Sure is." He gunned his motor. "You need anything, call the station."

Matt cut his own engine and rose from the car. He waited for Judy Leigh to push herself out and draw the mini-umbrella from her purse. As they walked the gravel path, she asked, "What are we doing here?"

"Probably just wasting our time. But I have to be sure." He opened the front door. "Watch out for the bomb pit there."

She shied away from the squarish hole dug in the floor. "That was for a bomb?"

"Yes." Matt shut the door. He stood there tasting the air. Waiting.

Then the shadows in the corner between the hallway and the kitchen coalesced.

Judy Leigh gasped and gripped both hands tightly around her stomach.

Allen Pecard stepped into the rain-washed light of his own living room. "You're late, Agent Kelly."

"I'd almost given up hope," Allen Pecard said.

Matt told him about getting zapped. "My brain still feels partly disconnected. Like some key synapses got permanently fried."

"I can assure you from personal experience that this will fade."

Judy Leigh was jammed into the living room's far corner, her gaze racing back and forth between the two men. "Aren't you going to arrest him?"

"He didn't do it."

Pecard gave him that tight glimmer of humor. "When did you arrive at this realization?"

"When you came through the door. Until then it was just a guess."

Judy Leigh said, "Maybe you're certain, but I'd be a lot more comfortable if you'd at least take out your gun."

Matt continued, "The guy spoke when he shot me with the stun gun. It's bothered me ever since. It could've been you. But I wondered."

Judy was still not convinced. "Why can't they be working together?"

"Everything about Pecard's life is based on solitude. I never liked the idea that he'd suddenly brought in a partner."

Pecard found that uncomfortable enough to turn his attention to the woman still cowering in the corner. "Who is your companion?"

"Judy Leigh, *Baltimore Times.*"

Pecard raised an open palm. His left forearm was bandaged where his sweatshirt rode up. "I don't make it a practice to attack expectant mothers, Ms. Leigh."

Matt asked, "You took a hit?"

Pecard pulled down the sleeve. "Our assailant is quite good."

"This being Porter Reeves. Also known as Richard Grimes."

"I am impressed, Agent Kelly."

"You want to tell me how you got involved?"

Pecard crossed the room and eased himself into a high-backed chair from which he could see the front door. "Where is the deputy?"

"Having dinner."

He kept his face angled so as to watch both Matt and the world beyond the room. "In the run-up to the final U.S. withdrawal from Vietnam, I was based at the British embassy in Manila."

"Military intelligence."

"Such as it was. We received word of a substantial cache passing through certain dealers in a regular and disturbing pattern. Manila to London and beyond. Artwork, jewelry, gold, antiques. We questioned the local man and received almost nothing, save that the goods came from Saigon."

"So you traveled over and worked with our guys." Matt motioned for Judy Leigh to sit. She chose a chair by the rear door. As far from Pecard as she could be and remain in the room. Matt asked, "Was that Bannister?"

"Bryan was already on the case. Apparently a team were trading bogus passports and travel permits for major payouts. Which they then smuggled out to the Philippines on flights ferrying combat troops on R & R."

"Barry Simms."

"Or another cohort."

"Which brings us to Porter Reeves."

"Porter Reeves was what you might describe as a serious burnout. A number of snipers were. Senior staff kept the best constantly on the move. And Porter was quite good at his work. He liaised with intel and various ground units, flying about, doing his work, then taking leave. He would turn up in Saigon and blow an enlisted man's annual salary in one week. Then he hopped back up-country again. We started track-ing him, waiting to see who else we could pull into our net."

"You got too close."

"Porter took out my partner. I am utterly certain it was him, but there was no proof. Just an impossible shot from fifteen hundred yards, and my best mate was gone. I managed to save Bannister. Barely." Pecard fingered the scar on his neck. "Porter gave me this. Before I was out of the hospital, Porter took a hit. Everything began shutting down. I was pulled out. End of story."

Rain painted gentle streaks upon the window. Allen Pecard still looked intent and severe. But exhaustion etched his features into caverns not even the rain could ease.

"My father," Matt said.

Allen Pecard gave no indication he had heard. "Last spring, I received a call from an ally within the craft. He had attended a major MIA rally, where to his astonishment he had spotted Porter Reeves. Coming from anyone else, I would have put such news down to momentary strain. But my ally does not make such errors. I began checking out what I could. Naturally, no one in Washington took me seriously. After Bannister was assigned here, he helped some. All unofficially, of course."

Pecard began tapping his fingers on the glass, almost mimicking the sound of pattering rain. "And then something rather strange occurred. I began hearing my name bandied about. In places and circumstances where I had never been. It was the only evidence I had that I was on the right trail. Porter Reeves considered me enough of a threat to set me up."

Matt repeated his question. "How does my father figure into this?"

"We were fairly certain the scam originated from your father's division. But we did not have a name. We never did." Pecard looked at him square on. "And I do not deal in suppositions, Agent Kelly. Neither then nor now."

"My father knew Porter Reeves before the war. They were in this together. They had to be."

"The only thing I can say for certain is this. From the beginning, Porter Reeves has laid out a trail he *wants* us to follow. He could have taken your father out any time he wished."

Matt worked that over, the seconds marked down by the falling rain and the beat of Pecard's fingers upon the glass. "Today is November third, right?"

DAVIS BUNN

"I haven't a clue."

Judy Leigh said, "That's correct. Why?"

"It was the day of the ambush. The date's on my dad's commendation. The one Reeves stole from our house."

Pecard pushed himself from the chair, wincing as he did so. "In that case we must be off."

"Where to?"

"I've been hiding in the crawl space under the roof, hoping you'd show up, pondering where Porter was aiming us. I think I might just know. But I need to go make certain. Can you give me a lift up the road?"

Matt's response was cut off by the ringing of his phone. It was Connie, who said, "You've got to get back out here."

"You've found something?"

Connie replied, "The guy. Your killer. Everything."

Allen Pecard directed them down the highway to a ranger trail above Gunpowder Falls. He waited until Matt completed his call to Bryan Bannister, then explained that he had known about the arrest warrant for him as soon as it was issued, but would not say how, except that the warning had not come from Bannister's office. Pecard had Matt drop him by a derelict Grand Marquis. As he slipped from the car, he said, "I will report in two hours."

Matt checked his watch. Noon. "You sure you don't want backup?"

Pecard gave him that peculiar look of his, the one of such intensity Matt could feel the skin of his face being peeled back. "You said it yourself. I operate best alone."

Matt waited while Pecard's car started with a deep rumble and rolled out of cover. As they left the forest clearing, it began to rain so heavily the drumbeats on the car's roof became a constant rush. Matt halted by the highway turnoff and rubbed his face.

Judy Leigh said, "Let me drive."

"I'm okay."

"You men." She said it like she'd had a lot of practice. She reached into her purse and came up with her collapsible umbrella. "You can slide over the console."

Matt would have argued, but she was already extending her umbrella and rising from the car. Matt had the choice of either moving or forcing her to stand in the rain. Matt levered himself into the passenger seat. She scrambled inside. "It's really pouring."

"Seat controls are on the door."

"I know how to handle a Beemer." She strapped the belt carefully around her middle and gunned the motor. "The way you guys go on, you'd think we were missing a gene."

Matt wanted to stay awake and gauge her ability. But with the seat tilted back he was so comfortable, the rushing rain so smooth, the world slipped out of his grasp and he was gone.

The next thing he knew was Judy Leigh saying, "Matt."

He struggled upright. Rubbed his face. Tried to work the numbers on his watch into focus.

"Man, somebody better warn your nearest and dearest, they're in for some serious noise." Judy Leigh had the seat back far enough to keep her tummy well clear of the wheel. Which meant she drove with her arms stretched almost horizontal. "We're talking metal shop."

There was a sack of sandwiches in the backseat, an empty drink in her holder, a wrapper on the center console. "How long was I out?"

"Hour and a half. The traffic just glued shut a couple of times." She turned off the valley road into the gravel track leading back into the Hollows. "How do you feel?"

"Better." He turned to his side window and closed out what was bound to be up ahead. He had not had the nightmare. In fact, it had not been a dream in the normal sense. A single image had come and gone in an instant before she had woken him. A hint of something he needed to remember. Something vital. But it was gone now. And all it left behind was a feeling of mortal dread.

The rain had stopped by the time Judy parked them inside the corral. But the storm was all around them as they rose from the car. The air was so full of moisture it bathed his clothes and hair in the time it took to approach the house.

Connie appeared from around back. She wore a blue police poncho with the hood thrown back. Her trousers and her poncho were both streaked with mud. She reported, "The forensics guys are having a field day."

Matt took small comfort in watching her move. A splash of color and life in an otherwise bleak day. "Has Bannister gotten here yet?"

There was a growing calmness about her, a subtle shift in internal winds. "He just called to say he's five minutes out."

Matt carried the sandwich bag and led them into the house's sterile front room. Over sandwiches he briefed her on his contact with Pecard. Found himself extremely grateful for the trust she showed by not criticizing his decision to let Pecard remain on the loose. Instead, she simply asked, "Where is Pecard now?"

The sound of a car scrunching down the track drew them back outside. "He wanted to check out a possible site where Reeves might have taken my father. He's supposed to call in at two."

Bryan Bannister drove a silver Lincoln LS that gleamed almost white in the rain. He maneuvered it into the pasture and parked alongside Matt. He walked to where Matt and Connie waited. The trees to each side dripped noisily. Thunder rumbled overhead.

Bannister said, "He didn't want to come."

Matt glanced at the car. Sol Greene remained seated with his arms crossed, staring sullenly out the side window so as not to look their way. "But he came."

"Only when I invited to cuff him and take him downtown." Bannister took a deep breath. "This weather reminds me of Nam. Air so thick you could drink it. Different smells, though. The odors in the delta would knock your head off."

Connie said, "There's some stuff I found that'll take you right back."

He pointed at the house. "In there?"

"No, the house is clean."

Bannister's gaze and speech held to a hollow core. "I still can't believe . . ."

Matt said, "This house is rented to Richard Grimes, aka Porter Reeves. He's the real killer."

That sharpened Bannister's day. "You've found conclusive evidence?"

"Out back," Connie confirmed.

Matt said, "I've spoken to Pecard."

"Where is he?"

"I better not say."

"No." Bannister heaved a breath he'd been holding for days. "You're sure? This is solid?"

"Pecard is clean," Matt replied. "You were right all along."

Connie said, "You haven't even seen the evidence yet."

"I don't need to. Pecard had nothing to do with my mother's death or the attacks on my father and D'Amico."

Bannister turned for the car. "What say we collect my ride-along and have ourselves a look at what you've found."

———

Connie led them around the house. Judy Leigh took rear guard. Sol moved forward only because Matt and Bryan Bannister tracked along behind him, showing him nothing but stern resolve. "I still don't know what this is about."

"Easier if we show you," Matt said.

"Do I need my lawyer?"

"We're just after your help in finding Pop." Sol stumbled on an exposed root. Matt gripped his arm and kept him from falling. Sol ripped his arm free. "Sol, we have a lead. We need your help in explaining how this is tied to Pop."

The young patrol officers were spinning out yellow police tape, sealing off the area. A portly man stood by a pile of rocks dislodged from the cliff face, talking in low, excited tones to a young woman in heavy black spectacles. They both wore hairnets, paper booties, and blue coveralls marked POLICE. Their clothes were streaked with red clay. The woman pushed her glasses back up her nose, smudging her forehead with the dirt she had on her gloves. Neither of them noticed.

The portly man broke off the conversation when he saw Connie. "These your people?"

"Agent Matt Kelly, Agent Bryan Bannister. Sol Greene and Judy Leigh are helping with our inquiries."

The portly guy handed the young woman his forensics case and helped her sling his camera around her neck. "You guys know the drill, right? This is still an active site. Don't touch. Don't take. We clear?"

"Yes sir."

He turned back to the young woman. "Get another shot of everything under the lights, just to be sure. I'll be back soon as I make the calls. But first go get them some suits." To the four he explained, "You don't want to go in there without protective gear."

The young woman came back with four sealed plastic carry bags. Each contained a disposable coverall of paper felt, gloves, hairnet, and booties. Connie declined, saying she was already wearing as much mud as one girl could. Sol protested bitterly until offered the alternative of ruining his clothes.

They followed Connie along a fresh trail toward the cliff face, back to where a shrub and a roll of metal fencing had formerly blocked the entrance to a cave. The raw stone rose sheer and glistening. High overhead, pines shifted sullenly in the rising wind, casting down their wet burden. Storm clouds swirled and boiled. They were surrounded by the sounds of dripping water and the smell of wet earth.

"You mind giving me a hand?" The young woman gave Matt and Connie battery-powered floor lamps.

"I'm not going in there," Sol said. "No way."

Matt sensed more than nervousness over the unknown. "You know what's in there?"

Bannister's gaze tightened down to narrow slits. He had noticed it as well. "Mr. Greene, do you have any information regarding the whereabouts of Paul Kelly?"

Matt resisted the urge to shake his head. That wasn't it.

Sol rounded on the FBI agent. "Are you *nuts?*"

"Come on," Matt said. "Inside."

The mouth was actually a triangular crevice. Matt had to stoop slightly. The air inside was instantly cooler. And sweeter. A distinct odor clung to the air and the rocks. The young forensics lady switched on her light and said, "It opens up just ahead."

"Seemed a lot farther my first time in," Connie said from in front of Matt. "I almost gave in to the heebies before I was through."

Thirty paces on, the defile opened into a cave shaped like an oval stone tent. The center was floored in cool pink sand. A bedroll lay beside a glowing Coleman lantern. Cans of food and a green military mess kit were stowed in a packing crate.

"I want to get out of here," Sol said weakly.

The sweet odor was stronger, almost a funk. Matt turned on his lantern and played it over the source. One wall of the cave was lined with empty Dole pineapple juice cans. Stacked up higher than Matt. Hundreds of them.

"Some guys back from the camps, they fixate." Bannister's voice was stronger now. Calmer. Finding great solace in being right about his friend. "They dreamed about something while they were held. Now it becomes an obsession."

Sol turned and stumbled against Matt. "I'm leaving."

"Not yet."

"I can't breathe."

Connie said softly, "Over here."

All three lights focused on the cave's far side. A third of the cave had been turned into a shrine. Two giant collages stood to each side of the largest POW-MIA flag Matt had ever seen.

"Guys who only came back partway, a lot of them fixate on the idea of MIAs." Bannister again. "Partly over the friends they left behind, or so the psych officers tell us. Partly over what they left of themselves back there. Here, but still missing."

Sol started for the entrance. Matt gripped his arm and pulled him forward.

"No."

"Look, Sol."

The left-hand collage was dedicated to Megan Kelly and her son. Mostly Megan. Hundreds and hundreds of pictures, going back decades. Matt's mother laughed and smiled and waved from across the divide.

The right-hand collage was all Paul Kelly. Many were from the current campaign. Every picture was defiled. Burned. Shot. Splintered. Slashed. Angry words formed ribbons of hate across the collection.

Matt pressed, "Why is Porter Reeves after my father, Sol?"

Sol feebly shook at Matt's grip. Said nothing.

"Pop was involved in the trade of false American documents, wasn't he."

Sol's breath drew in sharply. "How . . ."

"It doesn't matter how I know." Matt dropped his hand. Shock had robbed Sol of the power to struggle. "Pop was involved with Porter Reeves and Barry Simms in the illegal sale of bogus U.S. passports for gold and jewelry."

"None of that was ever proven!"

"Did Porter think my father set him up? Is that it? Then why didn't he just shoot Pop and be done with it? Why did he wait so long to retaliate?"

"Porter was a wild man! Who knows what he thought?" Sol jerked now, but against chains only he could see. "He defined burnout. But they wouldn't send him back. He was too good at his job. So they shipped him to Paul's squadron because Paul was an old buddy. Paul could control him. At least, that's what—"

Judy Leigh had slipped in behind them. Her camera flashed, throwing them into sharp silhouette with the collage as background. Sol flinched, looked at her closely, then drew back in real alarm. "You're that reporter! The one that was dogging Matt!"

"Judy Leigh."

Comprehension dawned. He shrilled at Matt so loudly the sound tore at the rocks. "We're in the campaign's last day!"

"Pop was involved with the trade," Matt persisted. "You didn't know exactly what we were after, but soon as you heard the investigation was pointed toward Vietnam, you—"

"Did you hear a single word of anything I've said? The election is *tomorrow*!"

"Sol, Pop is gone."

He was breathing so hard his throat rasped. "You don't know that."

"Sol—"

"You want anything more, you call my lawyer!" He stormed away, only to wheel about at the entrance and scream, *"Bring me my candidate!"*

The wind had accelerated while they were inside the rock. Fitful puffs managed to find their way down to where they stood. They were all breathing easier now that they were outside the self-made prison of Porter Reeves.

Bannister studied the trees shaking in cautionary unison overhead. "I need to have the federal attorney dismiss the warrant against Pecard, and I need to talk to the local DA responsible for Calvin Hogue's arrest. You know who that was?"

Connie gave Matt a chance to respond. But he had turned around and was studying the cave entrance. "Riva Pratt," she said. "She won't like you calling. She was out here and left when the house came up clean."

"I'll speak to my guy first, have him help bring her around."

"You think maybe you could speak with somebody about getting Chief Bernstein reinstated?"

"It would be a pleasure." Bannister unfolded his phone but did not dial. He asked Matt, "What's the matter?"

"Pecard was supposed to phone me at two."

Bannister checked his watch. It was half past three. "Allen is never late."

Matt continued to study the cave's entrance. Saw the collages again. He would probably see them for years.

"Something's wrong," Bannister said.

Connie kept watching him. "Matt?"

Matt said softly, "Of course."

"Are you okay?"

He was already moving. "I know where Pop is."

———

They took Matt's car. Judy Leigh was not the least bothered by being left behind. The cave promised limitless headlines. Plus Bannister was staying put until the DA arrived. Hannah Bernstein had been reached at D'Amico's bedside and was coming as well. The prospect of Riva Pratt dining on a false arrest and Hannah Bernstein reflecting on false dismissal brightened even this sullen day. At least for the reporter.

The rain closed in as they wound back along the high border of the Patapsco River Valley. The entrance to the 695 Beltway was blocked by a quarter mile of stalled traffic. Connie said, "Cross over to Frederick. Look for the Highway 144 sign."

The change in Connie filtered through his mental clamor. "You're different somehow."

She waited through several beats of the windshield wipers to reply, "I've been talking to Lucas." She looked over. "You want me to drive?"

"This helps me think." Matt watched as she returned her attention to the side window. She held to a core of calmness that not even the day's tumult could shift. It unsettled him. Why, he could not say. He tried to dismiss it as a day overloaded with psychic jolts and failed.

Traffic inside the city was slow but moving. Matt took Liberty Heights to Fulton, then went west on Franklin. Following the path of least resistance. Traffic snarled as they approached the central train station, so he took a right onto Martin Luther King. They passed Bolton Hill at a crawl. Then it hit him.

"Sol Greene," Matt said. "He's the answer."

Connie turned from her inspection of the rain-washed window. "The man we just let walk."

"Nothing to hold him on." The calm in her gaze rocked him, and the mystery made it worse. "If only I knew the reason."

She gave him nothing but steady. "Matt, what you've been through, don't you think it would help to talk it out?"

Matt kept himself from saying it. How often he had heard the very same thing. And all the different ways it'd been said. All his frozen years were reflected in her gaze.

Which was probably why he missed the oncoming danger until they were on Hanover Street and approaching water.

Matt pulled as far over as the high curb permitted and put on his flashers. "What time is it?"

"Almost four." A horn blared behind them. "We're blocking the bridge traffic."

Matt turned on his lights and sat on his horn. "This could be a little tricky."

He started into his U-turn, then halted when a truck in the inside lane roared past in a spray of water and horn and diesel and near death. Matt nosed farther out, pushing the BMW in front of an angry SUV, and gunned onto the central divide. Cars streaming off the Vietnam Memorial Bridge blared horns and flashed lights. Matt kept going. The car's underbelly scraped on the concrete divide and held for a moment, until Matt floored it. They spun and bounced and careened over with a final clatter. "Sounds like that cost me either a tailpipe or a bumper."

Connie released her hold on the car door and roof. "You want to explain that?"

"Pecard is so late it has to be major."

"And?"

"Bannister said it. I know it. Pecard is never late. Something is so wrong he can't make contact. If I'm right about the spot, I'm wrong about the approach. Everybody on and off the bridge can be seen from the site. I need to find a back door."

She looked at him a long moment. "Where are we headed?"

"Cherry Hill Park."

————

They swung past the Wright Industrial Zone on Washington, then headed east on Patapsco. As they approached where the road crossed the Patapsco River estuary, the CST rail sidled in close to the highway. Connie said, "We can park here and hoof it."

"You'll get soaked."

She gave him a cop's look. Then it was gone. Replaced by that same disconcerting calm. "Let's go do this."

The city park area was split by the Vietnam Memorial Bridge. North was the Middle Branch Park with its marina and rowing club. South was Cherry Hill Park. Between the two, jammed up tight against the point where the bridge left the water and met land, was the Vietnam Memorial.

They crossed the rail lines and took the trail that ran by the Patapsco River estuary. Up ahead the Hanover Highway traffic sliced high streamers and hit the bridge link with regular bass thunks. The rain cleared momentarily, long enough for Connie to spot the POW-MIA flag streaming black and wet upon the high ridge. "Of course."

They found the Grand Marquis at the entrance to the memorial's small parking lot. The exit ramp swung down at a very steep angle from the point where bridge met land. A tall central hedge masked the curve. The road had a pair of speed bumps just before the parking lot entrance. Pecard's old clunker stood by the second speed bump. Three of the tires were off the road. The car had crashed into a poplar. The side window and front windshield were totally shattered. Glass littered the bushes, the car hood, the wet empty seat. The driver's headrest was stained with something dark.

Connie said, "Windscreens don't shatter like this from gunfire."

Matt spotted the metal protruding from beneath the bushes. He picked up an aluminum bat. "Call for backup."

Connie reached for her phone, then realized he was moving on. "We need to wait."

"My father is up there." He dropped the bat and kept going. "Aim for the flag."

The first rule of engagement they taught at FLETSE was two words. The instructors all said it over and over, drilling it into the thickest skull: *Speed kills.*

Matt did everything by the book. He avoided a clear view of the ridge. He crossed the parking lot moving from cover to cover. He crouched at the base of the hill and waited through a clear moment, watching the three flags rattle the tall metal poles.

Rainsqualls snaked across the water, gray pillars that came with a soft rushing sound. When the next one dumped its drenching chill, Matt snaked uphill on his belly.

Even so, when he was about two-thirds of the way up, a shot from nowhere plowed a muddy ditch about ten inches from his face. He rolled back, pawing the dirt from his eyes.

A voice called from somewhere overhead, "Time to rise and shine, Kelly!"

Matt scrambled into the rain ditch that ran alongside the walkway. He had no idea if he was out of the shooter's line of sight. The rushing water sluiced the mud and grit from his eyes.

The pavement sparked to his left. Whatever sound the silenced rifle made was carried away in the wind and the rain. "You don't listen so good, do you, boy!"

The shooter had to be positioned on a bridge stanchion. Matt spiraled over so that he lay on his back in the frigid stream. He strained his neck and squinted against the flow. The bridge traffic thundered past. But he saw nothing. If he could not see, then neither could the shooter.

The voice shouted, "Paul! Tell the boy to get on up!"

"Don't do it, son! Get out of here!"

Something whanged on metal, a hard clanging that caused his father to cry out in either fear or pain. The shooter yelled, "You do what I say! The both of you!"

Matt stayed where he was. The next squall approached with the hiss of a million water snakes. Just as it hit land, he sprang.

A bullet whipped the sidewalk. Matt jinked slightly to his left, like he was aiming back downhill. But the sidewalk gave him purchase, enough to switch around and accelerate at the same time. He sprinted straight uphill, leaped over the ring's outer border of shrubs, tumbled, crawled, and halted by the stone wall that rimmed the memorial.

A bullet chipped off the stone by his head. Matt hugged the knee-high wall and scrambled to his left. It was a largely futile move. A trained sniper would sweep his scope back and forth along the wall, finger on the trigger, ready to blast away at the first sign. Especially now that the squall was passing.

The sibilant rush of sound gradually softened to pattering drops off the trees between the flagpoles. Matt hissed out, "Pop!"

The shooter yelled, "Don't call him that!"

Paul Kelly sounded hollow. "You shouldn't have come."

"Tell me your status."

"What for? It'll only get you killed too."

Another voice came in. Low and slightly slurred. "We're roped to the MIA flagpole."

"Pecard."

"Three claymores are wired around the base. He's fused—"

The shooter yelled out, "This is your last chance to come clean, Kelly! Tell the boy who you really are!"

"You're insane."

The shooter cackled. "No argument there. Losing your woman, watching her steal your boy. Learning she's given him to a scum who'd shoot his own man in the back. Yeah, that'd drive you insane."

"I never shot—" Paul Kelly's voice broke off as the flagpole clanked again. He moaned.

"Tell him!" The voice sounded slightly nearer, but it was hard to tell with the shifting wind. "Tell him how Megan wouldn't even let me have the boy tested to see if he was mine! She promised she'd call the cops if I even showed up at your door!"

"I don't know what you're talking about!"

Matt gripped the stone with both hands, took two tight breaths, and pitched his voice into a high familiar shrill. His mother's voice. The one she used when irate enough for her raw beginnings to emerge. "Porter Reeves! You stop that and *behave!*"

The only sound was the thumping rush of traffic on the bridge.

Matt knew he was too tense and too breathless to give his best. But the words came easy enough, drawn from his mother's stock phrases. "Haven't you learned anything in all these years?"

The response was fainter now. "Megan?"

"Why did you hurt me so? What did I ever give you but my best?"

"You left me! You married him!" The voice rose so high it broke and shattered. "You wouldn't let me claim my boy!"

"He isn't yours!" Matt heard the next soft rush of rain, pushed off the wall far enough to see the incoming veil. "Now you come down here so I can talk to you. Right this instant!"

The hardest downpour of the day hit then. Matt rolled over the wall and sprinted across the inner circle to where the flagpoles rose at its center. Expecting at any moment to be torn apart by incoming fire.

The two men were roped back-to-back. Claymores were positioned under both of them. Paul Kelly watched his approach in horrified disbelief. "That was you?"

Pecard's hair was parted by a slice that ran pink in the rain. His face was slack, his eyes unfocused. Matt examined the knots, hissed, "Knife."

Pecard had to form his tongue carefully around each word. "Rear pocket."

Matt dug it out and clawed at the clasp. He forced his fingers to unlock and pried out a blade. Went to work on the top rope. Pecard slipped off the pole, gasped with the release of pressure from his lungs. He began crawling away on his elbows. Matt sawed at the next rope.

There was a soft metallic click. And the feel of something colder and harder than the rain on his neck. "You think you're the only one who can use rain for cover, boy?"

———

Porter Reeves was an inch or so shorter than Matt. He had the same hyper-leanness of Allen Pecard, the same ornery tautness to his features. Only with Porter everything was magnified to an impossible degree. Impossible for a man to have a face like a stone ridge, where his eyes peered like furious beasts from two caves. Impossible to have a frame that powerful, emanating that much energy, and be so pale. Cadaverous. Even his mouth looked emaciated, just a slit in the bottom half of his face. "You're not half-bad, kid."

Porter Reeves held a military-issue forty-five in one hand and an electronic trigger in his other. He motioned with his pistol. "Slide on over here. Keep both hands where I can see them. Don't want you getting maimed with old Dad here."

He spiked that last word with a kick to Paul Kelly's side. "Go on. Tell him."

When Matt tried to deflect a second kick, Porter Reeves cocked the pistol. "Do that again and I'll take Kelly out real slow. Now move out of range." He waited until Matt had crawled a ways off, then kicked Paul Kelly again. Watching Matt as he did so.

Paul Kelly grunted but made no other sound.

"Go on, tell him. Else I'll cap that knee. Then you'll tell him. Only louder."

"Tell him what." Even pale with bone-deep cold and drenched, Paul Kelly was still a handsome man. "That you were always crazy? That your antics risked the lives of all my men?"

The living skull leaned closer. "You triggered the mine that took me out, then you left me to die!"

"What are you talking about?"

Matt watched as Paul Kelly showed him the same open scorn he'd given his son. His son. All the years Matt had wondered why his father couldn't just accept him for who he was. Stop racing from job to job, medal to medal in the business world. Slow down and let them be a family. It all came clear. That and more.

Paul Kelly said, "There was a firefight. You were on point. The mine went off. I saw you go down."

"You saw? I was ten feet from that mine when it blew." The cackle was somewhere between a laugh and a sob. "*You shot it off.*"

"I *should* have shot you. I knew you were running some kind of scam. But I couldn't prove it. All I did was call in the chopper. Sol went out to check for wounded. The chopper landed. We—"

"You left me for the Cong!"

"Listen to me! Sol checked you! My job was to save my men!"

Porter Reeves shouted so hard his neck corded from his shoulders to his ears. "*I was one of your men!*"

"It wasn't him." Matt was so cold, so detached, he could not claim the words as his own. Not until the two men stared at him. Matt said, "Pop didn't fire the weapon."

"I told you. Don't call him that." But the beast was back in the cave.

"Think for a second. Pop wasn't involved in your scam, was he?" When Porter didn't respond, Matt pressed. "If Pop had known, he'd have had you arrested, right? Not shot. He just said he was trying to get you taken off his roster."

"I knew it." Paul Kelly glared at his assailant. "The rumors from HQ were right. You conned those people."

"Shut up, Kelly." But Porter Reeves didn't put any fire into it. "Go on, kid."

"Pop sent Sol Greene to check for survivors. Sol checked you. He left you."

Porter Reeves said, "But Sol was . . ."

"Your partner. I know." And he did. Finally. "If anybody was going to fire a gun and set off a land mine, it would have been your partner in crime, right? The guy who was terrified you were going to get yourself arrested, and him too."

Paul Kelly gaped in horror at his son. "Sol?"

Allen Pecard grunted from his spot by the stone ring. It could have been a laugh. Or a cough. His eyes were shut. But Matt was fairly certain he was listening.

"Sol Greene and Porter Reeves were partners in a scam with Barry Simms. They offered safe passage and fake American IDs to rich Vietnamese desperate to get out. They were making a fortune." Matt pointed through the rain. "Pecard was investigating the scam. Porter took out Pecard's partner. Porter was wild, spending money, sending up flares. Sol must have decided it was best to sacrifice one of their own."

Porter Reeves opened his mouth, the effort of drawing breath turning each lungful into a tight scream. "Kelly . . ."

"Pop didn't know a thing," Matt said. Which wasn't exactly true. His father had known about Megan and Porter. And never forgot. Or forgave. Either of them.

Two women and a man appeared by the perimeter wall. Spread out at forty-five-degree angles. Connie shouted, "Police! Drop your weapons! *Now!*"

Bannister swung over the wall, his gun staying trained on Reeves. Hannah Bernstein added her voice. "Step away from these men!"

Porter Reeves shut his eyes briefly. For an instant a world of weariness flooded his frame. A dark wave of poisonous regret. Then he opened his eyes and right hand at the same moment. Letting his pistol drop to the sodden earth.

"He's got the trigger!" Matt scrambled up, preparing for attack. Knowing it was futile.

Porter Reeves turned slightly, looking at Matt. Then he stepped toward Paul Kelly.

Matt did the only thing he could to save his father. He leaped across the wet earth. Landed hard upon Paul Kelly. Gripped him tight. And shut his eyes against the blast to come.

"*Get off him!*"

A hand like a tree limb struck his neck. Matt only clung harder.

Then he heard three officers take Porter down. Still Matt held on, unable to accept that they had survived until Hannah Bernstein patted his shoulder and said, "It's over."

Lucas watched Hannah Bernstein work her phone. She had stopped by home to dry off and change into a gray pinstriped jacket with a high Nehru collar and a long row of gray cloth buttons. Matching skirt. Stockings. Lace-up shoes with a hint of heel, but still flat enough for real work. Which was what she had just returned from. Helping to bring a hardened criminal to justice. Talking with the press. Talking with the mayor's office. Being reinstated. His boss again.

Only she wasn't acting like a boss right now. She was pulling off her shoes. Setting them on the floor by his hospital bed. Smiling as she shut her phone. "This has been some day."

"Make yourself at home, why don't you." But Lucas was smiling too. "Guess I'll have to go back to being respectful again."

"Absolutely. My new lieutenant is definitely charged with setting the proper example for our troops." She was watching closely as she said it. "You'll do it, won't you. Take the job."

"There's the matter of the exam."

She waved it aside. Absolutely of no importance. "Will you?"

He looked at her. Nobody would guess that this woman had just come back from duking it out with a killer. Her hair framed a strong yet open face, eyes as clear as the sky outside his window. Winter eyes. Full of icy fire. "It felt good backing up the rookies, giving them support, trusting them to do the frontline work."

"Then you'll do it?"

"Yes, Hannah. If that's what you really want."

"I want this. A lot." She watched him ease up in bed, saw the wince. "You need something?"

"I'm okay. The therapist worked me over today, is all." He leaned forward for her to punch his pillow into submission. "Thanks. I've been hit before; I ought to know the drill by now. Before the hit, I was strong and fast and pretty much invulnerable. After, I was just scared."

He waited for her to say something like *Shouldn't you rest?* or *Is this really what we need to be talking about right now?* Any number of things that all would have added up to deflection. But Hannah didn't do that. Instead, she reached over and took his hand.

Lucas started to look down. But he stopped himself. He was afraid if he made a big deal of it she'd pull her hand away. And he liked it there. A lot. It felt like it belonged.

Hannah asked, "Is that when you became religious?"

"In a way. I thought I'd put the darkness behind me. I got on with life. I loved June so much. But I knew it was still there. The dark. I spent a long time in denial. You know?"

Hannah's features showed the kind of sorrow that turned her old. She whispered, "Do I ever."

"My faith is very important to me, Hannah."

The words hung there in the air between them. She looked nice sitting there, holding his hand. Softer. She said, "I've never known anybody like you, Lucas. And I've known a lot of people."

He saw the slight hesitation over that last word and knew she had started to say *men*. Known a lot of men. "I understand."

"I like the difference in you." And just left it there. He saw her taste several unspoken thoughts, saw her give a minute shake of her head. And he understood that as well.

"How about going out on a date with me, Hannah?"

She didn't draw her hand away, which was what he had been half-expecting. Instead she cocked her head to one side, letting the hair fall over her shoulder. And suddenly Lucas was looking back in years, to a much younger woman, one who was both shy and extremely appealing. "I'm your boss."

He gripped her tighter. "Nobody's perfect."

The wind was still building as Matt parked in the alley behind his father's house. Every surface was slick from the day's drenching, but the rain had passed for now. The wind carried a thin blade of frost. Faint traces of wintry blue appeared overhead, there and gone as fast as the changing afternoon light. His father's campaign bus glistened and mirrored the shifting season. The TV crews were gone, off chasing other sirens. The rain had shunted away the onlookers. The wind had erased the autumn colors. The street was empty and bare.

He stood by his car and waited as Bryan Bannister pulled in behind him, and then a second car of Bannister's agents. Connie and Judy Leigh rose from the car. Matt walked back to where his father sat in Bannister's rear seat. Paul Kelly was wrapped in an emergency blanket left by the ambulance that had taken Porter Reeves away. He rolled down his window and said, "I thought we were going to the hospital."

"There's something we need to take care of first," Matt replied. "And I was going to get you some dry clothes. Unless you want to—"

"No." His father glanced at the house, then turned away. "No."

Matt did not insist. Pecard watched him with his unbandaged eye. Bannister had wanted Pecard to take the ambo straight to Maryland General. Pecard had looked at Matt then the same way as now. Too ornery and British to plead. So Matt had asked for him, and Bannister had agreed to this one stop.

Matt signaled to Connie. Together they headed for the carriage house. He entered and found Sol seated behind his desk. Stacks of flyers and campaign posters and press announcements and time sheets filled every surface. Sol stared at the greaseboard covering the side wall. Across the top was written, "Campaign Timetable." The next day, Tuesday, was blanked out in red.

"Sol."

He turned slowly. "Any news?"

"Pop is outside."

Sol tried hard to work up some enthusiasm. "Is he okay?"

"Cold. Bruised. Maybe a cracked rib. Otherwise okay. We're taking him to the hospital."

Matt and Connie followed him outside. They all did. Judy Leigh burrowed into her voluminous purse and got digital snaps of the reunion. Sol was nervous and agitated. Paul Kelly remained wrapped in a blue ambo blanket and tensely refused to make eye contact.

"Sol." Matt grabbed his arm. "Come along this way."

Sol let Matt draw him over to the car's other side. "He's going to be okay, right? I mean, sure, we won't do anything outdoors tomorrow. But a taped interview, that's doable. Hospital bedside, to be played on the morning show, asking people to get out and support . . ."

Sol expelled the remainder of his words unshaped. Allen Pecard's window rolled down. Up close his face looked severely battered. One eye was closed and taped. His jaw was distorted. The line across his forehead was clotted and raw. It clearly hurt him to be there. Pecard watched as Bannister approached and said, "Sol Greene, you are under arrest for the sale of false American passports, extortion, and the attempted murder of Porter Reeves."

"What?" Sol tried hard for outrage. "How bogus is this? That was thirty years ago!"

Connie stepped forward, jangling her cuffs. "Place your hands behind your back, Mr. Greene."

"This is totally—"

"Hands behind your back." This time she helped him.

"My lawyer will have me released in an hour! I'm suing you for assault!"

"I doubt that," Matt replied. "We're going to ask the judge to hold you over without bail until the full ownership of Downtown is unraveled."

His father stopped his glare at the front window and looked over to see his campaign manager sag.

"Ian Reeves was right about one thing," Matt said to his father. "Some people never *want* to change."

His father just looked at him.

"A good campaign manager has to know where the money is, right, Sol? Cash and lots of it. So you found some of Baltimore's underworld, offered them a way to go legit. Big, splashy, make them a power in the city overnight."

Sol gave him a killer's glare. "You rescued your father just to ruin him?"

"What was it about the deal that you needed national influence for, Sol? My guess is two things. Inner-city housing grants, and rights to turn the old military harbor into a huge new yacht basin. What would they be worth, Sol? Enough to convince your old friend he needed to form a trust and put it in your hands and run for national office, I bet."

Sol spotted Judy Leigh writing furiously and clamped down. "I want my lawyer *now*."

———

Pecard twisted in his seat far enough to watch Connie deliver the suspect to the federal agents, then said, "I owe you quite a considerable debt."

"Not now, not ever."

He tightened the muscles that still worked into a partial smile. "Never refuse a debt, Agent Kelly. Haven't I taught you anything?"

Matt shook the man's hand, then walked around to where Bryan Bannister was waiting. "Thank you."

"Hey, I'm the one doing the owing here." Bannister pointed with his chin back at the car. "He saved my life. Pecard."

"A Major Stafford is head of base security at Upper Heyford. You might want to check and see if he was based in Manila during the war."

"He was involved in the scam?"

"Not in Nam. The British contacts were clear about that. Porter Reeves drank with him and possibly bought illegal weaponry from him. My guess is, Porter Reeves obtained the information leading to the

National Guard Armory heist from Stafford as well. But those two were close enough for Porter to be certain Stafford was not in Nam. If he had been, Porter would have known, and Stafford would have wound up suffering the same fate as Barry Simms."

Bannister nodded thoughtfully. "They give medals in your division?"

"Never heard of one."

"Well, they ought to." He offered Matt his hand. "Anytime, anywhere, Kelly. I mean that."

"In that case, I'd like to ask that you let Baltimore Homicide share the press on this collar."

"Far as I'm concerned, it's you and them. We just played ride-along."

Matt stepped back to where his father stared at him through the open window. Paul Kelly said, "I suppose you're expecting me to thank you."

"No, Pop."

"My best friend destroyed, the worst day of my past reawakened, my business gone, my future, my wife. How could anyone expect me to be grateful for anything?"

Connie was the only one looking his way. She had stepped over to where Matt could see her clearly. Showing him that disconcertingly deep gaze. "Nobody does, Pop."

"You're going to accuse me now? Ask me what I know about all this? How I could have trusted my oldest and best friend?"

"Bannister might want to talk with you about that. But I won't."

Paul Kelly struggled over the next item. "I wanted to tell you. But your mother . . ."

Matt found himself recalling that night in the kitchen. How his father had attempted an apology. The first ever. And left Matt convicted by his inability to offer anything in response. He could blame his father all he wanted. But the truth was brilliantly scripted upon the city and the dull gray sky. He had nothing to offer even when the chance came. Matt said quietly, "You did what you thought was best."

As usual, Matt's refusal to argue only heightened his father's ire. "Who *are* you?"

Connie moved slightly closer. Matt did not need to look up to feel the strength of her caring concern. The gift was so powerful he could reach across the void and touch his father's shoulder. "I'm your son."

Matt dropped Judy Leigh at the newspaper and then drove Connie home. Throughout the silent journey, he remained locked onto the exchange with his father. He could not say why he had spoken as he had. The words hung there before him. The touch to his father's arm. Such a feeble gesture, so paltry the words. Thirty years in the making.

It was not until Matt turned onto Connie's street that he acknowledged the underlying current. Connie sat there beside him, enveloped in the same disconcerting serenity.

He parked the car, cut off the motor, and turned to her. She met his gaze. And waited.

Where Megan Kelly had worked her way beneath his barriers with words, Connie was doing so with silence. This was a harder struggle, for she gave him nothing to defend against. He could not argue with her, nor barricade himself against questions she did not ask.

The exchange with his father was now coupled to this growing awareness over Connie. As he left the car and walked her to her front door, every false relationship he had known paraded before his eyes. The implacable rhythm at the hands of one woman after another. Different lady, same story. Meet, heat, defeat. Their accusations tossed like farewell grenades.

Only not this time. The difference was palpable. Connie unlocked her front door and then just stood looking at him with that dark calm.

She was not going to tell him good-bye. He knew that with a certainty that rocked his world.

Matt turned away from the suffocation, not from her. He walked back down the street and continued on past his car, a lone pilgrim so lost he could not even drive away.

At the corner stood a solitary maple, sheltered from the day's winds, still emblazoned with a final autumn song. On the opposite corner the lights of a bar sputtered and flickered and gleamed. If only he had learned to be a drinking man.

He watched his fingers trace a line down the tree's irregular surface. The image from his sleep in the car with Judy Leigh returned to him then. Sharper now than when he had first dreamed it. And he understood the dread he had felt.

The dream had been a single image. He was seated on a park bench. Connie was beside him. They ate ice cream from a cup. She held the spoon, he the container. She fed him, then herself. She had been so very happy. Not in the way of one who laughed. Down deep. In her very bones. In her *soul*. And it had been because of him. He had done this thing. He had given her such peace and fulfillment that this simple act of sharing a cup of ice cream had been utterly complete for her. She had looked at him with the tenderness of a woman unafraid to share her love.

A wind touched the leaves then, a soft sigh of lost breath. The leaves might have shifted. But all Matt heard was the call of crystal chimes.

He dropped his arm. He turned around. Connie still stood on the street in front of her house. He started back. She watched him return, motionless. Trapped in the helpless amber he had created around her and them.

He stopped in front of her. He wanted to take her and hold her until the air left both their bodies.

So he fought harder than he ever had in his entire life. The words were scarcely a whisper. "I don't want to get it wrong again this time. With you."

He was trembling so hard he doubted she caught everything he said. "You don't know. You can't. I've never, I haven't . . ." He felt the inevitable defeat swallow him, a great dark maw of winter blasting down and taking him whole. "I have to go."

"No, Matt." She was so calm, this woman. She reached for his hand. "There's no need to run. Not this time."

He looked down at her hand. Watched her join it with her other. And knew so long as she held him, he would never be able to leave.

"Just do this. Okay? Take a deep breath. Will you do that? Just breathe. Okay. Again. That's it. Nice and easy and deep. Good. Okay. Now I want you just to unlock that muscle. The one you've got clenched up so tight. Let it go. I'll be there. It's okay. I'm not going away and neither are you. Feel that muscle unclench?"

"Yes." He was so scared. But the power of her voice overwhelmed his ability to remain as he was, as he always had been. Here on this street, the winter wind could not touch him. The years of holding back meant nothing. All was washed away by her soothing concern.

"Okay. Breathe once more for me. Good." She smiled softly then. Confident in him. And them. "Now tell me what it was you wanted to say."

ACKNOWLEDGMENTS

Dealing with cops and security forces is a lesson in reality. I have been gifted with some of the finest teachers around. Special thanks must go to Detective Melisa Anderson and Detective Michael Hammel of Baltimore's homocide division, and Major James Rood and Detective Elizabeth Geiselman with Baltimore's organized crime squad. Thanks also to Dr. Patricia Aronica-Pollak and Jerry Dziecichowicz with the Office of the Medical Examiner. And to Richard Feser, patrol officer with the Washington, D.C., police, for helping me learn what questions I needed to ask.

Debbie Bernstein was formerly in State Department Intelligence, and a key reason for why this book came into being. Clare Lopez is a senior intelligence consultant to Homeland Security, and served in CIA ops for a number of years. Bruce Stofko is a special agent with the FBI. Nick Eftiamiades with State Department Intel kindly walked me through the FLETSE training school. Heartfelt thanks to all these great people. It has been a genuine honor.

Frank and Ruth Protokowicz and Jeff Leach are lifetime Baltimore residents and supplied much of the details that made the city live for me and hopefully on the page. Laura Vozzella and Doug Donovan are reporters with the *Baltimore Sun* and helped enormously. As did Hannah Lee Byron and Fran Carmen of the Baltimore Film Office, together with Kristen Zissel of the Baltimore Visitors' Association, and most especially Jack Gerbes and Kathi Ash of the Maryland Film Commission.

Thanks also to Sean O'Keefe, President of Union Pictures, and to Alan Nevins of The Firm. It was great working with you both on this concept.

Special thanks must also go to my publisher, Allen Arnold, and my editor, Ami McConnell. They represent a tremendous team at WestBow. It is great working with you guys and coming to know you as friends.

Lynda Atkins is a former adjutant with the Royal Air Force and kindly helped structure the UK military base scenes, as did former RAF navigator Brian Spurway. Christopher Compston is a senior judge with the Oxford Crown Court, and a new friend.

Heartfelt thanks to Isabella, my darling wife, whose guidance and wisdom and confidence in my meager abilities shine from every book.

This book is dedicated to all the great folks who call Charm City home.

Go birds.

/